Contents

Appendixes

Introduction

For me, football is the tired grass field beside Roosevelt Elementary School in the small Wisconsin town where I grew up. That's where my classmates and I spent many of our winter weekend afternoons and summer evenings. I can't quite tell you how well I scored in my third-grade math class or the first girl I had a crush on, but the memories of catching touchdown passes and dirtying my best school clothes on that field are still fresh in my mind. Football can have that everlasting effect on a person.

Football is a simple game of gains and losses, yet it's so much more. As a spectator, the experience can be every bit as everlasting—as real and moving—as the experiences of playing the game. Soon you'll agree.

While reading this book, you'll begin to understand why the sport has captivated its millions of fans all over the world.

How to Use This Book

This book is divided into five parts, each of which dissects a different aspect of football and combines to make you a more astute student of the game.

Part 1, The Basics, discusses football's history; covers the basic terminology and equipment; and takes a close look at the game's coaches, managers, and officials.

Part 2, We Got the Ball, explores the offensive side of the ball. It gives a detailed explanation for each position's objectives and limitations, and it covers the strategy, rules, and statistics important only to the offense.

Part 3, They Got the Ball, tackles the defense, breaking down each position and examining the defensive strategy, rules, and statistics.

Part 4, The "Other" Third of the Team, covers special teams—the kicking and punting game and all the coverage units. Same as with offense and defense, Part 4 discusses special teams strategy, rules, and statistics.

Part 5, A Spectacle at Every Level, features the different levels of play—professional, college, high school, and youth; how each is organized; and what it has to offer to the fan. This part also discusses the many ways fans can interact with the game, including fantasy football.

In the backfield, you'll find a glossary of football-related terms and also a resources appendix to help you gain extra yards with your football knowledge.

Extras

Throughout the book you'll find a number of elements providing insight or a fun nugget of information. Here's a quick description of the different kinds of information you'll find:

FUN FACT

These bits of trivia are fun to share with friends and enhance your football knowledge.

GRIDIRON GAB

These boxes contain clear explanations of terms that may be new to you.

PENALTY

Check these boxes for notes about rules that impact football players or coaches.

QUICK HIT

These boxes offer tips to help you better understand the action during the game.

WORDS OF WISDOM

Here you'll find timeless quotes from some of football's legendary coaches and players.

Acknowledgments

First I must thank my agent, Marilyn Allen of the Allen O'Shea Literary Agency, who is responsible for connecting me with this project. Writers often speak of how agents aren't accessible or compassionate; I guess those writers don't know Marilyn. She's a splendid lady and a true writer's agent.

To all the good people at Alpha Books—you have my gratitude for helping guide this project, especially Mike Sanders for his patience, Christy Wagner for her careful treatment of each sentence, and Kayla Dugger for helping bring it all together.

A special thanks to my stepfather, Mike Fadden, who has always been there for me and has asked little in return. To my older brother, Chris, who built the foundation on which my love of football continues to grow, and to my younger brother, Paul, who lives the way we all should.

To Bill Berry and William "Pete" Kelley, both of whom served as mentors, but more importantly, became lifelong friends. Much thanks to Steve Hill, Brian Toelle, Phil Tubbs, and Mark DeYoung, for offering input on this book.

To Bryan Van Stippen, my collaborator, business partner, and the greatest friend a guy could have.

To Jada and Isis, each an equal owner of my heart, and to their mother and my partner, Lisa, for making me whole and keeping me sane—love the three of you more than a single paragraph or an entire manuscript will allow me to express.

And to my two biggest fans—my mom, Kay, and my Aunt Belle—I dedicate this book to the both of you.

Trademarks

The Basics

Football is inescapable. It's an American treasure. One of the great spectacles of our time. But boil it down, and what more do you have than an open field, a ball, and a couple dozen men willing to batter and bloody themselves for the thrill of it all?

Part 1 covers the game's history, its rules, the playing field and equipment, the coaches, and the referees.

In other words, the basics.

A Game for the Masses

In This Chapter

- Why football is America's most popular sport
- How the game came to be
- Important chapters in the history of the game
- The men who put football on the map

For many of its fans, football is second only to breathing. It's what they think about, talk about, cry about, and yearn for. It bonds fans with nothing in common but the team they share, and it divides people who would otherwise get along just fine.

Football does not discriminate, and it knows no boundaries. Men and women of all ages and social and cultural backgrounds are passionate about it, and its popularity continues to grow in places far away from its origin.

To begin to understand the game—how it's organized and how it's played—one must first begin to understand where it came from.

The Greatest Game on Earth

Had gladiators lived in modern times, there's a good chance they would have chosen football over all other competitions. For the athlete, football challenges the individual's strength, speed, endurance, and intelligence. For the fan, it has everything a viewer thirsts for: drama, scoring, and loud collisions.

Although no longer the blood-and-guts game it once was during its formative years, today's football is still one of the most barbaric sports that exist. But make no mistake; football is not merely a game for thrill-seekers. The game's chesslike qualities and complex offensive and defensive systems make it a favorite for intellectual sports fans, too.

Sellout crowds and merchandise sales suggest the popularity of football is rivaled by no other spectator sport. In terms of fantasy sports, there's fantasy football and then there's everything else. And the game's biggest event of the year, the Super Bowl, draws one of the largest television viewing audiences of any program, sports programming or otherwise.

But before football became king of the U.S. sporting world, it needed to be perfected over several decades of trial and error.

The Origins of Football

American football, as opposed to *futbol* (soccer) as the rest of the world knows it, dates to the middle of the nineteenth century, when college clubs began to explore variations of rugby and soccer.

An 1869 game between Rutgers and Princeton is usually credited with being the first American football contest, although the game's historians often debate this. In its first quarter-century, football spread rapidly throughout the East Coast, mastered first by the Ivy League schools.

FUN FACT

Harvard, Princeton, and Yale were the three dominant schools during the game's formative years. In all but two years between 1880 and 1900, one of those three schools was recognized as the unofficial national champion of college football.

Throughout the 1870s and 1880s, Yale's Walter Camp helped transform the game by incorporating a number of rule changes that distinguished football from rugby. Camp is credited for establishing the line of scrimmage, inventing the center-quarterback exchange, and developing many of the scoring rules leagues use today.

Later, Camp began to recognize the best collegiate players in the country. Camp's squads were the first All-American teams. For all of his contributions, Camp is often referred to as the "father of American football."

WINNER OF THE WEEK Sochi is a study in opposites. She can't stand the cold, but she loves to play in the rain. She's been known to let out a delighted squeak, but she doesn't purr. The frisky kitty loves to play fetch, reports her person, Wendy Cook of Tampa, Florida. "She will bring you her toys when she wants to play," Wendy says. "Sochi is a real character."

20 · Monday · November *2023*

Other innovators helped shape the game through its first half-century of existence, men like Amos Alonzo Stagg, Glenn "Pop" Warner, and Knute Rockne. Bit by bit, football evolved.

And notice I said "men" in the preceding paragraph. One of the first observations a fan new to football will make is how few women are involved at every level. The game is played, officiated, coached, and managed by men, almost exclusively. Fortunately, the number of female spectators increases each year, and one of fantasy football's largest-growing demographics is its female players.

Early Era Rules and Equipment

Believe it or not, the first balls used were closer in resemblance to a medicine ball than to the ball fans are familiar with today. Footballs were round, heavy, and difficult to throw. Even if players had wanted to throw the ball, it wouldn't have mattered; the forward pass didn't become legal until the early 1900s and was not used widespread until after World War I.

The first few decades of organized football more closely resembled rugby, with players wearing thick sweaters instead of jerseys and relying on very little protective equipment, if any at all. Players began wearing head protection in the 1890s, but it wasn't until the 1940s that pro football required all players to wear a leather helmet.

Scoring was also much different when football first began: a touchdown was worth fewer points, and, as is the case with rugby, extra points and field goals counted the most.

PENALTY!

One of the early rules of football stated that when the offense failed to complete a pass it would be forced to turn the ball over to the opponent, same as would be the case with a fumble or an interception.

Key Points in Football History

The game of football has developed more rapidly than perhaps any other mainstream organized sport. Not much more than 100 years old, football has transcended from being a game for college club teams to the most watched sport in America. Several key moments in time have helped make the game what it is today.

A Nod to Teddy

The game of football was responsible for serious injuries (even casualties) in its formative years, so U.S. president Teddy Roosevelt decided to intervene.

Roosevelt was a fan of the game but understood rules would be needed to preserve it long term. Upon his recommendation, a number of changes were introduced in the 1906 season that helped reduce the number of serious injuries.

The First "Modern" Season

The year 1912 can be remembered for helping add excitement to the game. Rule changes before the start of the college season that year increased the points given for touchdowns to 6, removed limitations on forward passing, and shortened the field of play.

A Friendly Game of Catch

The great Knute Rockne was one of football's first innovators of the modern passing game. Although it cannot be said that Rockne invented the forward pass, nor can it be said that his Notre Dame teams were the first to use the pass regularly, Rockne's contribution to the advancement of the pass is often viewed above all others.

During the summer of 1913, Rockne and his college teammate, quarterback Gus Dorais, spent time on the shores of Lake Erie. The two played catch and spoke at length about the forward pass and how it could be used. The duo used the play effectively in Notre Dame's win over Army that season, bringing widespread attention to a play that had been legally used in college football since the 1906 season.

 FUN FACT

In the 1920s and 1930s, collegiate players such as Michigan quarterback Bennie Friedman, Texas Christian quarterback Sammy Baugh, and Alabama split end Don Hutson would further the advancement of the forward pass.

Establishing the Pro Game

The Roaring '20s were a time of celebration and unlimited possibilities, yet somehow pro football was struggling to gain its legs. As excitement for the college game spread, owners of the American Professional Football Association were finding it difficult to earn a profit. Through its first few years, the league changed its name three times, finally settling on the National Football League (NFL) in 1922. The only team that survived the transitional period was the Decatur Staleys, later renamed the Chicago Bears.

By 1932, the number of pro football teams had been reduced to eight, but the league finally had stable franchises to build around.

The Season That Changed the Game for Good

Few things that happened on the field make 1946 notable. But a couple of events made it a landmark year for football, especially the pro game. The Cleveland Rams relocated their franchise to Los Angeles that year, making them the first NFL team of the modern era to play west of the Mississippi River. Four years later, the San Francisco 49ers would join them.

That 1946 season the Rams also added African American players Kenny Washington and Woody Strode to their roster—a year before the great Jackie Robinson integrated Major League Baseball. African Americans had played pro football before, but by 1934, African Americans had disappeared; Washington and Strode were part of a movement that would help place an African American on every NFL roster by 1962.

 FUN FACT

Kenny Washington played in the same backfield as Jackie Robinson at UCLA. That team was among college football's most integrated at the time, and Robinson was so talented, many believed he could have played pro football instead of baseball.

The Television Era

What made the game of football the most profitable, most watched sport in America? Television.

With just a dozen pro franchises in existence in the mid-1950s, the buzz about the greatest game in the world was spreading slowly. Radio could give the details of a baseball game, but it couldn't offer the full effect of a bone-crushing hit or a fingertip catch. Television exposed football's violence and broadcast its odd characters to a much larger audience.

The game credited for being the most pivotal in the growth of the sport was the 1958 NFL championship game between the Baltimore Colts and the New York Giants. The game has the distinction of being the first championship game to be decided in *sudden death overtime*. Baltimore won, 23–17.

GRIDIRON GAB

When the score is tied at the end of four quarters, NFL teams go into **sudden death overtime,** and the first team to score wins. This is treated the same as any other quarter, with 15 minutes on the clock and time-outs given to each team. A coin toss determines possession. If the clock runs out in sudden death overtime of a regular season game, the game is then ruled a tie; if it runs out in a playoff game, the teams play another overtime (and so on) until one team scores.

Pete Rozelle, who served as the NFL's commissioner from 1960 to 1989, helped increase the demand for broadcasting pro football games. Under Rozelle's leadership, the game's audience increased significantly, much thanks to the power of broadcast games.

One League, Booming Business

By 1960, the popularity of pro football had begun to pique the interests of other businessmen. The American Football League (AFL) was started that year, and it catered to a number of West Coast markets not being serviced by the NFL. The AFL experienced tremendous growth throughout the decade and proved able to compete for the best talent. In time, however, AFL owners felt compelled to join the NFL instead of waging a war over viewers and players. In 1970, the two leagues merged, increasing the number of NFL teams from 16 to 26.

Perhaps the greatest thing to come from the two leagues pooling together was the Super Bowl. During its first four years, the Super Bowl pitted the AFL champion against the NFL champion. Now it hosts the winners from the league's two conferences.

All this growth, as well as the birth of *Monday Night Football* in 1970, helped pro football reach new heights of success.

Since the AFL–NFL merger, other pro leagues have tried to compete with the NFL, including the United States Football League (USFL), which lured high-profile college stars with big-dollar contracts in the 1980s. The USFL eventually folded out of financial hardship and frustration, and its top players were allowed entrance into the NFL. Of all the attempts since the AFL, no rival league has managed to mix the right formula to stay afloat.

FUN FACT

The most vocal owner—and sometimes spokesman—for the USFL was a savvy New York businessman who managed to sign two of college football's greatest players, Herschel Walker and Doug Flutie, to his team, the New Jersey Generals. The owner's name? Donald Trump.

Today, because of the decisions made during its formative years, the NFL has experienced steady financial growth in a period when other professional sports leagues have suffered losses and experienced declines in game attendance.

Names to Know and Performances to Remember

Who started pro football? The simple answer is William "Pudge" Heffelfinger, a former standout for Yale who was paid the handsome sum of $500 to play for the Allegheny Athletic Association in its 1892 contest with the Pittsburgh Athletic Club. The investment paid off, as ledgers later showed the Association had made a net profit of more than $600, and because a Heffelfinger touchdown helped Allegheny win the game.

No one really can say just how great Jim Thorpe was. Having played collegiately for coach Pop Warner during the early years of the twentieth century, Thorpe helped the Carlisle Indians compete with the finest college programs of the time. Opponents considered him difficult to catch and even more challenging to bring to the ground. Thorpe later played football professionally and was the first president of the American Professional Football Association, which later became the NFL. Sportswriters would later call him the greatest athlete of the first half of the twentieth century.

WORDS OF WISDOM

What's the secret of running? Just show 'em a leg, then take it away.

—Jim Thorpe

One of the early era's often forgotten great backs was Ohio State's Chic Harley, who was dominant for coach Jack Wilce's clubs of the World War I era. Harley could do everything, and his impact on Ohio State was so great that he's often credited for helping justify the spending for The Horseshoe, the stadium where the Buckeyes still play home games.

Before Harley, a pair of Midwestern backs had ruled the college football landscape at the turn of the century. Willie Heston was the focal point of Fielding Yost's "Point a Minute" Michigan squads, while the University of Chicago's Walter Eckersall helped Amos Alonzo Stagg to outstanding seasons in 1905 and 1906.

Another Big Ten legend from Harley's time was University of Illinois halfback Harold "Red" Grange—often referred to as the Galloping Ghost. Upon leaving Champaign, Grange was signed to a pro contract by George Halas's Chicago Bears, and Grange's presence helped stimulate interest in the pro game. He is often considered the NFL's first true superstar.

In the 1920s, it was not uncommon for football players to pick up extra games on *barnstorming tours*. During one such tour in 1926, fullback Ernie Nevers played in all 29 games for the Duluth Eskimos, and according to legend, was on the field for 1,711 of a possible 1,740 minutes of play.

GRIDIRON GAB

A **barnstorming tour** is a phrase used when a team plays a lot of games in a condensed amount of time during a road trip. This is most common for less-strenuous sports such as baseball and basketball, but in football's early era, professional teams went on barnstorming tours as a way to earn extra revenue and gain more exposure.

The Least You Need to Know

- Walter Camp is considered the father of American football.
- The shape of the ball and the rulebook made football a game fought mostly on the ground in its infancy.
- Television has helped make football the most popular game in America.
- The first pro football player was Pudge Heffelfinger; the first pro football star was Red Grange.

A Game of Inches

In This Chapter

- The officials and what they're responsible for
- How players line up on both sides of the ball
- Basic offensive and defensive strategy
- How teams score points

Football is a game of exactitude. Every yard counts—or, to go a step further, every inch counts—and players are willing to trade blows and exert all their energy just to gain a little ground. Often, a single inch can make all the difference.

To help keep everything aboveboard, officials watch the action and rule on player behavior. But those guys don't decide the outcome. Football is won and lost based on the strategic decisions the coaches and players make in trying to gain yards.

The Basic Rules of Football

To boil down football to its most basic form, the objective of the team in possession of the ball, the offense, is to advance it to the other team's goal; the objective of the defense, of course, is to stop the offense. The team that scores the most points by the end of the game wins.

Football is a series of plays, or downs, when all the action takes place. On every down, both teams position 11 players along an imaginary line, called the line of scrimmage, which runs perpendicular to the tip of the football closest to the offense's end zone, from sideline to sideline. Seven offensive players must be stationed along the line, facing forward, while the rest of the offense must be at least 1 yard behind the line of scrimmage. The defense can place as many men along the line of scrimmage as it chooses, with the rest of its players stationed at various depths to protect against both running and passing plays.

To start the play on each down, the center snaps the ball between his legs to the quarterback. Every offensive player must be set, or in a stationary position, before the snap of the football; any motion on the part of an offensive player will result in a penalty. Likewise, the defense cannot cross the line of scrimmage before the snap, nor can it use physical motion or verbal baiting to provoke an offensive player to move early.

To advance the ball, either by run or pass, the offensive team must retain possession of the ball at all times. If a player loses the ball or it somehow becomes free within the field of play, it's labeled a fumble, and either team is able to gain possession of it. If a defender secures the ball while it's traveling forward through the air, it is ruled an interception, and the defensive team is awarded possession of the ball (and can advance it). If the ball is thrown forward and neither an offensive nor defensive player catches it before it reaches the ground, it is labeled an incompletion, and the ball reverts to the offense at the last place it was spotted.

The offense has four plays, or downs, to achieve a first down, needing 10 or more yards to do so. If it's successful, it gets another four plays to reach another first down. By gaining first downs and retaining control of the ball, the offense works its way toward the goal line.

Simple stuff, right? It gets more complicated. Read on.

The Game Officials and Their Roles

The men running around the field wearing zebra-striped suits and caps are called game officials. It's the officials' job to ensure the game is played by the rules. They throw yellow flags when players break certain rules or when players conduct themselves in an unsportsmanlike manner. They blow their whistles to stop the action on the field, as well as to start and stop the game clock. And officials explain their rulings to the coaches.

PENALTY!

At no time are players or coaches allowed to make physical contact with a member of the officiating crew during a ruling dispute. If this happens, the player or coach may get ejected from the game and be asked to leave the playing field.

An official needs a good pair of eyes, a quick-working mind, and thick skin. Fans, coaches, and players test all three qualities on game day.

Let's review each official and his responsibilities during the game.

The Referee

This official is the most important of the seven-man NFL officiating crew. The referee has the final say on all penalties and game-management decisions and is the person who communicates with the audience. Positioned behind the offense's back-field, the referee's primary responsibility on each play is to watch the quarterback; on kicking downs, he watches the kicker or punter.

After a flag has been thrown, the official who saw the penalty will communicate what happened to the referee. The referee is also the person responsible for managing instant replay, wherever appropriate, and for tossing the coin at the start of each game.

QUICK HIT

It's easy to pick out the referee from the rest of the officiating crew. He's the one wearing a white cap. The others wear black caps.

The Umpire

The umpire is the number-two man in charge on the field. He mirrors the referee on each play, standing behind the linebackers and observing the linemen on both sides of the ball.

The Head Linesman

Positioned on either sideline and on the line of scrimmage, the head linesman watches to be sure no players move or line up improperly prior to the snap of the ball. During the play, he observes the action along his sideline and helps *spot the ball* after the play is completed.

GRIDIRON GAB

When the officials **spot the ball,** they determine the yardage mark where the ball was ruled down on the prior play, whether on a tackle, a fumble, or a play that went out of bounds.

The Line Judge

Positioned on the opposite sideline from the head linesman, the line judge also helps watch presnap penalties. In addition, the line judge is responsible for monitoring the action along his sideline and ensuring the offense has the correct number of players on the field.

The Side Judge

The side judge lines up along the same sideline as the head linesman, only he's positioned near the defensive *backfield*. His primary roles are to count defensive players on the field and watch for penalties on passing downs.

GRIDIRON GAB

The **backfield** is the area where the offensive (or defensive) backs line up prior to the start of each play.

The Field Judge

Also positioned near the defensive backfield, the field judge is along the same sideline as the line judge. He, too, counts defensive players. Along with the back judge, the field judge helps determine whether field goal attempts are successful.

The Back Judge

The back judge stands in the field of play, behind the defensive backs. Along with the side judge and field judge, he helps monitor action downfield (away from the line of scrimmage) between offensive and defensive players. It's the back judge's job to watch the play clock to be sure the offense doesn't use too much time to get the snap off.

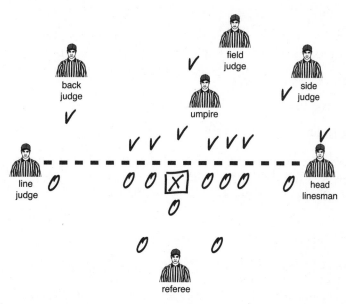

Each member of the seven-person NFL officiating crew is assigned a place to stand at the snap of the ball and specific things to look for during the action on each play.

The Lineups

The key number to know about the lineup is 11. Every unit—offense, defense, special teams—uses 11 players in some arrangement.

Countless combinations exist for offensive and defensive lineups, but they all follow the same basic structure—each unit has three tiers to which a number of players are stationed.

Offensive Lineups

Here are the three tiers to the offensive lineup:

- Linemen, positioned along the line of scrimmage
- Backs, bunched together in a variety of formations inside the backfield, a few yards behind the line of scrimmage
- Ends/receivers, lined up wide of where the ball is snapped, either on the line of scrimmage or a yard behind it

The offensive lineup must have no fewer than five linemen mixed with a quarterback and a combination of backs and receivers.

There are three types of linemen to know:

- The *center* lines up over the football.
- *Guards* line up on either side of the center.
- *Tackles* line up on the outside shoulder of the guards.

The quarterback is positioned directly behind the center, while running backs are positioned behind the line in any number of formations.

Now for the ends:

- An end positioned next to a tackle is labeled a *tight end*.
- Ends spread out away from the tackle are called *split ends*.
- Any player other than the tight end who lines up outside the tackle and is eligible to catch a pass can be categorized as a *wide receiver* (including the split end).

Offenses vary, but many pro-style offenses position two running backs behind the quarterback, with a tight end and a pair of wide receivers.

```
   O              O   O  [X]  O   O   O
   WR            LT  LG       RG  RT  TE
                            O                   O
                            QB                  WR

                      O        O
                      HB       FB
```

Players can be arranged in many ways on offense, but the pro-style formation is one of the most common.

Defensive Lineups

Like the offense, the defensive lineup varies based on the coaching staff's preferences. What makes all defenses similar, though, are the three tiers to which players belong:

- Defensive linemen, positioned along the line of scrimmage across from the offensive linemen

- Linebackers, stationed a few yards behind the defensive linemen

- Defensive backs, lined up across from the wide receivers and also several yards behind the linebackers

Teams use a number of combinations, but a standard pro football defense will use either three defensive linemen paired with four linebackers (called a 3–4), or four defensive linemen paired with three linebackers (4–3). Virtually all pro teams position four men in the secondary, or the defensive backfield.

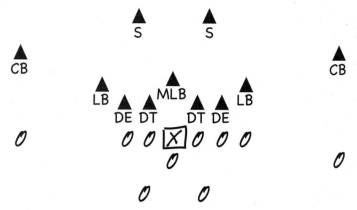

In the 4–3 defense, four linemen are positioned along the line of scrimmage with three linebackers a few yards behind them. To defend against the pass, this defense relies on two cornerbacks and two safeties.

 FUN FACT

At the high school level, it's common to see teams use three defensive backs to put more defenders near the line of scrimmage. (More on high school football in Chapter 27.)

Within the defensive line are two key position subsets:

- Defensive ends
- Defensive tackles

The ends are positioned at both ends of the line, while the tackles are inside. Another interior lineman used is a nose guard, or nose tackle, who is situated directly over the center.

Teams have special lineups for kicking or receiving a kick. I cover this in Part 4. The most important thing to know now, though, is that, like offense and defense, each special teams unit includes 11 players, each one with an assigned role.

What Happens on Game Day

Much of the important action on game day takes place before the game clock begins. While fans are sitting in the parking lot, grilling hamburgers and scarfing down potato chips, players in each locker room are getting their wrists or shoes taped up and getting mentally prepared for the job they have to do.

A team's pregame routine is timed down to the minute from the time it arrives at the stadium to the kickoff, and each detail is carefully planned. Injured players test out whatever is of concern to see if they can play that day. Coaches remind players of the week's game plan and emphasize points of importance. The game officials talk to each head coach to see if he has any items worth noting ahead of time, such as *trick plays*.

GRIDIRON GAB

A **trick play** defies traditional (and conservative) strategy. These plays often produce either fantastic or disastrous results for the team that employs them.

Another thing that happens on game day is the presentation of team captains. Most teams select three or four players to be the captains, and often the same players serve this role in practice and for every game of the season. Captains walk to the middle of the field for a coin toss to determine which team gets the ball to start the game.

The visiting team is asked to call the coin in the air. The winner of the coin toss is allowed to choose from one of three options:

- To kick the ball to the opponent in the first half

- To receive the kick from the opponent

- To defer, forcing the opponent to make a decision now

In almost all instances, teams choose either to receive the ball or defer, allowing them the option to choose at the start of the second half.

FUN FACT

During a 1998 NFL game played on Thanksgiving between the Pittsburgh Steelers and Detroit Lions, a Steelers captain called tails on the coin toss prior to overtime. When the coin came up tails, the referee mistakenly awarded the ball to the Lions, believing the Steelers player had called heads. Despite protesting from the Steelers bench, the Lions got the ball and scored first to win the game.

Referees also look to the captains when the opposing team has committed a penalty. The captain is responsible for choosing whether to accept or decline the penalty. Usually the captain looks to the sideline coaching staff for guidance before informing the referee of the team's decision.

The loser of the toss is given the opportunity to pick which end zone they would like to defend. This can be valuable in games where wind is a factor. A team with its back to the wind has a decided advantage over a team having to play into the wind, especially if that team likes to pass the football.

Finally, before an opening kickoff commences the action, the lineups for each team are announced, and, at most stadiums and for all levels of play, the national anthem is performed.

After all the pregame activity has wrapped up, it's time for the game to begin.

Defining the Possession

When the offensive team takes control of the football, it begins a new possession, or series. For as long as the offense has the ball, that particular possession continues.

To keep the football, and continue the possession, an offensive team is given four plays, or downs, to advance the ball 10 or more yards. If successful, the offense achieves a first down and a fresh set of four downs to advance the ball another 10 yards. If, after four downs, the offense has failed to move the ball 10 yards, the opposing team is given control of the ball. Or as is more common, the offense is allowed to punt the ball to the opposing team (almost always done on fourth down).

In either case, the other team takes control of the football and begins their possession.

The Game Clock and Quarters

Football is a game of quarters and halves. A pro football contest, for example, consists of four 15-minute quarters. After the first and third quarters, a short break is allowed, and the teams trade the directions they are facing on the field. At the conclusion of the first two quarters (the end of the first half), players from both teams are given an extended break, called halftime.

At the end of the first or third quarters, the play resumes the following quarter where it left off. At the start of a new half, the play begins with a kickoff.

The game clock is more important in football than perhaps any other contest. It runs without interruption during each play and when a ball carrier has been tackled inside the field of play.

After the clock winds to zero at the end of each quarter, it is reset to begin the next quarter.

The game clock stops when …

- A runner goes out of bounds before being tackled.

- A team has scored or a change of possession takes place.

- The offense throws an incomplete pass.

- One team calls a time-out.

- An official's decision needs to be reviewed.

- A player on the field is injured and requires attention.

- A quarter or half ends, or at the two-minute warning prior to the half's or game's end.

Football also uses a play clock, which starts when the game officials spot the ball and signal the start of the next down. Depending on the level of play, the offense will then have roughly 30 seconds to get everyone set along the line of scrimmage and begin the play.

The play clock helps keep the game moving and forces coaches and players to be well organized for competition.

FUN FACT

In some states, high school football uses a *running clock* when one team is leading the other by a large margin in the second half. This rule is designed to limit one team from piling on more points and to reduce the threat of injury in a lopsided game. When a running clock is at work, the clock will not stop for any reason other than a time-out, an injury, or if the referee instructs the game clock operator to stop it.

The Offense's Basic Objectives

It would be easy to say the offense's only objective is to put points on the board, but it goes beyond that. Sure, scoring is what decides the winner and loser of each contest, but to score, an offense must first advance the football through a series of successful plays.

Most coaches will tell you that a long possession resulting in points is preferred over a quick possession providing the same result. When a team is able to keep the ball, it shows dominance over the opponent and creates a mental advantage for the offense; it also helps wear down the opposing team's defense.

Teams use a variety of rushing and passing plays to advance the ball. The offense's objective is always to keep moving, and as it approaches the goal line, its number of plays increases, allowing for more chances to score.

Also, by controlling the football, the offense is able to keep the opposing team's offense off the field and thus disrupt that team's rhythm. The longer a team sits, the more stagnant it can become.

So you could say that in football, in some regard, the journey can be as important as the final destination.

The Defense's Basic Objectives

For the defense, the mission is clear: prevent the offense from advancing the football. Easier said than done.

The offense has all the advantages, which makes the defense's job all the more difficult. The offense knows when the ball will be snapped and where the play is going. It's the defensive coach's job to predict what the offense has up its sleeve and to position defenders in the right spot to stop their opponents.

To accomplish this, some defenses act more like offenses, using a variety of stunts to disrupt the offense and force it into making mistakes. (This is discussed in more detail in Chapter 19.)

Whenever the offense fails to gain a first down, it can be considered a victory for the defense. The fewer total yards the offense travels during its possession, the bigger the victory for the defense. And when the defense gains possession of the ball off a turnover, well, that's icing on the cake.

Scoring Methods

Part of what makes football fun for new fans is its simple scoring system. There are only a handful of ways for a team to put points on the board.

The vast majority of points are scored by the offense, but the defense and special teams can score points, too. Teams that capitalize in those areas tend to win ballgames.

Let's review the ways football teams are able to score points, with an explanation for each method.

How the Offense Scores

The offense has four methods of scoring points:

- A touchdown, worth 6 points
- A field goal, worth 3 points
- A 2-point conversion, worth—you guessed it—2 points
- An extra point, worth 1 point

Of course, every offense wishes to score touchdowns rather than field goals. To do so, an offensive player must cross the opposing team's goal line while maintaining possession of the football. Teams can accomplish this by either passing or rushing with the football, or having a player fall on top of a loose ball in the end zone.

When an offense has gotten near the goal line but is faced with unfriendly circumstances on fourth down, the coach is likely to order a field goal. This forces the placekicker (sometimes just called the kicker) to successfully kick the ball through the uprights, or goal posts, for 3 points.

QUICK HIT

Teams can score 3 points on a drop kick. To successfully complete a drop kick, a player must drop the ball and let it hit the ground before kicking it through the uprights. The modern football's shape makes it a difficult kick, and it's rarely attempted at any level.

After every touchdown, the ball is placed at the 2-yard line where the offense has the choice of kicking the ball through the uprights for an extra point, or passing or running it over the goal line for 2 points. Most pro and college teams choose to kick the extra point unless the coach feels it's in his best interest to go for the 2-point conversion.

FUN FACT

At the high school and college levels, the ball is placed on the 3-yard line for a point after attempt.

How the Defense Scores

The defense has two methods of scoring points, although defensive scoring is far less common:

- A touchdown, worth 6 points
- A safety, worth 2 points

Like the offense, whenever a defensive player crosses his opponent's goal line with the football, his team is awarded 6 points. This can happen when a defender intercepts a pass or collects a fumble and advances it over the goal line.

A safety most commonly occurs when a defensive player tackles an offensive player inside the offense's own end zone. It can also be the result of an offensive player running out of bounds in his own end zone and when the offense is called for a holding penalty in the end zone.

Safeties are rare because offenses usually do all they can to keep their players outside the end zone when faced with the possibility of giving up the safety. Another plus for the defense: following the safety, the offense is forced to punt, or kick, the ball from its 20-yard line back to the team that just scored the safety.

 FUN FACT

The popular term for when a defender picks up a fumble and returns it for a score is *scoop-and-score*. An interception returned for a score is often referred to as a *pick-six*.

Field goal and extra point attempts are considered part of special teams scoring, even though they're often credited as offensive points. The special teams can also score a touchdown by returning a kick or a punt to the end zone, or by blocking a kick or punt and returning the fumbled ball to the end zone. If a team blocks a punt out of the back of the end zone, 2 points are awarded for a safety.

The Least You Need to Know

- Each of the game officials is responsible for watching a particular area of the field.
- At the start of each play, the offense and defense position their players around an imaginary line called the line of scrimmage.
- The offense has four downs to advance the ball 10 or more yards. This continues until the offense fails to do so or scores.
- There are many ways a team can score—on offense, defense, and special teams—but nothing trumps a touchdown.

It All Comes Down to the Fundamentals

In This Chapter

- The different types of blocks
- How to pass and catch the ball properly
- The different stances players use at the start of each play
- The quarterback's moves

No matter how talented a team is, or how lucky it is over the course of a season, it won't have success if its players don't adhere to the game's fundamentals.

Every team must block and tackle well. The passers must throw properly and the receivers catch properly. The things players learn at the very basic levels of the game carry through all the way up to the professional game, and the teams that fail to take care of the fundamentals—doing the very basic things the right way—are the teams that fail to reach their goals. It's that simple.

Blocking

Every offensive football player must block, not just the big guys stretched across the offensive line. Sometimes even the quarterback can become an active blocker and must sacrifice his body for the sake of a few extra yards.

The skill position players—those players who line up either in the offensive backfield or at wide receiver—not only have to block, but they're also the difference-makers between good plays and big plays. When teams have wide receivers who block well, they tend to have success running plays to the outside, where sometimes the only thing standing between a running back and the end zone are his receiver teammate and the defender lined up over the receiver.

Blocking is technique, heart, and attitude. Players must practice the art of blocking to get better at it, and continue to practice it to stay good at it.

Every position uses different types of blocks, each with its own proper technique. The stalk block and drive block are two of the most common blocking types.

The Stalk Block

For wide receivers and other players blocking in open space, away from the line of scrimmage, a stalk block is an effective method of keeping an opposing defender away from the ball carrier. Stalk blocking requires the offensive player to read when the defender intends to make a play for the ball carrier and then stop, or break down, in front of the defender using a series of chopping steps and punching motions toward him.

The Drive Block

Anyone coming out of a stance to block a defender within reach can use the drive block. Its principles are based on power: get low into the defender, and use leverage to drive him backward.

It's all science: mass + velocity = momentum. On run plays coming through the offensive line, linemen use the drive block to clear space in an otherwise crowded area. Guards are the best at it; they are positioned low to the ground with a strong base to drive with.

The Trap Block

Trap blocking is a favorite of high school and college programs. One lineman allows his defender to go free. Thinking the lineman missed a block or forgot about him, the defender then pushes toward the offensive backfield, where a lineman coming from the other side (a pulling guard or tackle) catches him by surprise.

Trap blocks give the pulling lineman a good angle to block with. The offense usually runs through the point of the trap, waiting for the trapped defender to get cleared out by the pulling lineman.

The Reach Block

When a lineman desires to block the defender one spot down from him on either side, he must make a reach block. This requires that he get out of his stance quickly to reach the assigned defender.

The Slide Block

When the line, as a unit, each takes a horizontal step left or right, it's called slide protection. This can assist when a passer rolls out in that direction, or for counter plays where the protection slides left and the ball carrier fakes that direction before cutting back to the right.

Man-on-Man Blocking

Linemen take on the players lined up over them, or directly across the line of scrimmage, in man-on-man or big-on-big blocking. In some cases, a lineman has two players lined up on him, or no one at all.

To remedy this, at the start of the snap, the line counts off the defense, so each lineman knows who he has on that play.

Zone Blocking

The opposite of man-on-man, zone blocking has proven effective for small, more agile linemen at the pro level, but has also been incorporated throughout all levels. Players like it because the assignment never changes, regardless of what arrangement the defense puts its men in.

 FUN FACT

Zone blocking was popularized by Alex Gibbs, an offensive line coach who helped make the Denver Broncos one of the NFL's most dominant rushing teams in the 1990s and early 2000s.

The general concept is that linemen don't block an assigned man in a zone blocking scheme, but rather protect an area. Coaches tell them not to let anyone cross their face, which simply means no defender must be permitted past or through their area of turf.

If a lineman doesn't have a defender in his area, he's asked to help assist a nearby lineman.

Tackling

A defensive player's primary objective is to tackle the player with the ball. The defense works as a unit to do this and must take the proper angle when pursuing the person with the ball. When it's time to make the play, however, it's all about having good technique and finishing the job.

To tackle properly, a player should have his head in front of the ball carrier's body and his arms wrapped around the player's waist. To avoid neck injuries, the tackler's head should always be up and never down. When the tackler has a good grasp on the ball carrier, he squeezes him tight and powers him to the ground.

The tackler's legs act as the base from which he draws power on the tackle, and his arms are merely tools to hold the ball carrier tight. If a defender tries to *arm tackle* a player, he often loses his grasp and is unsuccessful.

GRIDIRON GAB

An **arm tackle** occurs when a defender does not use proper form to bring down a ball carrier, using only one arm. These tackles are dangerous for the defender and far less successful than a textbook tackle.

To limit injuries, all levels of the game have made certain types of tackles illegal. Defenders are not allowed to grab any part of the helmet or to attack the neck area to bring a ball carrier to the ground. One illegal tackle, called a horse collar, occurs when a defender reaches inside the back of a player's uniform and pulls him down.

Passing

Legendary Ohio State coach Woody Hayes liked to say, only three things can happen on a pass, and two of them ain't good. The point is that passers must be perfect with the ball; otherwise, an incompletion or turnover awaits. Successful passing begins with the proper throw.

When the ball leaves the quarterback's hand just right, it spirals through the air without disruption. A pass that spirals travels farther and is easier for the intended receiver to catch. If a quarterback fails to put the right spin on the ball, he'll throw a *duck*, which hangs in the air and is vulnerable to being intercepted by the defense.

> **GRIDIRON GAB**
>
> A **duck** is a pass that lacks a good spiral and wobbles through the air after it leaves the quarterback's hand.

To get a good spiral, the quarterback must grip the football with his throwing hand in such a way that it's comfortable to hold but spins tightly off his fingertips upon release.

Some quarterbacks put all four fingers along the laces of the ball. Most position two or three fingers on the laces and the index finger somewhere closer to the nose of the ball. The thumb goes on the other side.

When ready to throw, the quarterback turns his nonthrowing shoulder toward his target and winds the ball back to his ear and then follows through to throw it, snapping his wrist as he releases the ball. If a ball is thrown properly, the throwing hand—or more specifically, the thumb on the throwing hand—will point downward after the release.

Catching

Catching the football the right way can hurt. It burns the fingertips, especially if the ball's coming from a quarterback who *puts a lot of mustard on the ball*. But catching the ball with the hands is important, as balls caught with the body or uniform tend to bounce off and result in dropped passes.

> **GRIDIRON GAB**
>
> **Putting mustard on the ball** refers to when a quarterback throws a football will a lot of velocity, versus making a soft pass.

To catch a pass thrown waist high or higher, a receiver creates a triangle with his hands, touching the tips of both of his index fingers and his thumbs. He should try to look the ball in through that window. For passes thrown lower than waist high, the receiver should keep his palms up, with his pinkies next to one another.

For both styles of catches, the receiver must also hold his arms away from his body and keep his elbows bent. This helps create a cushion away from his body so he can absorb the velocity of the pass. His fingers should always be relaxed and bent.

The Proper Stance

Each position has a bit different stance, but at the core of every great stance are balance, comfort, and the ability to explode upon the snap of the ball.

The *two-*, *three-*, and *four-point stances* are all common for linemen. Each point represents a player's limb that comes in contact with the ground:

- In a two-point stance, the player stands comfortably with his knees bent and his hands resting on both knees.
- In a three-point stance, a player has both legs anchored and one hand on the ground to push off with.
- The four-point stance puts a player on all fours. This offers him the potential to get in low on the opponent but is a difficult stance to stand up from.

Offensive linemen mostly use a three-point stance but occasionally may favor a two-point stance for pass plays because it allows them to get into their pass protection quicker.

Interior defensive linemen use the three- or four-point stance, while defensive ends use either a three-point or a variation of a two-point stance.

WORDS OF WISDOM

Build your empire on the firm foundation of fundamentals.

—Legendary college coach Lou Holtz

Both linebackers and running backs prefer the two-point stance because it allows them good vision of the playing field at the time of the snap, and because it is easy to move out of. Some running backs, particularly the fullback, favor a three-point stance for its explosiveness.

The receivers and defensive backs almost always line up in a two-point stance. For wide receivers, the stance is a bit different. They stand with one leg out in front of the other, arms draped to their sides, knees bent. This allows them to explode off the snap into their pass route—the steps, moves, and direction in which a receiver runs on a passing down to reach the intended location where he can catch the football. The defensive backs stand in a two-point stance, except their feet are tighter together than a linebacker's or lineman's would be in a two-point stance to allow the defensive back to backpedal as he covers the pass route.

At the line of scrimmage and behind, or *under* the center, the quarterback is almost in a seated stance, bending down to accept the ball when it's snapped. The quarterback must be able to make a quick step away from the center after securing the football so he doesn't get tangled as the center comes out of his stance.

GRIDIRON GAB

In football, **over** and **under** mostly refer to a player's positioning on the field. A defensive lineman, for example, may line up over an offensive lineman, meaning he is directly across from that player.

The Quarterback Drop

On passing downs, quarterbacks under center must take a series of steps to set up in the *pocket*. Depending on the play, or the level of protection he has, the quarterback takes a different number of steps.

GRIDIRON GAB

The **pocket** is the imaginary zone where the quarterback sets up to pass the ball. It's as wide as the distance between where his two offensive tackles line up and stretches several yards deep behind the line of scrimmage.

A quarterback uses a *one-* or *two-step drop* for passes that need to get out quickly, such as outside screens and slant routes (see Chapter 9 for a list of passing routes). The quarterback simply takes one step back after receiving the snap from center, turns, and fires the ball at his intended target. As simple as it sounds, quarterbacks often have the most difficulty perfecting this drop.

For a *three-step drop*, the quarterback takes three steps away from center, using the third step to plant with. This drop is good for quick-striking teams that use a lot of intermediate passes, such as curls or comeback routes, and crossing patterns.

The *five-step* and *seven-step drops* are used to set up deeper routes that take the receivers longer to get into. The farther away a quarterback is from the line, the more vulnerable he is to outside pass rushers, but the better he can see the field.

Pro and college teams favor a five-step drop but have plays requiring all varieties. High school teams use all drops as well, but tend to throw more short passes and therefore use shorter drops.

The Least You Need to Know

- Offensive players use a variety of blocks to keep defenders away from the ball carrier.
- A good tackle should have but one goal: to (legally) stop the ball carrier's motion.
- Players catch with their hands, not their bodies.
- Many different types of stances are all used to serve a different purpose for the offensive or defensive player.

Player Accessories

In This Chapter

- All the protective gear players wear
- The uniform and its numbering system
- Sacred property—the playbook
- Other equipment you might see

Without his uniform, pads, and helmet, a football player would be just a man. With those things, however, he can be a warrior. But a player's attire offers more than just protection from harm and a feeling of invincibility. It provides him with an identity and bonds him with the other players on his team.

Fans know their players by the emblems on the helmet and the stripes on the uniform. Those colors tell the fans, "This is my team," and a player's number tells his fans, "This is my guy."

Player equipment has been evolving since the start of the game and will continue to evolve as designers find new ways of dressing and protecting the players underneath all that attire.

The Protective Pads

There was a time in football lore when padding made a player seem soft, not tough. Today's players know better, and pro teams are especially concerned with providing each player with the most effective pads because each player represents an investment the team is trying to protect.

All of a player's essential joints or areas of vulnerability are protected by a different pad. Shoulder pads are designed to protect a player's shoulders and sternum areas. There are different sizes of shoulder pads to accommodate different positions. For example, a quarterback's shoulder pads allow for more arm mobility—something a lineman may not need.

The elbow, knee, and hip pads are all lightweight but effective in limiting the risk of injury to those areas.

Quarterbacks, running backs, wide receivers, and other players who may be vulnerable to taking hits to the rib cage wear flak jackets (lightweight undershirts that offer extra padding).

The Head Gear

Nothing is more worth protecting than a player's head. The helmet he wears contains special padding inside to absorb hits and reduce the threat of him sustaining a concussion. Modern helmets can be inflated in different spots to achieve a perfect fit all around. The team's training staff can add or release air to get a tight and comfortable fit.

The helmet's chinstrap buckles on both sides of the helmet near the ear hole and helps keep everything snug. Players wear a mouth guard to limit potential damage to the mouth and teeth and also to further prevent the possibility of sustaining a concussion.

PENALTY!

Players can be penalized if their chinstrap isn't buckled or if they're not wearing their mouth guard prior to the snap of the ball.

To protect the player's face, each helmet has a facemask. The mask helps keep objects from injuring a player's eyes, nose, or mouth. For many years, quarterbacks, punters, and kickers wore helmets with just a single bar across the front to protect their face. The idea was that fewer bars on the facemask allowed the player to have better vision. For safety reasons, leagues no longer allow the single-bar facemasks.

Some players wear visors in their helmets. This windshieldlike screen offers a player's eyes additional protection.

The Uniform

When the home team takes the field, the first things fans will identify are the colors on the player uniforms. Each pro team has its own set of colors and designs, and that makes each uniform unique. (That's mostly true of college and high school football, too, although the number of teams at those levels makes it nearly impossible not to duplicate certain patterns.) Each team has two sets of uniforms: colored dress for home games and white dress for away games.

QUICK HIT

The silver star on the helmet helps give the Dallas Cowboys one the most recognizable uniforms in the NFL. The University of Notre Dame's golden helmet helps distinguish that team from other college programs.

The top portion of the uniform, the jersey, stretches over the shoulder pads and tucks into the pants, which meet the socks at a point just below the knees.

Jerseys feature numbers on the front and back, and at most levels, the player's last name is also located on the back, across the top of the numbers. Numbers run from 1 to 99, and different positions are required to wear certain numbers. For example, a lineman is not able to wear a jersey number in the 20s, just as a running back may not wear a jersey number in the 70s.

FUN FACT

Hall of Fame center Jim Otto wore the number 00 during his playing days in Oakland in the 1960s and 1970s. The NFL no longer allows players to wear 0 or 00.

Here's a quick breakdown of which NFL players may wear which numbers:

1 through 9	Quarterbacks, punters, and kickers
10 through 19	Quarterbacks, punters, kickers, and wide receivers
20 through 39	Running backs and defensive backs
40 through 49	Running backs, defensive backs, and tight ends
50 through 59	Linebackers and offensive linemen
60 through 79	Offensive and defensive linemen
80 through 89	Wide receivers and tight ends
90 through 99	Defensive linemen and linebackers

What an NFL player wears in addition to the assigned uniform is scrutinized heavily by a monitor hired to ensure each uniform is in compliance with league rules. For example, players cannot wear torn sleeves or excessive jewelry. If a player tapes up his shoes, the tape must be the same color as the shoe or transparent. The league is very strict about these things, and the fines grow in amount for players who become repeat offenders.

The NFL has strict policies about wearing branding of any kind, so players cannot wear arm bands or socks with unauthorized logos. It also fines players large sums of money for writing personal messages on any portion of their uniform.

The Footwear

Players wear special shoes with cleats designed to grip the surface of the field and make it easier for the player to change direction.

Cleat sizes range generally from $\frac{1}{2}$ to 1 inch, and each cleat can be screwed in or out of the player's shoe and replaced with another.

Teams carry different-size cleats for all kinds of game conditions and field surfaces. For muddy or wet conditions, a player will use a longer cleat, which offers him more grip on the unstable and slippery surface. For dry and faster surfaces, such as artificial turf, a player is more likely to use a shorter cleat that allows him to run faster.

Different positions have different traction needs. Linemen, for example, care more about stable footing and less about raw speed, so a longer cleat is a better fit. Running backs and wide receivers, on the other hand, care about the ability to run fast and change direction quickly, so whenever possible, they'll use a smaller cleat.

It's not uncommon to see players change cleats during a game as the weather changes, or if the original cleat becomes ineffective.

The Playbook

Of course, no football player is complete without his playbook. This sacred book, often a three-ring binder, contains the formations, play assignments, and terminology unique to that team's system for offense or defense. Without it, a player wouldn't know in which direction to start running.

Players study the playbook and are often quizzed on where they need to be and what their role is on each play. Some teams have very complex systems, and therefore have a playbook that's thicker than the Manhattan telephone directory. Other teams make a point of keeping things simple and easy to understand and have much lighter playbooks.

When first-year players, or rookies, arrive at camp, the playbook is the first thing handed to them, and when a player is cut from the roster, the playbook is the one thing the team insists on collecting before the player is free to leave the locker room. The playbook is top secret stuff, not to be shared with outsiders.

Other Player Equipment and Gadgets

Football is always evolving, and officials are constantly searching for ways to make the players safer, to help them perform better, and to make the game more technologically savvy.

Let's take a look at some of the latest equipment and gadgets you might see your favorite player using.

Football Gloves

It used to be that gloves were for cold-weather games, but players at every position now wear specialized football gloves on game days. The gloves are light and thin and offer a special tacky surface for holding the football.

Wide receivers most commonly wear gloves to take a little of the sting off of catching sharply thrown passes. For some receivers, though, the gloves can eliminate a player's natural feel for the football and result in dropped balls.

 FUN FACT

NFL Most Valuable Player and Super Bowl winner Kurt Warner was one of the rare quarterbacks who preferred wearing gloves to pass the football. The majority of quarterbacks feel most comfortable gripping the ball with their bare hands.

There is little downside to wearing gloves for defenders or special teams players. Still some do, and some do not. It's a matter of preference ... unless the game is in frigid conditions, in which case gloves become a matter of necessity.

The Wrist Coach

Players use wrist coaches to help them decipher plays during the game. These wristbandlike devices contain small sheets of paper tucked inside a plastic sleeve. Think of it as a cheat sheet. When a coach calls in the play, the wrist coach gives the quarterback specific instruction so he can relay it to the other players in the huddle. Some high school and college programs with complex playbooks require all their offensive players wear a wrist coach, and defensive players (usually just the captain) also use wrist coaches for defensive play calls.

Eye Black and Nasal Strips

Some players at all levels choose to use eye black for games during which the sun or stadium lights might impact their vision. The greasy substance is applied below each eye to reduce glare.

Players sometimes also use nasal strips. These band-aid-like strips help open the nasal passage, allowing the player to breathe better during the game.

The Helmet Transmitter

The NFL allows transmitting devices to be placed inside the helmets of one offensive and one defensive player. This allows coaches to communicate with the player without the use of hand signals.

Before this technology, coaches needed to signal formations and plays to the quarterback or defensive captain on each down—a system still used by most high school and college programs. The transmitter has made communicating easier and reduced the threat of coaches being able to "steal" the opposing team's signals before each play.

The player wearing the transmitter is identified with a green dot on the back of his helmet, and only one coach is allowed to speak to the player throughout the game. The coach can communicate with the player for 15 seconds prior to the start of each play.

The Least You Need to Know

- The padding and air pockets in a football player's helmet can be adjusted to custom fit each player and maximize protection.
- Only certain positions can wear certain numbers on uniforms.
- Players use different-length spikes based on the position they play and the condition of the field.
- The size and complexity of the playbook depends on the team.
- Wrist coaches and helmet transmitters ease the flow of communication between coaches and players on the field.

The Playing Field and Equipment

In This Chapter

- All about the ball
- The lines and markings on the field and what they mean
- The importance of the red zone
- The different types of fields and stadiums

In the field of play, virtually anything goes in the fast and sometimes violent world of football. But when a player steps just a foot outside those lines, he is forced to live by the rules of the rest of society.

The playing field's outer boundaries provide structure for the game and give shape to the strategy coaches employ. The field's many lines act as checkpoints for teams on the move, and its unique numbering system and all its special zones help give the game mystique.

The Ball

The football is distinct because it's one of the few balls that's not perfectly round. Called a pigskin because a pig's bladder was once used as partial material, a football has an inflated rubber inner skin with a leather outer coating. It measures approximately 11 inches from point to point, with a circumference of roughly 21 inches the short way around the ball, and roughly 28 inches the long way around. A regulation football weighs between 14 and 15 ounces.

QUICK HIT

Fans may see quarterbacks and kickers attempting to squeeze a football before the start of the game or during a break in the action. This is to soften up the ball's hard surface, if only a little, to make it easier to handle.

The football fits comfortably into the crook of a ball carrier's arm, making it more difficult for defenders to pry out of his grasp than, say, a round ball would be.

The modern football was designed to throw. At the top side of the ball are eight white laces that hold the ball together and help quarterbacks grip the ball. Without the laces, quarterbacks would have a difficult time putting the proper spin on the ball to create a spiral throw.

In professional football, it's the home team's responsibility to supply enough game balls for the contest. If the stadium is open to the elements (has no enclosing roof), the home team must prepare 36 balls. (In case rain or snow causes balls to get wet and slick, teams want more dry balls ready to use.) In a domed stadium, the home team need only prepare 24 balls.

FUN FACT

Prior to the start of each game, game officials inspect each of the designated game balls to ensure they're properly inflated and of the right dimensions.

The Field Dimensions

First, the basics:

- The length of the football field is 120 yards, or 360 feet, with 10 yards allotted on both ends to create each team's end zone.

- So not counting the end zones, the playing field is 100 yards long.

- The width of the football field measures 53⅓ yards, or 160 feet.

The lines that create the boundaries for the field all have special names:

- The *sidelines* outline the outer edges of each of the longest sides of the playing field.

- The *end lines* outline the outer edges of each of the shortest sides of the playing field.

- The *goal lines* are marked 10 yards inside the end lines on both ends of the field.

Any activity outside of the end lines or the sidelines is ruled out of bounds.

With the exception of leagues that use special rules, such as the Arena and Canadian Leagues, every football playing field—high school, college, and professional—is the same size.

The Yard Markers

Lines are painted to outline the field and mark every 5-yard interval on the 100-yard field of play, thus giving the field its nickname, gridiron. The middle of the field lengthwise is designated as the 50-yard line, and the yard numbers count backward on both sides as they head toward each goal line. This is important, as it gives each team an equal amount of territory to defend.

Two lines of hash marks are located 1 yard apart running parallel to each sideline. When a play is blown dead, or ruled over, outside the hash mark, either because the ball carrier was tackled or he went out of bounds, the ball is spotted, or placed, on the nearest hash mark on the yard line where the player was spotted. By moving the ball back to the hash mark, and thus back toward the middle of the field, it opens the entire field to the offense at the start of each play. If the play is ruled dead *inside* the hash marks, the ball is spotted where the runner was ruled down.

The orange markers surrounding each end zone are called pylons. They stand roughly 1 foot high and are anchored by the bean-bag-like filler material inside.

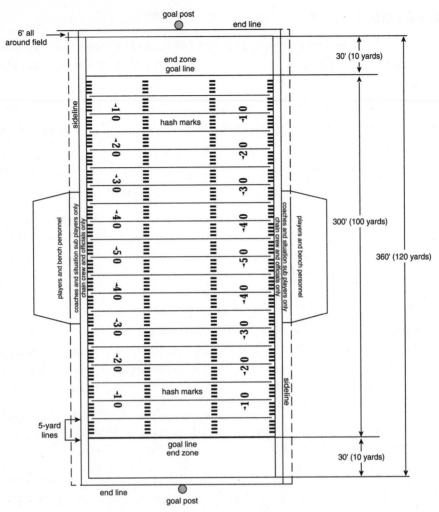

Other than a few minor exceptions, the football field fans see at the local high school is the same as the fields used by college and professional teams.

The Invisible Areas on the Field

Some of the areas most important to the game are not officially marked on the field. Instead, these are zones that have been created to better strategize or explain the game. Let's take a look.

The Red Zone

When teams are positioned anywhere within 20 yards of the opponent's goal line, they are said to be in the red zone, a place on the field offering high-percentage scoring potential.

Getting into the red zone is an accomplishment of sorts. It puts the defense on its heels and offers confidence to the offense knowing that a field goal is all but assured.

Coaches (and fans) expect their team to score anytime it reaches this magical destination, and they are often bitterly disappointed when the team fails to walk away with at least 3 points.

 FUN FACT

Like many terms used in football, *red zone* is also a term used in military actions, designating an area under attack.

The Pocket

The quarterback's comfort zone is called the pocket. In this area directly behind and guarded by the offensive line, the quarterback has maximum pass protection to search for open receivers to throw to.

When a quarterback is flushed from the pocket—usually due to defenders chasing after him—he is forced to make plays with his feet or more difficult throws while on the run.

Sometimes you might hear game announcers refer to a collapsing pocket. This simply means the defense has broken through the offense's blockers, shrinking the area where the quarterback has to work.

A pocket passer is a quarterback who operates most comfortably from the pocket. (Some quarterbacks are most comfortable making plays on the run, away from the pocket.)

The Flats

The flats are the areas between the hash marks and the sidelines on both sides of the playing field, not too far beyond the line of scrimmage.

It's an area where offenses like to throw the ball because fewer defenders are stationed in the flats, thus presenting the quarterback with good odds of completing a pass.

Turf Styles

At one time, football field surfaces came in a few options: grass, dirt, or sand. Grass fields were inexpensive to grow but challenging to maintain. In cities like San Francisco, for example, harsh weather wears heavy on a grass field, often leading to sloppy conditions. For teams that have fast players, this can be a problem.

The development of synthetic surfaces helped change the game—and reduced the amount of upkeep needed to manage the field. No more fixing areas of sod, no more painting the lines each week, and no more mud fields.

Artificial turf, first developed in the 1960s, is a more compact surface that allows players to run faster than they can on grass. Over time, though, those same players began to favor grass again for its forgiving surface. When a player attempts to plant his foot into the artificial turf to make a cut, it sticks, often making the player's knees and ankles vulnerable to serious injury. Players also commonly get *turf toe* playing on artificial surfaces.

GRIDIRON GAB

Turf toe is a nagging injury athletes suffer to their big toe area during the course of play. It can hold football players out of action for several weeks because it makes running and normal athletic movements extremely painful.

Modern advancements have helped make artificial surfaces safer and more grasslike. Now many stadiums use field turf, which has fibers that closely resemble blades of grass and a filler made of sand and rubber that offers the same cushion effect natural turf does.

The Sidelines

Each team is given one side of the field where its coaches, players, medical staff, and equipment are kept during the game. Even farther from the field are benches where linemen sit by other linemen, linebackers sit by linebackers, the quarterback talks to his receivers, and coaches relay teaching points.

It's also where the trainers attend to injured players and where coaches grab the attention of the game officials following a bad call.

The Goal Posts

Positioned in the middle of each end line is a goal post. It consists of three parts:

- A thick post that's planted in the turf
- A crossbar
- Two uprights

The crossbar is 18½ feet long, parallel to the end line, and 10 feet above the ground. At each end of it is an upright measuring 20 feet tall.

> **FUN FACT**
>
> The height of each upright is irrelevant. As far as the rules are concerned, each upright stretches to the clouds. No matter how high a kicker kicks the football, it must cross over the crossbar and inside the uprights.

For many years, the goal posts were positioned at the front end of the goal line, but too many players ran into the post and the risk of injury was too big to ignore. (And organizers hoped to encourage more touchdown attempts and fewer field goals.) In 1974, the goal posts were relocated to the back of the end zone.

Other Objects Seen on Game Day

A number of other tools or devices are used on game day to enhance the fans' viewing experience, or to make life easier on the players.

The Kicking Tee

One team kicks the ball to the opponent after each score and at the start of both halves. The rubber object used to hold the ball while the kicker gets ready to propel it high into the air and deep down the field is called a tee. The tee has three pegs that rest on the ground and a few angled prongs on top to hold the ball in place before the kicker sends it sailing.

After the ball is kicked, a designated person from the kicking team (usually a ball boy) runs onto the field to remove it from the field and dashes back to the sideline while play continues. (And if you're curious: the ball boy doesn't cause a penalty for too many people on the field. That penalty only applies to the number of *players* on the field.)

The Chain and the First Down Marker

For many years, viewers needed to rely on an orange stripe placed on each sideline to tell them where their team needed to get to in order to gain a first down. Technology has made this easier, thanks to an invisible line the behind-the-scenes TV people add so television viewers can see the first down line. While this works for TV viewers, the people on the field of play can't see the added line.

The only exact measurement on the field is the chain. Managed by three individuals called the chain gang, the chain consists of two posts—one to mark, or spot, the original line of scrimmage and the other to spot the first down—and a chain measuring exactly 10 yards long that runs between the markers. Another person in the chain gang carries a separate marker not attached to the chain that's positioned wherever the ball is spotted for that particular play.

In situations too close for the game officials to call, the chain gang brings the chain onto the field for a measurement. If any part of the football touches the most forward-pointing chain, a first down is awarded.

QUICK HIT

Coaches often ask for a measurement if they think their team has achieved (or denied the other team of) a first down, but the game officials ultimately decide when to bring the chain gang onto the field.

Football Stadiums

There's no better way to watch a football game than to be in the stadium, squeezed in among tens of thousands of other fans. The noise and the smells of the football stadium can definitely intensify the experience.

Outdoor stadiums offer the rough-and-tough feel of football of yesteryear. Indoor stadiums offer comfort and environment control. Both have their perks.

In terms of capacity, most NFL stadiums hold between 60,000 to 70,000 fans, while several college football stadiums hold more than 100,000 fans.

QUICK HIT

A number of the largest American football stadiums belong to college teams in the Big Ten conference. Penn State's Beaver Stadium has a capacity of more than 107,000, followed by the University of Michigan (106,000) and Ohio State (102,000).

Beyond the field and the stands, every football stadium has features that make it unique and special. Considered architectural masterpieces, today's stadiums have become more and more lavish with their details and amenities. In 2009, the Dallas Cowboys opened a state-of-the-art $1 billion stadium that can house 80,000 fans on game days, with additional capacity outside the stadium, and the world's largest high-definition television screen.

The Least You Need to Know

- The outer boundaries of a football field are 120 yards long and $53\frac{1}{3}$ yards wide.
- The hash marks give game officials a place to spot the football near the middle of the field.
- Artificial surfaces can lead to playing injuries; grass is preferred, but it's difficult for teams to maintain.
- The goal post is the forklike structure at the back of the end zone where kickers aim to make successful extra point and field goal attempts.
- The average pro football stadium holds between 60,000 to 70,000 fans; the biggest football stadiums belong to universities.

The Men Pulling the Strings

In This Chapter

- The many things a head coach manages
- Assistant coaches—team micromanagers
- What the owner and the team's management oversee
- Important men worth knowing

Every ship needs a captain, right? Well, a football team wouldn't leave the shoreline without a head coach to push it on its way. The coach is the one who nurtures the team from infancy to adulthood, teaching it all it needs to know about X's and O's, proper technique, and finding inner strength when times get tough.

Coaches come in all shapes, sizes, and temperaments. But each must earn the respect of his players, whether he's well liked or not. Not every coach needs to be fierce or intimidating, or even have been a successful player; great coaches merely need to be great teachers, able to share a common message and get every player and coach in the organization to buy into executing the plan.

Any coach will tell you it's a tough life. The hours are long, even for high school coaches, and the profession takes a toll on a coach's personal relationships away from the game. It's common for a coach to work into the late hours of the night, studying game film, scripting new plays, hoping to gain a competitive advantage.

But for any coach, the reward of seeing his team win on game day always outweighs the sacrifice.

The Head Coach

In some camps, the head coach is the loudest barker on the field; in others, he lets his many assistants do the barking for him. Whatever his style or personality, a head coach must be accountable for getting his team to act as one functioning unit on the field. When the team wins games, people label the coach a genius; when they lose games, regardless of the reason, the coach is the one held most responsible.

To succeed as a coach requires practice, coordination, practice, teaching, practice, strategizing, and, well … more practice.

Coaches are obsessed with getting things right. It's not uncommon for a coach to spend hours upon hours going over a single play until his team understands it as well as the play can possibly be understood. And even then, he'll insist on the play being repeated during practice.

FUN FACT

In March 2010, Calvin Coolidge Senior High School in Washington, D.C., hired 29-year-old Natalie Randolph to be its head coach. At the time, Randolph was believed to be the country's only female head coach of a varsity football program.

The head coach is the figurehead for the team, even though he's rarely the "boss" of the club. At the college and pro level, the head coach is often as much of a local celebrity to the fans as his top players. Head coaches have television programs, serve as company spokesmen, and receive invites to black-tie affairs.

But there's little time for play because coaches have an assortment of duties that keep them plenty busy.

The one duty most identify with the coach is to motivate his players before each game and during the halftime break. Good coaches can use words to motivate a lesser team to overcome the odds and to bring a better team back from the grip of despair. Not every great coach is a great public speaker, but those who possess the quality are able to work wonders other coaches cannot.

FUN FACT

The most famous speech a coach ever delivered was prior to Notre Dame's clash with Army in 1928. Notre Dame head coach Knute Rockne shared with his men a request former Fighting Irish star George Gipp had shared on his deathbed in 1920. Whenever times got tough, Gipp told Rockne, have your men dig deep, and "Win just one for the Gipper." Notre Dame defeated a previously unbeaten Army squad that afternoon, 12–6. The speech was immortalized in the 1940 film *Knute Rockne, All American.*

Hollywood has dramatized the head coach as the team's inspirational leader, the man whose words can get the men in uniform to act. But head coaches are responsible for much more than giving pregame speeches. Here are a few of a head coach's many tasks:

- Develop, or endorse, a system of strategy for all facets of the team

- Learn the upcoming opponent's tendencies, or habits, on offense and defense and script a plan to counterattack them

- Select a starting lineup that will best perform against the opponent

- Manage the game clock and make the crucial strategic decisions during the game

- Speak to the press, often both before and after each game

- Evaluate each player's development, both during the season and in the off-season

Coaches never finish everything on their long to-do list because there are always ways to help the team prepare, improve, and, ultimately, succeed. Head coaches are driven by success—or have a deep fear of failure—and thus feel the need to work harder than their peers to ensure their team will reach its goals.

PENALTY!

No head coach's appearance was more distinct than Tom Landry, who wore a fedora and overcoat for much of the time he served as the coach of the Dallas Cowboys, from 1960 to 1989. Due to strict league dress codes, today's NFL coaches are prohibited from wearing more formal attire such as suits, ties, or a fedora.

The Assistant Coaches

No one coach can do it all. To run a successful program, he must delegate responsibilities to his staff of assistant coaches, each one overseeing a different aspect of the team.

There are different levels of assistants:

- *Coordinators* manage one of the three facets of the game—offense, defense, and special teams.

- *Position coaches* work underneath the coordinators to manage only the individual positions.

On game days, some assistant coaches are down on the sideline where they're able to interact with players, while others prefer to sit in a booth high up in the stands where they can get a better view of the action taking place on the field.

No matter where they sit, the primary goal of the entire coaching staff is to act as a single unit working on one wavelength to share the same message with the team's players.

The Coordinators

Football teams have offensive, defensive, and special teams coordinators to manage the three facets of the game. In some cases, a head coach serves as his own offensive or defensive coordinator, especially if he has a keen mind for that side of the ball. But because of the many demands placed on the head coach, he will usually put his faith in each of those individuals to manage the development, and sometimes strategy, for their respective area.

A coordinator develops players to fit into his philosophy, or style, and ensures each member of the unit understands his responsibilities and the overall goal for the unit.

A coordinator also studies the opponent's game film, often comparing notes with the head coach. On game day, the head coach may defer to the coordinator to act as the point of contact between the sideline and the players on the field. This can include having the offensive coordinator give the play to the quarterback prior to each snap, or the defensive coordinator signaling in the formation and assignment to the defensive captain prior to each play.

 QUICK HIT

Top-level professional coordinators can make millions of dollars each year without having to accept all the extra burdens that come with a head coaching post.

Managing one side of the team is no small task. To accomplish all that needs to get done, each coordinator has help ....

The Position Coaches

Below the coordinator on the coaching chain are the individual position coaches, each responsible for those players who play that particular position. A quarterback coach, for example, concerns himself only with the few quarterbacks on the roster and how each player is progressing. During practice, the position coaches are given one-on-one instructional time with their players, usually to work on something for that week's game plan.

The bigger the football program, the more individual position coaches it has on staff. For example, a high school or college team may have just one defensive line coach, while many NFL teams have coaches for both ends and tackles.

The position coach reports back to the rest of the coaching staff on player development. The position coach also offers his input to the head coach and general manager when they decide which players to keep and which to cut loose.

The Management

NFL coaches have enough to worry about while developing personnel and preparing for each opponent. So for the more administrative day-to-day tasks, a general manager comes into play. The general manager sits above the coach on the organization's chain of command.

A few of a pro football general manager's duties include the following:

- Hires and fires administrative staff, talent scouts, and the head coach
- Oversees all aspects of the scouting process
- Manages the selection and termination of all players
- Manages all player and staff contracts
- Speaks to media for matters pertaining to his responsibilities

Like the head coach, the general manager of an NFL team has plenty of help. For example, a team will employ a specialist to manage the team's salary and ensure it's within the budget allowed by the league. This individual, or someone else, represents the team in negotiations with players and reports back to the general manager.

 FUN FACT

A number of men have taken on the dual role of NFL coach and general manager, but few in recent years have been able to manage both jobs successfully. Mike Holmgren was able to coach the Seattle Seahawks to a Super Bowl, but only after he relinquished his role as general manager.

At the high school and college level, the general manager's role is served by the school's athletic director, who manages the logistical details for all the school's athletic programs. An athletic director is also often the buffer between the head coach and the school's administration, and he or she is responsible for managing budgets and travel arrangements.

The Scouts

Scouts watch endless hours of game film to gauge how well a particular player will perform at the next level. For professional scouts, the work involves long trips to college campuses across the country to establish relationships with coaching staff and get firsthand looks at potential new players.

At the college level, assistant coaches serve as the scouting team for the program. College programs usually focus first on recruiting the very best high school prospects from within the region, knowing those athletes may have a stronger bond with the program and thus will be more easily convinced to attend that school. Scouts also focus on targeted areas around the country where they have existing relationships with coaches and former players.

Teams tend to hire former players to serve in their scouting department, but anyone with an eye for talent and a passion for film study has the potential to become a football scout. Keeping the job is a matter of picking players who go on to have successful careers.

The Administration and Owners

Of course, pro teams have an owner looking to put a competitive product on the field (and make a profit each year as well). Owners fall into two general categories:

- Those who prefer to stay away from all the attention
- Those who thirst for the limelight as much as the players do

Both varieties have been proven to work in the NFL.

The owner's primary role is to offer his financial support and encouragement to the men he hired and has empowered to help the team get better. The owner must also act as an ambassador for pro football in his city and work with other owners from around the league to help make decisions aimed to improve the game and strengthen football's viability.

Some owners take a more active role in the organization. Oakland Raiders owner Al Davis, for example, has long kept a say in the team's day-to-day operations and has retained control over some of the key decisions. Davis was the team's coach for many years, and he's always been its most visible spokesman.

FUN FACT

The Green Bay Packers are the only pro sports franchise that's publicly owned. When the club was struggling to stay afloat in the early 1920s, a group of local business leaders rallied with coach Curly Lambeau to establish financial stability. The Packers have held a number of stock sales through the franchise's existence, helping keep America's smallest-market club going.

College and high school teams cannot be owned, but rather, they represent the school and answer to its administration. At the high school level, most decisions are left up to the school's head coach. In matters where final say is needed, either the school district's superintendent or the school board may intervene.

In college, a strong football program can be a valuable asset in helping the university achieve its goals. Football programs can help drive enrollment and draw revenue to help support other athletic clubs. For these reasons, campus administrators keep a close watch on the program's development and often play a role in hiring and firing the coach. The school's chancellor or president may take an active role in the search for a new coach or defer to the athletic director.

And when necessary, the school's administration works with the National Collegiate Athletic Association (NCAA) to investigate alleged misconduct of that particular school's football program.

Names to Know

Vince Lombardi does not own the most wins or the greatest winning percentage in the history of professional football. He is, however, often considered the greatest football coach who ever lived, and along with leaders such as Winston Churchill and John F. Kennedy, he's one of the most quoted men in history. Lombardi led his Green Bay Packers teams to five NFL titles in the 1960s, including wins in the first two Super Bowls played.

WORDS OF WISDOM

I firmly believe that any man's finest hour, the greatest fulfillment of all that he holds dear, is the moment when he has worked his heart out in a good cause and lies exhausted on the field of battle—victorious.

—Vince Lombardi

Before Lombardi, the Packers had Curly Lambeau, who coached the team to six NFL titles, the first of which came in 1929. A native of Green Bay, Lambeau helped change the identity of the small Wisconsin city to what fans around the country know it as today: Title Town.

A rival to both men, George Halas was instrumental in helping grow the NFL. He served as the owner of the Chicago Bears for more than 60 years and as the team's coach for 40 of those years.

Amos Alonzo Stagg was a charter member of both the College Football and Basketball Hall of Fame. His University of Chicago football teams of the late 1800s and early 1900s were highly successful, and Stagg was one of the game's great innovators.

Before a plane crash ended his life in 1931, Knute Rockne had won 105 games and suffered just 12 defeats during his 13-year stay at the University of Notre Dame—a winning percentage no coach, at the pro or Division 1 college level, has been able to duplicate since.

Don Shula won 328 games—more than any other NFL coach. But he's best known for the 1972 season, during which he coached the Miami Dolphins to a perfect record of 16–0.

No coach in the history of the college game has won as many games or coached at a single university as long as Penn State's Joe Paterno, who began his tenure with the Nittany Lions in 1966.

Jerry Jones is one of the most visible owners in all of sports. He purchased the Dallas Cowboys for $150 million in 1989 and doubled the franchise's estimated worth in less than a decade. In 2009, Jones opened a $1 billion state-of-the-art stadium in Dallas.

The most successful coach in recent pro football history has been Bill Belichick, who failed in his first few attempts as a head coach before catching on with the New England Patriots. He is the only coach to have won three Super Bowls in a four-year span.

WORDS OF WISDOM

Anything easy ain't worth a damn!

—Woody Hayes, Ohio State coach from 1951 to 1978

The Least You Need to Know

- The most successful head coaches know how to delegate to their staff.
- Assistant coaches manage more concentrated areas of the team.
- A professional football team's general manager is responsible for finding (or firing) the head coach and assembling the talent.
- Don Shula won more games than any other coach in NFL history; Vince Lombardi is revered as the greatest coach to have ever lived.

We Got the Ball

Touchdowns. Field goals. Long drives and thrilling plays. Yep, the offensive side of the football has it all. Offensive players are also usually the most popular players among fans—and the ones bringing home the largest paychecks. If it all sounds like Hollywood, well, it is (close to it, anyhow).

Part 2 covers all the positions, strategies, penalties, and statistics that pertain to the offensive side of the ball.

The Quarterback Leads the Team

In This Chapter

- The qualities all quarterbacks need to succeed
- Pocket passers versus mobile quarterbacks
- What the cadence is all about
- The types of passes quarterbacks throw

Every team needs a hero. For the offense, 9 times out of 10, that hero is the quarterback. He's the guy whose picture female fans tack up on their wall, and who dads hope their sons will grow up to be like. It's the position kids dream about because the quarterback is the person in charge. He's the one who gets the glory, and the one who often gets chosen to go to Disneyland after his team wins the Super Bowl.

Not every player is cut out to play the position, however. A quarterback must execute perfectly in pressure situations, must have brains and guts, and must have a tolerance for pain. He's got to be Joe Cool, and few people are cool enough to stand behind the center and run the offense.

What They Do for the Team

Not only does the quarterback job description call for someone with intelligence and a strong arm to throw the ball with, but every great quarterback also must be a capable leader. The quarterback is the guy who rallies the offense when it's behind and who keeps everyone focused, no matter how bleak things look on the field.

The great quarterbacks have a quality that rubs off on the rest of the team. Have a winner at quarterback, and chances are your team can accomplish great things. Lack a good quarterback, and you better hold on because the season is going to be a bumpy ride.

FUN FACT

Randall Cunningham was one pro football's most effective running quarterbacks. He averaged 6.4 yards per carry and scored 35 rushing touchdowns during his career.

Another of the quarterback's primary tasks is to relay messages coming from the sideline coaching staff to the rest of the team in the huddle. After accepting the ball from the center, the quarterback sets up the play from there. He either gets the ball to the running back or sets up to pass the ball. He's the catalyst to everything that happens during each offensive play and the player most responsible for a team's success—or failure.

Different Types of Quarterbacks

You think of quarterbacks, and no one particular model comes to mind. That's because different types of quarterbacks bring the offense various advantages by doing different things. Think of Brett Favre, and you think of his arm. Think of Michael Vick, and you think of his feet.

The traditional quarterback, if such a thing exists, would have to be the pocket passer—a guy who sets up 3 to 5 yards behind the line of scrimmage, between where both tackles are positioned, and looks for open receivers to throw to. He must have the patience to wait for plays to develop, and he must have the courage to stand pat while the defense closes in on him.

Mobile quarterbacks are running backs who are able to play the quarterback position. They have excellent speed, can break tackles, and can see things open up down the field. Defenses have to respect a quarterback's option to throw the ball, which holds everyone in place and allows the quarterback to take off running with the ball for big gains. (If the defense chases after the quarterback, he passes over them; if they sit back and wait, he runs for positive yards.) That dual threat is difficult for defenses to prepare for and why more teams are starting to consider mobile quarterbacks.

No one type of quarterback is better than the other, and some offensive systems cater to one style or the other. It doesn't hurt to have both qualities, though, along with an understanding of when to rely on one skill or the other. That was Steve Young, the San Francisco 49ers quarterback of the 1990s, whose feet could make plays and whose arm was as strong and accurate as most any other quarterback in the league. The biggest asset Young had, though, was his brain. He understood when to throw and when to tuck the ball and run. That made him special.

Running the Huddle

In the offensive huddle before each play, no one is allowed to talk but the quarterback—one message, one messenger. And because the quarterback is the chosen player who gets to communicate with the coaching staff, he's the guy who gets to share the message with the others.

It's the quarterback's job to be sure he first understands the play he's been given and then communicates it well to all the other 10 players in the huddle. This may include the *snap count*, the blocking assignments for the offensive line, the lane where the running back and his blockers will attack, and the routes for the receivers.

 GRIDIRON GAB

The **snap count** tells all the players when to begin the play. If the center is to snap the ball the first time the quarterbacks says "Hut" or "Hike," the quarterback will say the play is "on one." If the snap is "on two," it means the ball is to be snapped on the second "Hut"; "on set" indicates to snap the ball on the word *set;* and so on.

The quarterback is also the person responsible for getting everyone in and out of the huddle efficiently, like a cowboy rounding up calves. After he has given the play to the rest of the team, he dismisses everyone from the huddle and they all jog to their spots on the field.

Barking the Cadence

Quarterbacks have to have guts, but they also need a throat able to belt out directions at the line of scrimmage. After breaking the huddle, the quarterback calls out the cadence, a string of colors, numbers, and other code words that offer additional instructions to the players.

Quarterbacks also can use the cadence as a weapon. When a quarterback varies the volume and patterns of his voice to try to draw the defense offside, that's called a hard count. This is commonly seen on third- or fourth-down plays when the offense only has a couple yards to go to get the first down.

PENALTY!

Quarterbacks love to use the cadence to pull defensive players offside. But if the quarterback moves too much during the delivery of his cadence or bobs his head to simulate the start of the snap in an attempt to draw the defense offside, the game officials may penalize him for presnap movement.

Soft-spoken quarterbacks simply cannot make it. The noise coming from the crowd and from both sidelines can drown out the whispers of a timid quarterback.

A quarterback must also be able to clearly annunciate his words. If the players cannot understand the cadence, all that loud talk will fall on deaf ears.

At the end of the cadence, the quarterback accepts the snap from the center and play begins!

Analyzing the Defense

After the snap on passing downs, the quarterback's eyes must tell him the safest place to throw the football. On each play, he has three, four, or sometimes five players running routes—the path or direction a receiver runs on a passing down so he can get to a place where he can catch the ball. The quarterback must identify where the mismatches are and which receiver has the best possible opportunity of making a big play.

He does this through a series of what are called reads. For each passing play, the quarterback has a list telling him the order in which to look at his receivers. The primary receiver on a passing down is the first person the quarterback reads. If the player is open when the quarterback spots him, it's probably already too late; a quarterback must anticipate the open receiver *before* he's open. If the primary receiver is covered, the quarterback will check down, or move, to the second receiver on his list, then the third, and so on. And he must do all this quickly—in a matter of a few seconds. For this reason, few quarterbacks are able to get through more than three checks on any given down.

FUN FACT

Dan Marino of the Miami Dolphins analyzed the defense about as well as any quarterback ever has, which is why he was able to pass for more than 400 touchdowns and 60,000 yards during his professional playing career.

The quarterback must also make decisions before the play based on what he sees. While coming out of the huddle, he evaluates where all 11 defenders are lined up and points out players to his teammates that they should be aware of.

If a quarterback steps up to the line of scrimmage and doesn't think the play he has called will work against the defense he sees, he'll often call an audible, another play from the playbook he believes will work better. The code he yells out alerts the offensive players that he has changed the play, and the cadence gives them the directions they need to execute it. Sometimes it's a bluff—a series of nonsense meant to confuse the defense. Sometimes it's not.

A few quarterbacks call all their plays at the line of scrimmage. Peyton Manning of the Indianapolis Colts, for example, uses a no-huddle offense. Rather than gathering his team in a huddle to deliver the play, he takes them straight to the line of scrimmage, where he waits to see what the defense offers and then shouts out the play and the cadence before the snap. This accomplishes three things:

- It allows the offense to control the tempo at which the game is played.

- It prevents the defense from substituting players.

- It gives the quarterback the opportunity to decide which play will work best for each defense he sees.

Not many coaches run a no-huddle offense, because few quarterbacks are trusted enough to operate it.

Passes, Long and Short

On most passing plays, quarterbacks can choose from three or four routes down the field, some short and some deep (see Chapter 9 for more on the different types of routes). It's the quarterback's job to decide which player to throw to, and to understand the needs of the play and the risks of each throw.

For example, if it's third down and the team needs 12 yards to gain a first down, a quarterback should not throw an 8-yard route to a receiver standing along the sideline with no extra room to run. He needs to throw the ball either to a receiver who is positioned past the first-down marker, or one with the potential to catch the ball and advance it to the first down.

Likewise, a quarterback is probably not going to throw a *bomb* on third down if the team only needs to advance the ball 3 yards and there's a shorter, easier throw to be made.

> **GRIDIRON GAB**
>
> A **bomb** is a pass thrown deep down the field to an intended receiver. Similarly, a *Hail Mary* is a desperation pass deep down the field, usually at the end of either half, in the hopes that a receiver will come down with the ball in the end zone.

Inexperienced quarterbacks, at every level, often make the mistake of trying to throw deeper than they should. Quarterbacks love to connect on the big play even when there's an open receiver somewhere else on the field who's closer.

Coaches must condition a quarterback to decide when to roll the dice and throw long, and when the team only needs for him to throw safer, shorter passes. Most often coaches prefer the latter.

Names to Know and Performances to Remember

No matter how many championships a quarterback wins, or how many passing yards and touchdowns he collects, that player will always be compared to Baltimore Colts quarterback Johnny Unitas, or Johnny U, as he is affectionately called.

For many, Unitas not only defines the position, but the game itself. With his crew cut, black high-top shoes, and crooked walking style, Unitas looked more like Frankenstein's monster than he did a starting quarterback. But there was never a finer field general, nor has any passer dominated his era quite like Unitas did in the 1950s and 1960s.

Unitas finished his career with 290 touchdowns and more than 40,000 yards, and from 1956 to 1960, he threw a touchdown pass in 47 consecutive games—a record that stands today.

One of college football's first great passers was Texas Christian's Davey O'Brien, who completed 110 of 194 passes his senior season. The mark O'Brien left on the college game was so great, in fact, that the Davey O'Brien Award was created to recognize the most outstanding collegiate quarterback each season.

The facts about John Elway's pro career are astounding: he took his Denver Broncos to 5 Super Bowls during his 16-year career, won 148 regular season games, and passed for 300 touchdowns and more than 50,000 yards. In Elway's final two seasons, his team ended the year on top, with Super Bowl victories in 1998 and 1999.

If a quarterback's number-one priority is to win, then Pittsburgh's Terry Bradshaw and San Francisco's Joe Montana are certainly two of the greatest to have ever played the position. Both men won four Super Bowl titles during their careers, and both won a lot of games during the regular season: Montana's team won 71.3 percent of the time, while Bradshaw's Steelers won 67.7 percent of the time.

FUN FACT

The game that made Joe Montana famous was the 1982 NFC Championship Game against the Dallas Cowboys. With 58 seconds remaining, and the 49ers trailing 27–21, Montana rolled from the pocket to his right, backing away from the Dallas defense. Just as he was running out of time—and out of room—Montana sailed the ball to the back of the end zone where Dwight Clark jumped up and caught it for the deciding score in the game. The play is often referred to as "The Catch," but it was a heck of a throw, too.

In terms of raw statistical numbers, Brett Favre is in a league all his own. Favre owns the NFL records for most career attempts, completions, yards, touchdowns, and games won by a quarterback. Oh yeah—he also owns the record for most passes intercepted.

The best quarterbacks of recent years have been Peyton Manning of the Indianapolis Colts and Tom Brady of the New England Patriots. Manning is on pace to break all of Favre's career passing records, while Brady is the most successful big-game quarterback of his generation.

WORDS OF WISDOM

Leadership must be demonstrated, not announced.

—Hall of Fame NFL quarterback Fran Tarkenton

The Least You Need to Know

- Quarterbacks can win games with their arm or their feet. All great quarterbacks should be intelligent and have excellent leadership skills.
- The quarterback acts like a coach on the field and is the only player allowed to talk in the offense's huddle.
- Quarterbacks are required to read the defense as the play transpires; if they don't like what they see before the snap, they can audible.
- Brett Favre holds most of the significant records for pro quarterbacks; Johnny Unitas is the person most identify with the position.

Running Backs Do a Little of Everything

In This Chapter

- Running back types and purposes
- A look at the fullback and what he does
- The tools a running back needs to be successful
- Some of the running plays teams use

Consider the running back the horse that drives the cart where the team needs to go. He's durable, reliable, powerful, and quick when he needs to be.

Of all the skill players, the running back, or back, is the hardest worker. He's never afforded a play off; when he isn't running with the ball and fighting off men twice his size, he's blocking them, running a passing route, or carrying out a fake. The running back is a tool the offense uses on each and every play.

Also true of running backs: they accept a lot of punishment. No other player on the team gets hit or tackled as often as the team's top running back, which is why so many backs retire not long after the age of 30.

What They Do for the Team

Running backs run, catch, and block …. Perhaps the more fitting question is: what *don't* running backs do?

A reliable running back handles the football 20 to 25 times each game, either carrying it on running plays or catching the ball out of the backfield on passing downs, and can account for a large chunk of the total yardage gained by the offense. When a running back is hot, the team often continues to feed him the ball on successive downs until he's stopped.

Some running backs catch a lot of passes, while others catch few, if any. But on passing downs, most any running back can act as a safety net for the quarterback. If no other receiver is open, the running back will find an open area, not far from the quarterback, and make himself available as the last receiving option so the quarterback doesn't have to take a sack from the defense. And on some passing downs, the running back is the first option for the quarterback to consider.

In addition to being one of the offense's lead playmakers, a running back must also serve as a blocker. On passing downs, the running back often is the quarterback's last protector and is forced to take on men much bigger than he. Making a block on a blitzing linebacker coming up the middle of the line, or a defensive back racing off the edge, is a matter of effort and pride. It's something not every back does well, and some backs simply refuse to put in the effort.

FUN FACT

Some of the greatest rushers in the history of the game were also some of the position's best blockers—men like Walter Payton and Emmitt Smith come to mind.

The running back is also his offense's best decoy. Teams fake to one back and then hand off to another, trying to get the defense to follow the first back and lose sight of the second. If a running back does his job and carries out the fake, he'll take a pounding from the confused defense, but it helps his team gain yards.

Fake runs are also an important ally of the passing game. Play-action fakes use a phony hand-off to the running back before the quarterback sets up to pass. If the fake is sold well, the defense converges on the rusher, which allows the receivers to get open down the field.

Different Types of Running Backs

There are different categories of running backs and different types of players within each category. The most common is the halfback, who is often just referred to as the running back, seeing that his primary role is to run with the ball. The fullback's primary job is to block for the running back (more on him in a bit).

Some running backs are large, powerful, and difficult for defenders to take down. These guys are given the ball when the offense has only a short distance to travel and can rely on the running back's power to push the pile forward. Other backs are small, quick, and difficult for defenders to catch. These guys are asked to help the team advance the ball down the field, but sometimes they're removed from the game on plays where their size might be a problem. Other backs are able receivers but cannot be counted on to carry the ball 20 times a game or in short-yardage downs.

The most successful backs to have played the game have a little of everything— enough speed to run away from defenders, reliable hands to catch the ball, and enough power to play on every down in every situation. These running backs are able to get into a rhythm without disruption.

Some teams use several running backs, called specialty backs, to get the job done. They might use a large and powerful runner for short-yardage and goal line situations, a quick back with good hands to catch passes on third-down plays, and a steady rusher to carry the ball on every other down. This way, every back has a smaller workload and can remain fresh throughout the game.

The Fullback and His Role

The fullback is a running back, too, but he serves a much different role from the guys who carry the football. In more primitive football times, the fullback was both a blocker and the team's primary rusher, hence the name *full*back. He did it all.

Now, though, fullbacks are used to be the lead blocker for the runner, or as extra protectors on passing plays. They tend to line up in a three-point stance, where the halfback more commonly stays in a two-point. Bigger than halfbacks, fullbacks tend to rely on strength and force more than speed and quickness.

 QUICK HIT

In most cases, fullbacks wear higher jersey numbers than other running backs. This is not a rule, just something teams and players have accepted over time.

Fullbacks rarely are given the opportunity to carry the football, and when they do, it's usually on short-yardage situations when they can use their bulk and muscle to push straight ahead for a few yards.

The fullback was an integral part of Bill Walsh's San Francisco teams of the 1980s, as both a pass receiver and an occasional ball carrier, but pro teams have gone away from utilizing the position in recent years due to a desire to get more every-down playmakers on the field.

Fearless and Forward Moving

Running backs have to run without fear, even though they act as prey for a pack of hungry predators (i.e., defenders) every time they touch the football. Being a running back takes a certain mind-set. The best ones don't see the defender in front of them; they see the defender as merely an obstacle to what's beyond him.

Running backs use *stiff arms*, or bull rush straight through opponents, if they have to. They do whatever it takes to get from point A to point B, regardless of who is in the way.

GRIDIRON GAB

A **stiff arm** is when the ball carrier uses his hand or arm to fend off a defender. The technique is legal only if the ball carrier does not make contact with the defender's facemask or head area.

The goal on every carry is for the back to gain as many yards as possible, all while protecting the football. Teams do not tolerate plays that lose yards, so a running back must always be pushing forward, first to the line of scrimmage and then beyond. At the end of each play, when he is about to get tackled, the running back makes a point of falling forward, rather than getting pushed backward, to gain extra yardage.

Read the Blocks, Run with Patience

Great running backs have good vision—they can see things happen before they really happen. Most of the time, a running back has only a split-second to make a decision, change direction, and sprint to daylight. He must rely on his vision to lead him to where he needs to go.

What is he looking for? Well, mostly a running back must see the direction where his blockers are trying to push defenders and anticipate where the opening will be at the moment he reaches the spot of attack. Running backs are taught to run behind their blockers and use them as a cushion from the defense.

With good vision comes patience. Impatient backs sometimes try to get through the hole before it's been opened, and without blocking they're left helpless against the defense. A patient runner understands that it's both him and his line gaining the yards, not just him alone. Sometimes backs need to slow down, or stop for a brief second, until everything comes into place.

Runs to the Outside and Through the Middle

Depending on the game situation, and the running back, running plays can go through the line (between the tackles) or around one side or the other. It makes the most sense to use speed backs to run to the outside, where speed is the greatest ally, and power backs to run between the tackles, where most of the linemen and other defenders have congested a small area. But executing the play properly matters more than having the right match.

When backs run between the tackles, it results in fewer plays where the running back loses yards. This is called *north-and-south running.*

Teams have backs run to the outside of the offensive line, on either side, when they think a running back's speed will get him to the sideline faster than the defense can catch up. This is called *getting to the corner.*

There are dozens of inside and outside runs, but teams at all levels usually include a core few in their playbook. Let's look at those now.

The Dive

On a dive play, the running back runs straight through a hole in the offensive line, usually through a hole created by the center and one of the guards, and behind a lead blocking fullback. This is meant to be a quick-striking power play, almost as if to say to the defense, "We're going to run right over you, and there's nothing you can do about it."

The Draw

On the draw, the offensive linemen, quarterback, and running back give the defense the look of a pass play, each dropping into position to protect the quarterback.

As the quarterback takes his drop, he quickly turns to hand to the running back, who sprints straight forward, running off either side of the center.

The Pitch

After receiving the snap from center, the quarterback pivots and tosses the ball underhand to a running back running parallel to the line of scrimmage in either direction. The pitch, or the underhand toss, gets the ball from the quarterback to the running back quickly and helps the back catch the outside edge sooner than he would be able to on a hand-off.

Before the pitch, teams often fake a hand-off to a back running between the tackles.

QUICK HIT

If the running back fails to secure the pitch from his quarterback, it's ruled a fumble because the ball is traveling away from the line of scrimmage.

The Counter

The quarterback fakes a hand-off or a pitch to a back heading in one direction and then hands the ball to another back heading through a hole in the line, hence the counter.

When teams run the pitch well, this play tends to be effective because the misdirection can be confusing for defenders, who bite on the first movement and miss the back coming through the line.

The Sweep

The sweep is one of the most recognizable outside runs. When executed properly, Hall of Fame coach Vince Lombardi argued, the play cannot be stopped.

The quarterback hands the ball to the halfback, with the fullback and both pulling guards leading the way out in front. The halfback runs parallel to the line of scrimmage until his blockers are in position and then the foursome makes a dash along the sideline area, sweeping around the edge of the line.

Names to Know and Performances to Remember

His name was as plain as any person to have ever played the game of football—Jim Brown. But during his time at Syracuse University, and in the NFL with the Cleveland Browns, there was nothing plain about Jim Brown. He was extraordinary. He ran over people or around them, and he finished his pro career with more rushing yards and touchdowns than any player to come before him.

Brown led the league in rushing eight times during his nine-year career, and he owns one of the highest yards per attempt career averages (5.2) among running backs in the history of the game. After finishing up the 1965 season, the 29-year-old Brown left the game of football to become a Hollywood movie star.

WORDS OF WISDOM

Looking back, Jim Brown was even better than I thought he was, and I thought he was the best.

—Hall of Fame Baltimore Colts defender Gino Marchetti

Walter Payton's nickname was Sweetness, but like Brown, Payton was a tough runner and a fierce competitor. He could dance around tacklers, or jump over them in search of the end zone. Off the field, Payton was well liked by his peers, and upon his untimely death in 1999, the NFL renamed its annual Man of the Year award in his honor.

The most desirable of all pro football records is arguably the one for having the most career rushing yards—a record held by Brown, then Payton, and now by Dallas Cowboys great Emmitt Smith, who gained 18,355 yards during his 15-year career. Smith was durable for Dallas during the 1990s and was an integral part in the team's three Super Bowl victories. Throughout his career, he was also one of the best pass protectors at his position.

Daryl Johnston helped Smith gain a lot of those yards by paving a safe road for Smith to travel. Nicknamed "Moose," Johnston defined the role of the fullback in the 1990s.

Many believe that had Barry Sanders continued his playing career, he, and not Smith, would be the NFL's all-time leading rusher. The Detroit Lions elusive back made defenders miss tackles like no one else to ever play football—at any position—and he is one of only six running backs to gain 2,000 or more yards in a single season.

In Super Bowl XXII, rookie running back Timmy Smith rushed for a record 204 yards on 22 attempts to help the Washington Redskins defeat the Denver Broncos. Smith is an enigma; he played in just 25 games during his abbreviated career, and he never again reached the success he had that one game.

Minnesota Vikings running back Adrian Peterson is one of the best running backs in the game today. In 2007, Peterson's rookie season, he set a new NFL record for most yards gained in a single game—296 against the San Diego Chargers.

Marshall Faulk is one of only a couple NFL running backs to have gained 1,000 yards rushing and 1,000 yards receiving in the same year. Faulk's versatility as a running back prompted other teams to begin to use their backs more often in the passing offense.

The Least You Need to Know

- Running backs are the primary rushers on the team, but they also assist in the passing game. Fullbacks act as lead blockers and sometimes get to run the ball.
- Vision is one of a running back's best assets. Without it, and the ability to act quickly, the running back won't travel far.
- Running backs must also have patience to wait for their blockers to open holes.
- To advance the ball, teams use a combination of runs through the middle of the offensive line and to the outside.
- Jim Brown is the greatest running back to ever play the game.

Wide Receivers Make the Biggest Plays

In This Chapter

- The types of receivers and their roles
- A look at the tight end
- Getting it right from the snap
- Choosing a pattern
- Receivers—the characters on the team

If the quarterback and his offensive line are the meat and potatoes of the offense, the receivers offer the seasoning to give the unit its flavor. Receivers are athletically gifted, often energetic, and sometimes brash—and they always believe they're wide open, regardless of how many defenders are in their vicinity.

Also called split ends, because they're split away from the core of the offense's formation, wide receivers can be positioned in a number of spots on the field to force defenses to adjust their alignment. Any player lined up outside the offensive linemen, on or off the line of scrimmage, is classified as a receiver. Receivers lined up off the line of scrimmage are called flankers, or sometimes slot receivers.

To get open on passing downs, receivers run pass patterns, or routes, carefully designed to put them in a position to catch the football. After the receiver catches the ball and tucks it safely into his armpit, he takes on the same mission as the running back—to elude oncoming defenders, break through tackles, and maneuver his way to the goal.

What They Do for the Team

What do they do? Three little words: they make plays. Or perhaps, more appropriate, receivers make *big* plays.

Whereas running backs eat up ground a few yards at a time rushing the ball, receivers collect yards in bunches by catching passes from the quarterback. When an offense has a long way to go to reach the first-down marker, or needs a lot of points in a short amount of time, the receiver is the best option to get there.

One of the receiver's important tasks is to act as a downfield blocker on rushing downs. When running backs get to the outside, or beyond the line of scrimmage, receivers are often in a position to make a key block to clear a path for the back to the end zone. Receivers are assigned to block cornerbacks and safeties on most downs but are occasionally asked to block an unsuspecting linebacker or defensive lineman. The most common block a receiver uses is the *stalk block*.

GRIDIRON GAB

Receivers use a **stalk block** to help shield a defender from the ball carrier. The receiver positions his body between the defender and his teammate's running lane and makes continual contact with the defender while jogging his feet in place.

On occasion, receivers run the ball on an end-around, or a reverse, aimed to take the play to the outside of the defense's attack. Offenses use these plays to take advantage of a receiver's speed.

The Different Types of Wide Receivers

Like every other position, receivers come in all shapes and sizes. Each has a distinct use, although some are better fitted for certain styles of offenses.

Receivers with great speed allow teams to pressure opposing defenses vertically, or deep down the field. These players are thrown a lot of long passes, or bombs, and are generally good for keeping the opposing safeties back and away from the line of scrimmage. Speed receivers make their yards in bunches.

Tall or physically gifted receivers can be effective on short-yard situations or when the offense is in the red zone. They can handle catching the ball in traffic and can jump over smaller, overmatched defenders.

FUN FACT

The great Oakland Raiders offenses of the 1970s and 1980s used speed receivers to set up a power running game, and vice versa. The team's slogan was "Speed kills," and its three Super Bowl titles during those two decades proved that to be true. Another speed receiver was 1964 Olympian and Dallas Cowboys great "Bullet" Bob Hayes, whose rare speed forced coaches to rethink how they defended against the pass.

Some receivers offer neither optimum size nor speed, but rather a good feel for how to find open areas in the opposing defense, and therefore are prone to success. They are preferred for their intelligence, sure hands, and reliability. These players are called possession receivers, which indicates they are the quarterback's primary target on most passing plays.

Possession receivers usually lead the team in catches, but they don't create as many big plays as the speed receivers or those who present a more favorable matchup due to size. Nonetheless, a team with a reliable possession receiver—or two—can use the pass effectively to move the ball down the field, just as a run-oriented team would do with its backs.

The Tight End and H-Back

Not a "wide" receiver, a tight end is nonetheless a valuable tool for the modern-day offense, providing added protection, run blocking, and another receiver for select passing downs. Tight ends are lined up next to the offensive tackle, on either end, and help create the strong side of the offense's formation. Teams sometimes use a second tight end to give the opponent a different look.

What makes using the tight end appealing for coaches is the rare blend of size and athleticism. Many tight ends stand as tall as the biggest players on the field, but also possess the running ability and agility of the team's best athletes. Linebackers are rarely as nimble as good pass-catching tight ends, and defensive backs—even the biggest of them—rarely match a tight end's size or physicality.

And just as there are many different types of wide receivers for coaches to consider, the same is true of this position. More-streamlined tight ends offer less help to their offensive line mates but are far more valuable as down-the-field receivers. Some teams prefer bigger, beefier tight ends who act almost as a third tackle rather than an extra receiver. When these tight ends are used on passing downs, it's usually on a short pattern.

The H-back, a hybrid of the tight end and fullback, is also used as a lead blocker, extra pass protector, and pass catcher. The difference between this position and the tight end is that the H-back is not always on the line of scrimmage; sometimes the H-back can be positioned off the line of scrimmage, directly behind the lineman, or in the backfield. Few offenses utilize the H-back, but those that do line up this player in a variety of spots, much like the wide receiver, and often relocate the player prior to the snap to help bring another body to the intended point of attack.

QUICK HIT

Other offensive linemen, besides tight ends, can become eligible receivers if they report to the referee prior to the play. When an ineligible lineman touches a pass before any other player, whether he is the intended target or not, it is ruled illegal touching.

It Starts with the Proper Stance and Release

Most passing plays are carefully timed down to parts of a second, making it important for a receiver to arrive at the same location on a given route at the same time each repetition. If a receiver doesn't explode off the line of scrimmage, or is held up by a defensive back, it disrupts that timing.

Because a team can only have seven players along the line of scrimmage, sometimes receivers are positioned a yard or two behind the line at the start of the play. Teams also do this to keep the receiver away from a defensive back to help the receiver get a clean release, or start, from the line.

But before the receiver can begin his motion up the field, he must first position his feet and hands properly before the start of the play. A proper stance accomplishes three fundamental objectives:

- Allows the receiver to be positioned comfortably while he awaits the snap of the ball

- Offers him a starting point from which he can explode, much like a sprinter coming out of his block at the start of a race

- Offers him the ability to combat a defensive back ready to press him

Most receivers use the stand-up stance, keeping both arms free, with the front leg bent directly below his forward-leaning chest and his back leg stretched out directly behind him with the heel off the ground. If a receiver fails to properly proportion his weight in his stance, he'll *false step*. Tight ends are usually in a three-point stance at the start of the play, the same as the rest of the team's offensive linemen.

GRIDIRON GAB

A **false step** occurs when a receiver does not advance forward on the first step of his release. To avoid this, receivers are trained to balance their body weight and use their front foot as an anchor from which to drive off of.

A receiver's release is the motion he makes coming out of his stance as he heads into his pattern on the play. A clean release means he's able to get into the pattern with little hassle from the defensive back. The tight end either tries to get a clean release or, in the case of play-action, "sells" a run block before releasing into his pattern.

Today's football rules have helped receivers gain an advantage over the defense. Defensive backs aren't permitted to make excessive contact with a receiver at any point beyond 5 yards past the line of scrimmage, meaning once the receiver maneuvers past the initial battle, he is free to roam without disruption the rest of the way.

Needed: Quick Feet

No matter how big a receiver is, every good one needs to be able to change direction quickly in order to lose the defender trying to cover him. This act is called creating separation, and its purpose is to establish a safe zone into which a quarterback can successfully pass the ball to the receiver.

To do this, receivers use a variety of tools. They may throw their head one direction before dashing in another, or they might run at variant speeds to throw off the defender. The most common technique for creating separation is called a break, accomplished when the receiver slows down his momentum to change direction. Having quick feet coming into (or advancing out of) the break is a receiver's best asset and can make up for a lack of speed or size.

Breaks can help a receiver get to any point of the field, but they commonly require 30-, 45-, 60-, or 90-degree-angle changes. Depending on the severity of the angle the change of direction requires, a receiver can use a number of different stepping methods to help him get to his destination point. For more severe cuts, a receiver uses a stutter step, a series of chopping steps, to slow down. For more obtuse cuts, a jab step can be used. This is a long stride used to help slow down a receiver's momentum.

No Easy Catches

No doubt about it, NFL receivers are paid big-dollar contracts because they're many times put in harm's way. They're also some of the more graceful athletes on the field, able to dive, leap, and tiptoe, all for the sake of making the play.

In the game of football, there are no easy plays for the receiver, just different grades of difficult ones. A catch made in the middle of the field requires a degree of toughness because that's where the majority of defenders swarm. A catch made near the sideline, or in the end zone, often requires a receiver to coordinate his feet with his play on the ball.

Next to the quarterback, the receiver is the most vulnerable offensive player to the viciousness of the game. Receivers are often facing the pass and therefore have their backs turned to the defense. So receivers must be fearless, able to focus on the play without worrying about the consequences. Sometimes, when a receiver is more worried about getting hit than catching the ball, he'll tense up and use *alligator arms* to catch the pass (often unsuccessfully).

GRIDIRON GAB

If a receiver is guilty of **alligator arms,** it means he made a lame attempt to catch the ball while bracing for an expected hit from a defender.

Many Patterns to Choose From

Like a magician with a deck of cards, a receiver's tricks are the countless patterns, or routes, he has at his disposal. There's the dig, the fade, the hook or hitch, the wheel, the skinny post, the whip, and so on. Clever names aside, the primary function of each pattern is to place the receiver in a position on the field where he can make a play.

Specific patterns are designed to beat specific coverages. For example, a deep-out route works well against a cover-2 defense because it places the receiver in a spot over top of the cornerback and away from and underneath the safety. When the defense is relaxed and playing off the receiver, a team may want to run a hitch, a short pattern whereby the receiver runs hard at the defender, then stops and runs back toward the quarterback.

For most offenses, the words and numbers that make up a play indicate which pattern each receiver will run. Offensive plays are designed to keep each receiver in the pattern at a comfortable distance from one another to spread out the defense and give the quarterback more options to throw to. A pattern tells the receiver how many yards to run to and is often broken down into a number of steps for each part of the route.

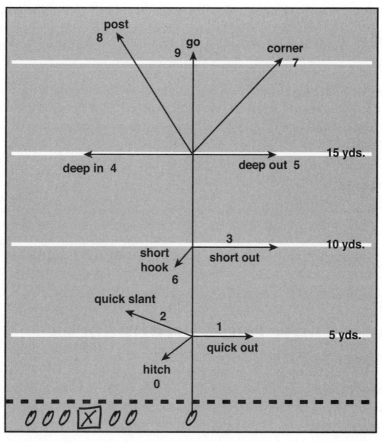

Many patterns are available for receivers to choose from.

Personality to Spare

Former Dallas Cowboys wide receiver Michael Irvin was known as "The Playmaker" because of his ability to come up big in critical game situations. Irvin danced, showboated, and spoke freely during interviews. He loved the cameras, and they loved him.

Wide receivers, perhaps more than any other position in football, add flair to the team—sometimes unwanted. They can act as the on-field cheerleaders and are usually the guys who perform crazy stunts after they score a touchdown. The receivers are the ones usually throwing tantrums on the sidelines of pro or college games because they're not getting the ball enough. Many of the game's all-time greats were also the most outspoken, charismatic performers of their respective eras.

In recent years, Randy Moss and Terrell Owens have been two of the game's more colorful characters. For both men, however, theatrics have created as many negative headlines as positive ones, and both, at one point or another, wore out their welcomes with their respective organizations or teammates.

It should be noted, though, that not every receiver is a showman. Receivers can be the vocal leader of the team, the veteran other players look up to, the quiet lead-by-example types, and the model for which the organization hopes all other players will strive to be.

 FUN FACT

Few receivers have performed as many creative or bizarre stunts as Terrell Owens. During a *Monday Night Football* game against the Seattle Seahawks in 2002, the then–San Francisco wide receiver caught a long touchdown pass and bolted to the back of the end zone. There, he pulled out a Sharpie marker he'd tucked away in his sock, signed the ball, and handed it to his financial adviser in the stands.

Names to Know and Performances to Remember

When Jerry Rice was eligible to enter pro football in the spring of 1985, many teams questioned his size and speed. More than a dozen teams passed on Rice before San Francisco selected him in the first round of the NFL Draft that year.

In 20 NFL seasons, Rice amassed 23,540 yards from scrimmage—more than any other offensive skill player in the history of the game. He holds numerous NFL records, including those for touchdowns scored in a career (208) and playoff game appearances (29). At the age of 40, Jerry Rice caught 92 passes for 1,211 yards and helped the Oakland Raiders earn a trip to Super Bowl XXXVII. One reason for his greatness was his knack for remaining injury-free; another was his well-documented work ethic. Every NFL receiver is now measured against that player initially thought to be too small and too slow.

Before Rice, Green Bay Packers great Don Hutson served as the benchmark for the position. During the 1942 season, he generated more receiving yards (1,211) than 4 of the league's 10 teams had gotten from their entire receiving corps.

The NFL's first great pass-catching tight end was the Chicago Bears' Mike Ditka, who later became one of the game's great coaches in the 1980s. Another tight end from Ditka's era, John Mackey, helped change the way teams utilized the position.

In a 1982 playoff game that reached blistering temperatures, exhausted and physically spent San Diego Chargers tight end Kellen Winslow Sr. was carried off the field by teammates after a thrilling overtime win over the Miami Dolphins. Winslow caught 13 passes and blocked a field goal in one of pro football's most memorable performances.

Marvin Harrison holds the NFL record for most catches in one season—143 catches for the Indianapolis Colts in 2002.

Of the few wide receivers to have been named the most valuable player of the Super Bowl, three played for the Pittsburgh Steelers: Lynn Swann in Super Bowl X, Hines Ward in Super Bowl XL, and Santonio Holmes in Super Bowl XLIII.

During his first season in the lineup at Texas Tech, Michael Crabtree caught 134 passes for 1,962 yards and 22 touchdowns.

 FUN FACT

Seattle Seahawks Hall of Fame wide receiver Steve Largent served in the U.S. House of Representatives from 1994 to 2002 for his native state of Oklahoma.

The Least You Need to Know

- Wide receivers are offensive players positioned farthest away from the quarterback at the start of the play. They can line up on or off the line of scrimmage.
- Tight ends are offensive linemen who act as receivers on passing downs. The best ones are too quick for linebackers to keep up with and too big for defensive backs to contend with.
- Wide receivers are graceful athletes, able to leap high and change direction quickly.
- Each pattern determines the distance and direction to where the wide receiver will set up to catch a pass.
- Hall of Famer Jerry Rice is the player to whom all other wide receivers are compared.

Offensive Linemen Do the Dirty Work

In This Chapter

- Offensive linemen and what they do
- Linemen's roles on passing downs and running plays
- Good linemen versus average ones

No matter how good the quarterback is, or how quick and fast his wide receivers and running backs are, the offense simply won't advance the football if it doesn't have a good offensive line.

What makes a lineman great? Well, size and strength count for a lot, but sometimes even the biggest and strongest guys on a football team fail to get the job done. What really matters is a good work ethic. Coaches love to see a lineman block until the officials blow the play dead, and they're absolutely thrilled to see a lineman running around the field in search of more people to block.

The linemen are the guys who bring a bag lunch to work, and who wear bib overalls to social occasions. They're salt-of-the-earth folk, and it's common to see all five of the starting linemen sitting together, usually in the same order they line up on the field. They're a unit within a unit, and sometimes they're a quirky bunch.

What They Do for the Team

Linemen block defenders, simple as that. They act as a wall to prevent pass rushers—usually defensive linemen, but sometimes linebackers and defensive backs, too—from getting to the quarterback on passing plays. And linemen open the holes and clear the way for the running backs.

The task, however, is much more demanding than the job description. To do their job effectively, linemen must take the proper angles to move defenders out of the way. They must understand about such things as leverage, explosion, and where a person's vulnerable points of attack are.

When things are going well for the offense, and it has a scoring lead, the linemen can also act as finishers in the game—beating on the opponent and frustrating defenders into submission.

The linemen, like the quarterback, must also be able to succeed on pressure downs. When faced with short-yardage or goal line situations, the offense almost always relies on the line to push back the defense just enough to get the necessary foot or yard for the first down or score. This is when linemen must dig down deep.

Tackles: The Biggest Guys on the Block

The outside protectors in the *tackle box* are the tackles, who line up on the outside shoulders of both guards. Tackles are often forced to contend with the defense's quickest pass rushers, the defensive ends, and must have nimble feet to move from their stance to a place where they can make a block.

GRIDIRON GAB

The **tackle box** is the area that includes the five offensive linemen.

Most pro football tackles stand 6-foot-4 or taller and weigh in excess of 300 pounds. Their bulk makes them difficult to get around, and their strength makes them near impossible to run over.

Each team has two tackles, one to line up on the left side of the line, and one on the right. The more important of the two is the tackle who protects the backside of the quarterback. In most cases, that's the left tackle because most quarterbacks are right-handed and turn their back to the left side of the line when preparing to pass the ball. The backside, or blindside, tackle holds a pass rusher if he has to protect his quarterback from absorbing a vicious hit. This level of responsibility also makes the tackle a valuable asset to the team and someone who usually collects a handsome paycheck.

Guards: Compact and Powerful

Lined up on either side of the center, the guards push hard off the line of scrimmage to create room for the running backs and must fend off pass rushers with an inside lane to the quarterback.

The average pro football guard stands a few inches shorter, and weighs a few pounds less, than a tackle.

Like tackles, guards must also be quick on their feet. Why? After the ball is snapped, teams often relocate, or pull, guards from the spot where they lined up to an area where the ball carrier is headed. Tackles can do the same, but it's not as common.

On pulling plays, guards are asked to lead block, taking on the first defender who poses a threat to the ball carrier. When a guard has the ability to pull out of his spot and maneuver to the point of attack, holes open up and good things happen for the offense.

When he stays put at his natural spot along the line, the guard must have the strength to hold off oncoming nose guards or defensive tackles—players often weighing more than he does.

Center: Captain of the Line

The center lines up directly over the football on every play and absorbs punishment, regardless of whether the play is near him or not. Centers must have thick skin, a solid base, and a quick mind—qualifications that make it one of the most demanding jobs on offense.

 FUN FACT

Because he is assigned to snap the football, the center is the only player, on either side of the ball, allowed to line up inside the neutral zone, the area that separates the offensive and defensive lines and measures the length of the football.

Before he can worry about blocking the defender lined up over him, a center must first deliver the ball safely to the quarterback to start the play. If the center doesn't place the ball properly, or if he pulls back too early to get his hands in position to make a block, it can result in a fumble.

The snap must be second nature to the center because a team can't afford to have an error during the center-to-quarterback exchange. Therefore, the relationship between the center and quarterback must be similar to that of the pitcher and catcher in baseball. The two are a single working unit on running and passing plays and must be in sync at all times.

It's the center who usually points out possible blitzers (a linebacker and/or defensive back poised to rush the quarterback) to his line mates, and he's also the one responsible for calling out blocking assignments at the line of scrimmage. He's in the middle, so he's the easiest for everyone to see and hear. He's also the unofficial captain of the line.

Centers are roughly the same size and shape as guards, and it's not uncommon for players to rotate between the two positions.

Protecting on Passing Downs

When the offense has a planned passing play, the linemen must come out of their three-point stance quickly to stand up and defend against the oncoming pass rush. Miss a block on a passing play, and a lineman could cost his team a sack or a turnover—or worse, put the quarterback at risk of injury.

> **PENALTY!**
>
> On passing plays, no ineligible lineman is allowed to cross the line of scrimmage before the quarterback throws the football. After the ball is in the air, however, linemen are free to roam anywhere in search of defenders to block.

Linemen may be large and strong, but their best tools for pass protection are their feet and hands. Linemen must shuffle to keep themselves in front of the quicker defenders coming at them, and by keeping their hands on their opponent, it creates a cushion that can be difficult for the defender to collapse.

Linemen are usually the last players to know when the quarterback has released the ball. Because things can happen on a play—a fumbled snap, no open receivers to throw to, etc.—it forces each lineman to block until the play is blown dead, or until there are no more defenders to demolish.

Pushing the Pile on Rushing Downs

Linemen don't block on rushing downs; they explode off the line, like a rodeo bull coming out of its pen. To pave a clear path for the ball carrier, each lineman has someone (or an area) he is assigned to block. To win the battle, the lineman aims to hit first, hit hardest, and hit with the best leverage to push his man back and away from the action.

Some linemen are better at this than others. Usually a tackle-guard combination is paired up on the left or right side of the line, and wherever those two are, that's often where the team runs its backs.

When a team needs a few yards—either to gain a first down or score a touchdown—the coaching staff or the quarterback calls on the line to dig deep and push the pile forward. It becomes a matter of pride, and great lines almost always get the necessary yards for their team.

FUN FACT

Many of the great running backs credit their success to the blocking of the men pushing piles in front of them. And some backs have offered their linemen more than a thank you. Dallas Cowboys running back Emmitt Smith bought each of his linemen a $5,000 Rolex watch after Smith won the first of three straight NFL rushing titles in 1991.

wind

uality they often look for is whether a player
all and round, sure, but they also want a guy
e street tough, necessarily. More like down-

e play and block every second the play
es a cheap shot at the quarterback, the
if to say, "If you mess with him, you mess

logical advantage over the opposition as
ive linemen scratch and punch and hold
he end of it all, the line that got the best
the field with its teammates victorious.

3756500974 9408

all field where the two lines wage
linemen dig into the turf, not

The comple

It...   t having an inner hatred for the
oppo   ground on every play. That's being
nasty!   ind

'A - 3233

Names to Know and Performances to Remember

The most famous offensive line in the history of football may have been the one that belonged to the Washington Redskins in the 1980s and early 1990s. Called "The Hogs," the line had personality and housed several of the game's best (and biggest) linemen of the era—men like guard Russ Grimm and tackle Joe Jacoby. From 1982 to 1991, Washington twice led the NFL in total offense and earned its way to four Super Bowls, with much thanks to The Hogs.

Coach Vince Lombardi had a wealth of great players during his time at Green Bay. According to Lombardi, though, the best player he ever coached was offensive tackle Forrest Gregg, who was invited to play in nine Pro Bowls during his 15-year career.

The greatest single-play effort from linemen may have occurred on December 31, 1967, during the NFL title game at Lambeau Field fans still refer to as the Ice Bowl. With the clock winding down, the temperature frigid, and the field frozen solid, the Green Bay Packers had one last play with which to score a touchdown. The team's quarterback, Bart Starr, kept the ball and ran behind center Ken Bowman and guard Jerry Kramer, who combined to push the Dallas Cowboys defense back enough for Starr to land in the end zone.

The Lombardi Award, given to college football's top lineman or linebacker since 1970, has rarely been given to an offensive lineman. Ohio State's Orlando Pace not only won it as an offensive tackle, but he became the first player at any position to win the award in consecutive seasons (1995 and 1996). Pace had a distinguished career in the NFL with the St. Louis Rams and was one of few linemen to be selected with the very first pick in the NFL Draft.

The tackle by whom all others are measured tends to be former Cincinnati Bengals star Anthony Muñoz, who was voted to the league's All-Pro team 11 years in a row from 1981 to 1991.

Another tackle whose career flourished in the 1980s was Jackie Slater, who played 20 seasons in the NFL, all of them for the Rams, first in Los Angeles before the team relocated to St. Louis.

The greatest guard who ever played? It's certainly up for debate, but it'd be difficult to argue against the New England Patriots' John Hannah, who was not only dominant but reliable. In 13 seasons, he only missed five games.

WORDS OF WISDOM

All that I accomplish is not because of me. It's because of God and the offensive line.

—Chicago Bears running back Walter Payton

The Least You Need to Know

- The tackle who protects the quarterback's blindside is often one of his team's most important—and highest-paid—players.
- Guards often pull to the point of attack to help create running room for the ball carrier.
- Size helps a lineman do his job; a nasty streak can give him that special edge.
- Washington's offensive line, labeled The Hogs, helped take the team to four Super Bowls during a 10-year span.

Traditional Offensive Formations

In This Chapter

- The shotgun and other formations
- A look at some of the systems offenses use
- Understanding the West Coast Offense
- Why teams use the goal line formation

Fans new to football often wonder why the offense lines up its men in different spots for different downs, or why some teams start the play with the quarterback away from the center versus directly behind him.

Different formations make football interesting. They can cater to a team's strengths, hide its weaknesses, or exploit a weakness in the opponent. Most importantly, they keep the other guys wondering, *What are they going to do next?*

Coaches are always searching for new ways to line up their guys, and coaches make no secret that they borrow from their peers all the time. If it works for that other team, maybe it will work for this one, too.

The Shotgun Formation

The shotgun is not so much a formation as it is an adjustment to where the quarterback lines up. Instead of accepting the ball directly from behind the center, the quarterback lines up 5 yards back, forcing the center to snap the ball to him through the air. This is called a shotgun snap.

The receivers and backs can line up in any number of spots, but most of the time the offense has only one running back in the backfield next to the quarterback because the shotgun is primarily a passing formation. Naturally, the draw play (remember that from Chapter 8?) is an effective run to use from this formation.

The shotgun formation creates an extra cushion to protect the quarterback from the defense. It also assists the passing game, eliminating the quarterback's need for a three- or five-step drop, and helps him get rid of the football sooner. When a team needs a lot of yards, it often drops into the shotgun formation to provide more time for the receivers to get downfield.

As with the regular snap, the center and quarterback must practice the shotgun snap in order for this formation to be run effectively. The quarterback expects to have the ball snapped crisply and delivered about chest-high. If the ball is snapped too high or low, the quarterback may fail to catch it, creating a fumble.

WORDS OF WISDOM

I want the big play. I don't want the little play, the average play. I want the big play. I'm not going to stay up all night trying to figure out how to gain 3 yards.

—Football coach and innovator Sid Gillman

The T Formation

In the T formation, three running backs are situated approximately 5 yards behind the quarterback at the start of the snap—a fullback directly behind him, and halfbacks on both sides of the fullback. The formation looks like the letter T, hence the name.

The traditional T has two tight ends on the line of scrimmage, but teams also run the split-T with one tight end and one wide receiver (the split end) on the other side. It's a formation primarily reserved for power running teams, although the split-T is more balanced and therefore good for both run and pass plays.

The T formation is one of football's oldest formations, used mostly today by high school and some college programs.

The Wishbone Formation

A distant relative of the T formation, the wishbone has the same look, only it brings the fullback closer to the quarterback at the start of the snap. The three backs in the backfield are positioned in an upside-down V, which resembles a wishbone.

Like the T formation, the tight ends and receivers can be mixed and matched along the line of scrimmage. The wishbone is another power running set, using a lot of options off of its three backs and quarterbacks in the running game. The triple option, made famous by the wishbone, allows for more blockers at the point of attack. Defenses are left guessing on every play as to which player will get the ball and where the play is headed. Eventually, the offense hopes, the defense will misstep, allowing for a large gain.

 FUN FACT

The wishbone was most famous during the 1970s, when college programs like the University of Texas and the University of Alabama used it with great success.

The I Formation

In the traditional I formation, the fullback and halfback are lined up directly behind the quarterback, with the fullback 5 yards behind and the halfback a couple yards behind the fullback. The I uses two wide receivers, both spread out wide, and a tight end.

In the offset variation of the I, the fullback is lined up behind either guard, anywhere from 3 to 5 yards off the line of scrimmage, with the halfback 5 to 7 yards directly behind the quarterback. Without having all its backs in a straight line, this variety may no longer look like the letter I, but the basic philosophies behind it are the same.

Many teams still use the I, and it's one of the few formations popular at every level of the game.

The Single Wing Formation

One of football's more popular offenses in the early part of the twentieth century, the single wing puts multiple blockers at the point of attack, either an extra lineman, the wing, or a lead blocker on the play. This formation uses an unbalanced line, with four linemen on one side of the center and two on the other.

The wing is positioned next to the tight end, 1 yard off the line of scrimmage. This creates the strong side of the line. The fullback and halfback are also lined up on the strong side. The ball is snapped to a back—either the quarterback or one of the running backs—situated 5 yards behind the line of scrimmage. Single wing teams often run behind lead blockers to the strong side of the field.

By using motion and fakes and counters, the single wing creates a lot of confusion, leaving defenses sometimes lost trying to figure out where the ball carrier is going to come from.

The Wildcat Formation

A descendant of the single wing that's become popular in recent years, the wildcat puts the running back in shotgun formation behind the center and snaps to him directly. The offense relies on presnap motion and the sweep play (turn back to Chapter 8 for a refresher of the sweep). As with the single wing, the line is unbalanced, creating a power side that's run behind most often.

Running offenses that snap directly to the halfback are effective because they bypass the need for a quarterback-to-running back exchange. Used mostly as a running formation, the running back is also asked to throw short passes on occasion.

The wildcat was first used by the Kansas State Wildcats under coach Bill Snyder in the 1990s.

FUN FACT

A variation of this offense is also called the razorback, named after the University of Arkansas teams that ran it with so much success, especially during the 2007 season when the team featured Darren McFadden and Felix Jones in the backfield.

The Spread Formation

The goal of the spread offense is what its name suggests: to spread out the offensive players across the width of the field so as to spread out the defense, create more room to run the football, and find open spots to pass into.

Usually the spread puts the quarterback in the shotgun formation, with one back in the backfield and wings on either side. The spread formation uses a lot of runs around the edge to try to stretch out the defense, thus leaving the middle of the defense vulnerable to runs between the tackles.

The Pro Set Formation

Named because it's been the offense of choice for professional football teams, the pro set features two running backs in the backfield, split on either side of the quarterback, with a tight end and two wide receivers spread out wide.

It's a balanced offense, favoring neither the run nor the pass. It's easy to do plays of either from the set, which makes it more difficult for defenders to predict what the play will be.

The backs are important to the passing game in the pro set offense because they're placed in a good spot to step up and help in pass protection, or slip out of the backfield to catch a pass.

The West Coast Offense

Legendary San Francisco 49ers coach Bill Walsh's system, improperly labeled the West Coast Offense, became one of the most popular offenses throughout collegiate and professional football in the 1980s and 1990s. Its base formation is the pro set formation, but its general philosophies differ from what most pro set teams prefer.

The general concept of the offense is to use high-percentage passing plays to advance the football, in much the same way a more conservative team would use running plays. Plays are well timed and require the team's quarterback and wide receivers to be in sync. Eventually, the short passes open up longer pass plays down the field.

The offense must also be able to run the football to balance its short passing game. This keeps defenses honest and guessing.

In Walsh's offense, the fullback and tight ends play an integral role in helping develop the short passing attack. Both must be capable receivers and sound blockers. All the players in the system must be intelligent to understand its complex playbook.

The "West Coast Offense" label was applied, even though it was a term meant to describe the vertical passing offenses of 1960s AFL coaches Sid Gillman and Al Davis.

Walsh's offense was a combination of the things he had learned as an assistant coach under Paul Brown in Cincinnati, and at other stops he made during his coaching career.

 FUN FACT

A number of Walsh's assistant coaches left San Francisco to accept head coaching jobs in other NFL cities, where they brought variations of his offense with them.

The Goal Line Formation

When teams need a yard or two, either for a first down or to get into the end zone, they often line up in a goal line formation, using three tight ends and two running backs, or vice versa.

The purpose of the goal line offense is to add bulk and power to the lineup, as if to say, "We're going to ram the ball straight at you!" It's all about pure brute force and will.

Most of the time, teams run out of this formation, but the quarterback can also pass, faking a hand-off to one of the backs and then passing to either a back or a tight end releasing from the line.

The Least You Need to Know

- In the shotgun formation, the quarterback lines up 5 yards behind the center. Teams use this to buy time when trying to pass the ball.
- The wildcat is a formation college and pro teams are using more often today. It's a descendant of the single wing, which was the game's most popular offense during the first half of the twentieth century.

- The pro set offense uses two backs, two wide receivers, and a tight end. Teams can throw or run easily from this formation.

- The West Coast Offense uses short passes and a running game to open up bigger plays downfield.

- A goal line offense crowds all the offensive players near the line of scrimmage. Teams use this when they're near the goal line or only need to gain a yard or two.

Offensive Strategic Tools

In This Chapter

- How motion and play-action help set up the offense
- Offensive trick plays
- Why teams try to manage the clock and field position
- Making game and scoring decisions

Players aren't the only tools a coach has with which to beat the opponent. There's trickery, strategy, and well-planned game management. Strategic tools often fit the coach's personality (for example, a conservative coach won't use a lot of trick plays) and over time, help define his legacy.

Each coach has his own set of rules and way of doing things. The best formula? No such thing. All that matters is what works and what doesn't, and even then, sometimes what worked yesterday doesn't work today. Football is always changing, and the sharpest coaches never stick to one way of licking the opponent; they change with the game.

The Numbering System

For running plays, offenses use a numbering system so players know who's getting the ball and through which hole he's running.

The lanes, or holes, between each lineman are designated with a number to tell the running back where to go after getting the hand-off. In most systems, holes to the left of the center have odd numbers (1, 3, 5, 7, etc.), and holes to the right have even numbers (2, 4, 6, 8, etc.). A play going directly over the center is 0.

Most teams also label their ball carriers. A fullback, for example, might be the 3 back, and the halfback the 2 back.

When a team wants to run its halfback between the left guard and left tackle, the play would be labeled a 23—the 2 for the halfback and the 3 for the hole. A fullback run to the outside of a tight end lined up on the right side of the line would be a 38—the 3 for the fullback and the 8 for the hole.

Obviously, defenses understand a 23 play, so the offense disguises the language of the play when it's called in from the sideline.

Motion

After all the offensive players are in the set position prior to the snap, the quarterback may put one player in motion, allowing him to run parallel to or away from the line of scrimmage. This player can move from one side of the field to the other if the offense so chooses and does not need to be set before the snap of the ball.

PENALTY!

If a player in motion makes even the slightest movement toward the line of scrimmage prior to the snap of the ball, he will be flagged 5 yards for illegal motion.

Motion is valuable in helping an offense change its strength, determined by the side of the ball where it has the most players lined up. By motioning a back or a receiver from one side to the other, it sometimes changes the strength to that side and opens up plays the defense doesn't have time to react to.

Teams are allowed only one player in motion on any given play. Any more than that will draw a penalty for an illegal shift (see Chapter 13 for a full description).

Play-Action

When teams have a good rushing game, play-action can be a valuable tool to help open the passing game.

The start to any play-action pass is a fake hand-off to a running back, who must sell to the defense that he has the football (when he sells it well, he gets clobbered).

Believing the running back has the ball, the linebackers and safeties run toward the line of scrimmage. After the fake, the quarterback looks quickly to find an open receiver.

Play-action passing must happen quickly; otherwise, it loses its effect. The key is for the quarterback and running back to fake out the defense.

Trick Plays

Kids draw up trick plays in the dirt every weekend. They're fun. "I'll throw the ball to Larry, he'll pitch it to Stevie, and he'll pitch it back to Marvin."

When these plays work, the designer of the play is a genius. When a play fails, it looks like a gobbled mess, and sometimes results in a turnover.

The Flea Flicker

On a flea flicker, the running back takes the handoff from the quarterback, runs straight forward into the line, then turns and pitches the ball back to the quarterback.

Having seen the running back get the ball and advance forward, the defense may be tempted to crowd the line of scrimmage. If this happens, the quarterback simply throws over top of the defenders to a receiver racing deep down the field.

The Halfback Pass

The quarterback gives the ball to a running back, who starts to run parallel to the line of scrimmage, usually with a lead blocker in front of him. At the last second, just as the converging defense surrounds him, the running back pulls up and searches for an open receiver down the field. Sometimes the quarterback becomes the receiver on the halfback pass, as few defenders know to keep track of him after he hands off the ball.

The key to this fake play is to be sure the linemen don't go downfield until the ball is thrown and to find a running back capable of passing the football.

The Hook and Lateral

Often called the hook and ladder play, the quarterback throws a quick pass to a receiver running a hook route. Another offensive player, often a running back or a slot receiver, trails the intended receiver on the play. Before the receiver with the ball is tackled, he *laterals* it to the trailing receiver.

> **GRIDIRON GAB**
>
> A **lateral** is any pass from one player to another that travels backward, away from the goal the offense is headed toward. Teams can use as many laterals as they care to on any given play, but if the ball winds up on the ground, it's ruled a fumble.

When timed perfectly, the hook and lateral is a difficult play for the defense to stop, as defenders are often caught off-guard and out of position to make a play on the trailing receiver.

The downside to this play: if the lateral isn't timed right, there's a good chance a fumble will occur.

The Statue of Liberty

After the quarterback takes the snap from the center, he drops back to pass, clutching the ball with both hands. He then raises his throwing arm as if to show he's ready to throw, but he keeps the ball in his nonthrowing hand. As he fakes the pass, he hands the ball to a player (usually a running back) who often accepts the ball behind the quarterback and runs in the opposite direction from where the pass is faked.

This play gets its name because, when executed properly, the quarterback has the appearance of the Statue of Liberty.

Boise State beat Oklahoma University using this play on a 2-point conversion in the 2007 Fiesta Bowl.

The Reverse

After the snap of the ball, the quarterback turns and hands it to either a back or a receiver heading in one direction, parallel to the line of scrimmage. Another player, coming from the opposite side of the field and heading in the opposite direction, then takes the ball from the original ball carrier and races toward the sideline.

This play works when defenses have a tendency to overpursue. If the defenders all follow the first ball carrier, they'll be out of position and unable to catch the second player handling the reverse.

In some offensive systems, especially at the high school level, this is a commonly used play. Most NFL teams avoid it, however, due to the athletic and disciplined defensive players of today.

Running the Two-Minute Drill

When an offense has control of the ball with little time remaining in either half, it may decide to operate the two-minute drill. This may not involve any plays different from what the offense usually runs or include any personnel not normally on the field. The two-minute drill is a state of mind—or better yet, a state of urgency.

Every week in practice, teams practice the two-minute drill. The coach gives his team a distance to travel and two minutes to get there. The team must advance the football while managing the clock at the same time. Receivers who catch passes are taught to get out of bounds if they're not able to advance the ball any farther. The quarterback and linemen must race to the line of scrimmage on every play to save time.

The goal, of course, is to move the ball far enough into the opponent's territory where the end zone is within reach or a field goal is likely. To do that, however, the offense must eat up chunks of yards little by little so it can continue to gain first downs and keep its drive alive. As the clock winds closer to zero, the panic and pressure of the situation intensifies, and the offense is more apt to try for larger gains.

 FUN FACT

No quarterback managed the two-minute drill better than San Francisco 49ers quarterback Joe Montana. On the final drive of Super Bowl XXIII, the 49ers took the ball at their 8-yard line with just more than three minutes left. Montana moved his team 92 yards in just under two minutes, hitting wide receiver John Taylor for the game-winning touchdown.

Managing Field Position

Psychologically, where a team starts with the football plays a big part in how well it performs. When a team is backed up against its goal line with a long field to work with, it feels pinned and uncomfortable, and the defense is motivated to make a stop. When a team has the ball with a short field to work with, it feels more secure, more confident, and the defense is left to feel pinned and under pressure.

The battle for field position is a chess game within a chess game, trading possessions until one team has a favorable spot from which to go on the attack.

Those coaches who play for field position are said to be conservative, but the most fitting word might be *patient*. A coach doesn't need to feel as though he has to score on every possession. Instead, a coach who plays for field position waits for the right moment to strike.

Ideally, a team would like for its opponents to begin drives on their 25-yard line, if not farther back. Favorable field position is anything from a team's own 40-yard line or better, with 60 or fewer yards to travel to reach the end zone.

Controlling the Clock

Coaches manage the game clock by speeding up or slowing down the tempo of the offense. When they need to move quickly to score points, the offense moves with efficiency and stops the clock whenever it can. To stop the clock and preserve the time remaining, players can run out of bounds, the coaching staff can use a time-out, or the quarterback can ground the ball into the turf immediately after the snap. (The latter is the same as an incompletion.)

PENALTY!

Teams hurrying to ground the ball are often flagged for a penalty because not everyone gets in a set position prior to the snap of the ball.

A team is given only three time-outs to use per half, so the other options are preferred when possible.

When the offense has the lead, and its coach wishes to milk the clock, he will use every available second on the play clock before having his center snap the ball, and he'll use running plays over passing plays to keep the clock going after each down.

If the other team is out of time-outs, and the number of remaining downs multiplied by the amount of time on the play clock for each down is greater than the amount of time remaining, the offense can go into the *victory formation*. In this formation, the quarterback stands behind the center, with players crowded in tight to protect him, and kneels down after receiving the snap. He'll do this a few times if he has to. The defense is left helpless as it watches the remaining time in the game wind down.

Risk Management

Coaches have to weigh risk versus reward just like any other decision-makers. For example, a coach rarely goes for it on fourth down and a yard to go when the ball is pinned back near his own goal line. The risk of failing on the attempt and giving the opponent a short field to work with is far too great.

However, a coach may go for it on fourth down and a yard to go when the ball is spotted at his opponent's 40-yard line (or closer) because he knows that if his team fails, the opponent would have to travel a considerable distance to put points on the board.

When trailing late in a game, a coach may have to choose between an *onside kick*—a high-risk, high-reward option wherein the kicker kicks the ball 10 or more yards to a spot where his teammates sprint to collect it—or *kicking the ball* deep to the opponent and hoping his defense can force a punt—this is a low-risk, less-reward option.

QUICK HIT

Teams don't disguise the fact that they intend to try an onside kick. Most of the time they position as many as six men on the side of the kicker to where the ball will be kicked. When the receiving team sees this, they know to be on guard.

Throughout each game, coaches face countless decisions involving varying degrees of risk. Sometimes coaches need to play it safe; other times they need to gamble. The best coaches have the ability to coach both ways and have the feel for what to do when each situation presents itself.

Risk management also factors heavily into decisions coaches make regarding scoring outcomes ….

Scoring Decisions

Depending on the score and how much time remains in the game, coaches must decide when to go for a touchdown instead of a field goal, or when to go for a 2-point conversion rather than take the extra point. If the coach makes the wrong decision, it can cost his team the win—maybe cost him his job, too—and there's little time for him to ponder.

There's no cut-and-dry system for making these decisions, and sometimes the wrong decision works out for the offense, thanks to other outside factors.

Many coaches carry a scoring sheet telling them when it's best to go for 2 points after a touchdown versus 1. You may think, *Why not always go for 2?* It's because a team's success rate on 2-point conversions is far less than it is kicking the extra point. In most cases, a coach won't consider the 2-point conversion until the fourth quarter. That's when all the mathematical outcomes are thought through on the sideline.

For example, if there's one minute remaining and a team is trailing by 2 points and scores a touchdown, it will want to go for the 2-point conversion because the touchdown gave the team a 4-point lead. An extra point would extend the lead to 5 points, whereas a 2-point conversion would extend the lead to 6. A 5-point lead is no better than a 4-point lead, but 6 points means the other team would need both a touchdown and an extra point to win.

Or if a team is trailing by 10 points with three remaining minutes and scores a touchdown, it will go for the extra point because the touchdown pulled the team within 4 points of its opponent. Either way, the team still needs at least a field goal. The extra point is a better percentage attempt than the 2-point conversion, so with little more to gain and plenty to lose, the offense goes with the safer bet.

Let's assume the offense has a 2-point lead and is at its opponent's 19-yard line. It's fourth down and 4 yards to go. In this scenario, the offense should choose to kick the field goal because if it fails on the fourth-down attempt, the opponent can win the game if it advances the ball into field goal territory. A touchdown would be best, but it's unlikely here. The field goal extends the team's lead to 5 points, forcing the opponent to score a touchdown to win the game, versus a field goal.

The ability to make the right decision is much like a poker player knowing how to read a hand; after seeing so many situations so many times, a coach starts to learn what the most likely outcomes are and knows what to do with whatever time is on the clock.

The Least You Need to Know

- To simplify the system, offenses number the ball carriers and the holes through which they run with the ball.
- Play-action passes help good running teams open their passing game.

- The two-minute drill requires the offense to move the ball quickly with limited time to work with.

- Teams use the victory formation to run out the final seconds of the game clock.

- Coaches often carry a sheet that tells them how to handle certain scoring situations.

Rulings That Affect the Offense

In This Chapter

- The signals officials make during a game
- The rulings called against the offense and the penalties for each
- How instant replay works and the plays eligible to be reviewed

For all that's said about football's violent side, its many rules make it a very organized and civilized game. Players can hit one another, but only in a proper manner. Quarterbacks can pass the ball, but only from certain spots on the field. Linemen can block defenders, but they can't hold, trip, or pull hair. You get the idea.

The truth is that the rulebook places the game officials in control of the game. And as much as the players, coaches, and fans hate to admit it, without the game officials, cheating and chaos would run rampant and disrupt the good-natured part of the game.

To keep the peace, and to communicate in a loud and hostile environment, officials use dozens of signals.

General Signals

The game officials make hand and arm motions during the entire football game, but not always to alert the players and coaches of a penalty. Sometimes the officials are making a ruling on a scoring play or communicating to the clock operator.

Let's review the signals officials make that have nothing to do with a player infraction.

Successful Score

The game official extends both arms skyward when the offense has scored a touchdown, converted a field goal or extra point, or made a successful 2-point attempt. Fans often mimic this to celebrate when their team scores a touchdown.

First Down

Whenever the offense successfully advances the ball 10 yards from the line of scrimmage, the game official turns to face the direction in which the offense is moving and extends one arm toward the goal.

Fourth Down

When the offense is faced with a fourth-down attempt, the game official holds one fist in the air, to alert the fans, players, and coaches that it's fourth down. Officials often use fingers to show second or third down.

Unsuccessful Attempt

If a pass is ruled incomplete, a field goal or extra point fails to go through the uprights, or if a 2-point conversion fails, the game official extends both arms in front of him and waves them back and forth to signal an unsuccessful attempt. The game officials also make this motion to show that a team has refused to accept a penalty.

Dead Ball

When the game official wishes to communicate that the clock was stopped when an infraction occurred, he gives the dead ball signal, simply holding one hand up high in the air.

QUICK HIT

When two or more officials make different calls on the same play, they gather together to discuss the play before offering a final ruling, often with the referee assisting the discussion. The goal of the conference is always to learn which official had the best vantage point on the play. After the conference, the referee clarifies the ruling to both teams and the viewers.

Begin (or Continue) the Game Clock

When the game official makes a circular motion with one straight arm, it means the game clock should be active. The official does this to start the clock or when a player is tackled near the sideline but not ruled out of the field of play.

Stop the Game Clock

The game official waves both arms over the top of his head to stop the clock, due to a break in the action, when a player is injured on the field, when a player has gone out of bounds, or when a team has called a time-out. The game official also makes this motion at the end of the first half or regulation.

Reset the Play Clock

Whenever the play clock is not properly set, the game official halts the action before the snap and requests that the clock operator reset the game clock, or set it to a certain number of seconds. To do this, he pushes upward repeatedly, with palms pointed up.

Loss of Down

When the game official puts both hands behind his head, it signals a loss of down. This is important to remember because some penalties, if accepted by the defense, allow the offense to replay the previous down. Loss-of-down penalties do not.

Bobbling the Ball

If a receiver isn't able to secure the football before establishing possession with his feet, usually on his way out of bounds, the game official makes a juggling like motion to indicate he did not make a clean catch.

Offensive Penalties

Even though the defense is the more aggressive of the two sides of the ball, having to claw and push its way to get to the ball carrier, the offense is flagged for just as many penalties, albeit less of the physical variety.

The following sections cover the key offensive penalties.

False Start

During the cadence, offensive players get into the set position, a stationary stance from where they are not allowed to move until the ball is snapped. When a player who is set moves before the snap, the offense receives a 5-yard penalty for a false start. The official signals this by making a rolling motion with his two arms in front of him.

Illegal Motion

One offensive player is allowed to be in motion while the other players are in a set position. However, if this player makes a move upfield before the snap of the ball, the offense receives a 5-yard illegal motion call. The official simply takes one arm at chest level and extends it outward.

Illegal Shift

If more than one player is in motion before the snap, the team receives a 5-yard penalty for an illegal shift. This signal is the same as with illegal motion, only the official uses both hands.

Illegal Formation

If the offense doesn't have enough men along the line of scrimmage, or if it has too many, the game official calls an illegal formation, which carries a 5-yard penalty. The official uses the same signal as false start for this penalty.

Holding

One of the most common offensive penalties, holding is also one of the most costly: 10 yards. The official holds one arm with a closed fist against his body with the arm grasping the wrist. They say offensive blockers are guilty of holding on every play, but what the game officials are looking for is to see if the defender is unable to break free from the blocker's grasp.

Illegal Use of the Hands

Like defensive players, offensive players cannot use their hands without restriction. Linemen and wide receivers often get flagged 10 yards for placing their hands on the face of a defender. The signal is the left hand out with the right hand grasping the left wrist.

Tripping

An offensive player is not allowed to trip a defensive player during the play. Offensive linemen commonly commit this foul when trying to prevent a pass rusher from getting to the quarterback. It may be worth saving their quarterback, but it costs the offense 10 yards. To signal this, the official stands on one leg while using the other to illustrate a tripping motion.

Chop Block

Another lineman no-no is the chop block, illustrated by a game official striking both of his legs while in a squatted position. This is a dangerous block, which is why it carries a 15-yard penalty. A lineman is guilty of a chop block when he makes a low block on a defender who is already physically engaged with another offensive player.

Illegal Substitution

When an offense brings in an ineligible player, or has too many men in the huddle or on the field at the time of the snap, it is given a 5-yard penalty. The official puts both hands on top of his head to signal this.

QUICK HIT

Teams generally get called for having too many men in the huddle when an inexperienced quarterback is on the field or in situations when the offense is moving at a frantic pace.

Pass Interference

This penalty is most commonly called on the defense, but the offense is not immune. The rules state than an offensive player may not interfere with a defender's right to make a play on a pass in the air. If he does, he'll be called for offensive pass interference, and his team will receive a 10-yard penalty. The signal for this is one fans dread seeing: the official pushes both palms out away from his body.

Illegal Forward Pass

An official makes this call if the quarterback throws the ball after he crosses the line of scrimmage, or if two forward passes are made on the same play. The result of the play is negated, and the offense is penalized 5 yards from the spot of the infraction and suffers a loss of down. The official signals this by waving one arm behind his back.

Ineligible Man Downfield

On passing downs before the ball is thrown, the offense can have only five of its players beyond the line of scrimmage. Any more than that, or any lineman downfield who does not qualify as an eligible receiver based on his uniform number, and the team is flagged for a 5-yard penalty. The official simply puts one hand on his head to signal this penalty.

Illegal Touching

If the official touches both shoulders with the tips of his fingers, it means an offensive player has made contact with the ball illegally. Usually this 5-yard penalty is called when a pass strikes an illegible lineman before touching an eligible receiver or defender.

Delay of Game

If the offense fails to snap the ball before the play clock expires, the team is flagged 5 yards. Game officials demonstrate this by folding their arms in front of their body. The officials also use this call when a player kicks a football or does something to disrupt the officials' ability to manage the game.

Intentional Grounding

Sometimes quarterbacks get into sticky situations. Whenever possible, a quarterback is better off throwing an incomplete pass than taking a sack for lost yardage. However, game officials flag a quarterback for intentional grounding if they deem no receiver was in the vicinity of where the quarterback was throwing the ball, and if the quarterback was neither inside the pocket nor got the ball back to the original line of scrimmage. The official illustrates this by taking both hands and making a slashing motion in front of his body. For this, the offense accepts both a 10-yard penalty and a loss of down.

Personal Foul

The personal foul call usually precedes another, more specific type of infraction on the offense. The official shows this by holding one arm out, head high, and striking it with a chopping motion using the other arm. For example, the game official may first signal a personal foul and then signal a chop block. The personal foul call can be used for any number of major infractions on the offense. All personal fouls carry a 15-yard penalty.

Unsportsmanlike Conduct

If an offensive player argues with an official, taunts or fights with a defensive player, or is guilty of excessively celebrating an important play or score, he may get flagged 15 yards for unsportsmanlike conduct. The official stretches both arms out away from each side, shoulder height.

Instant Replay

Not every play is able to be reviewed by game officials. Those that are can be subject to instant replay, a technology popularized during pro football's trial with it in the 1980s.

NFL rules allow coaches two opportunities to challenge a penalty or ruling each game. If the coach is successful with both challenges, a third is given.

When he wants to challenge a ruling, the coach throws a red flag onto the playing field and explains to the game officials what he wishes to challenge about the play. If the coach's challenge fails during the instant replay process, the coach is forced to sacrifice one of his team's valued time-outs.

The referee is given 60 seconds to review the play to determine if a mistake was made. The referee can decide one of three things:

- The right call was made on the field.

- The wrong call was made.

- There's not enough indisputable evidence to change the call.

If the referee does determine to reverse the call, he may also need to use instant replay to determine the spot of the ball and the time on the game clock.

In the final two minutes of both halves, coaches are not permitted to challenge calls; all reviews must come from the replay booth, where an assistant to the officials determines whether to review the play.

FUN FACT

One of the most memorable instant replay moments occurred during a 2002 playoff game between the New England Patriots and Oakland Raiders. Late in the game, the Raiders sacked New England quarterback Tom Brady, jarring the ball free. The game officials ruled the ball a fumble and gave Oakland possession. Instant replay helped the officials determine that the tuck rule applied, and the ball was returned to New England, who went on to win the game in overtime. The tuck rule states that a quarterback cannot fumble the ball when drawing the ball back to his body after making a throwing motion. Instead, the ball is treated the same as an incomplete pass.

Instant replay can be used to determine:

- If a receiver or defender made a successful reception
- If the quarterback was guilty of an illegal forward pass, or if a pass was travelling forward or backward
- If the quarterback was making a pass or guilty of a fumble
- If one team had too many men in the huddle or on the field at the time of the snap
- If a defender or ineligible receiver touched a pass, or if a player touched a kick or punt
- If the ball or a player was out of bounds
- To review all scoring plays

The Least You Need to Know

- In addition to using hand and arm signals to call penalties, game officials also use signals for a variety of other game situations.
- Rulings carry different penalties based on the severity of the infraction. Most are either 5, 10, or 15 yards.
- Instant replay is a tool game officials use to ensure the correct call was made. Not every play can be reviewed.

Offensive Statistics

In This Chapter

- Why statistics are so important
- Quarterback, running back, and wide receiver statistics
- The pancake block: an offensive lineman's favorite statistic
- The most prevalent statistics for team offense

There are statistics to keep track of everything, from how a player performs to how many minutes a team possesses the ball each game.

Offensive statistics are more widely used and appreciated than defensive statistics, especially those that track player performance. But statistics are more than just numbers on the back of a playing card; they have a life all their own.

Why Statistics Matter

Fans care about numbers. Actually, some fans are *obsessed* with numbers. They can recite yards and touchdowns from the current season and for players from many seasons ago. A number can cement a player's legacy or doom him forever.

Players and coaches care about statistics, too. Those numbers tell them who's doing well, who needs to improve, where the team has been successful, and where it's struggling.

Statistics are numbers, separated into many categories. Every pass a quarterback throws can influence a half-dozen or more of the statistics his fans and the coaches on his team pay attention to.

When players or coaches say only winning matters, not statistics, don't believe them. Sure, the ultimate objective of any game is to win, but it's the statistics that help influence the result of the game. And you can bet those same coaches and players use those numbers the next time it's their turn to negotiate a contract.

To qualify for any statistical category, a player must have a minimum number of units in that category. For example, if a running back runs the ball once and gains 14 yards, his average per attempt would be 14 yards. But until he accumulates a certain number of attempts, his numbers aren't included in the official list teams and media sites post each week.

Sometimes statistics can be misleading. Because a quarterback completes a lot of passes doesn't mean he's a great quarterback. It's a subjective science, enabling the interpreter to decide what's of relevance and what isn't.

Passing Statistics

Teams are protective over who they let pass the football, so besides trick plays, the quarterback accumulates all the passing numbers for the team. He does this through a variety of ways.

Attempts

Every time a quarterback throws a forward pass, it counts as one attempt, whether it is successful or incomplete, unless the play is nullified.

The average NFL quarterback throws between 450 and 500 passes per season, not including exhibition or playoff games. That amounts to about 30 passes each game.

Completions

A quarterback earns a completion whenever a receiver—a running back, wide receiver, tight end, or anyone else eligible—catches a pass.

FUN FACT

Brett Favre has completed more NFL passes than any other quarterback. The first receiver he completed a pass to was … himself. In 1992, Favre threw a ball that was batted backward. He caught it for a loss on the play.

More important than a quarterback's number of attempts or completions is his completion percentage, which is calculated by dividing the total number of completions by the total number of attempts.

An average completion percentage in the NFL is 60 percent. Any starting quarterback who completes 65 percent of his passes or better can be said to be having a fine year.

Passing Yards

In terms of statistics, a yard is a yard is a yard. The advancement of the football for a full 3 feet equals 1 yard on the stat sheet. Quarterbacks are measured by how many yards they pass for, but it doesn't matter how far they throw the football on any given play. For example, if a quarterback throws the ball 10 yards downfield to a receiver, who advances it another 20 yards before being tackled, the quarterback is given credit for 30 passing yards even though his pass only traveled a third of that distance.

The benchmark for starting quarterbacks in the NFL is 3,000 yards, or about 200 yards per game on average. Today it's becoming more common to see multiple quarterbacks pass for more than 4,000 yards in a season; before major rule changes were made in the late 1970s to make things easier on the passing game, very few quarterbacks in the history of professional football had passed for 4,000 or more yards in a single season.

Quarterbacks are also judged by the number of yards they average per passing attempt. This shows a level of productivity but is a better indicator of the team's passing offense as a whole than it is of a quarterback's prowess.

Touchdown Passes

When the passer throws the ball to a receiver who either catches it in the end zone or successfully advances it there, the quarterback is credited with a touchdown pass.

FUN FACT

In 2007, New England Patriots quarterback Tom Brady established a record by throwing 50 touchdown passes in one season. Besides Brady, only three players have thrown more than 40 touchdown passes in a single season. (The others are Peyton Manning, Dan Marino, and Kurt Warner.)

Roughly half of the NFL's quarterbacks throw 20 or more touchdowns in a season; only a handful throw more than 30 touchdowns each year.

Interceptions

No quarterback wishes to lead this category, but it's part of the game. Whenever a defender catches the football, the quarterback is charged with an interception.

Most quarterbacks average just less than 1 interception per game, or roughly 12 per season. Any more than that and the passer may find himself on the bench before too long.

Sometimes the interception isn't the quarterback's fault. A wide receiver may run the wrong route and therefore not be in the spot on the field where the quarterback expects him to be. Or a receiver may miss or fail to catch a perfectly thrown pass, allowing the defense the opportunity to catch the ball.

Unlike in baseball, where errors are determined on a subjective basis, interceptions are all credited to the quarterback, right or wrong.

QUICK HIT

Quarterbacks aren't always the biggest fans of throwing a Hail Mary at the end of a half or the game. While launching the ball into the end zone can provide the offense with a chance to score, often the pass is intercepted, adversely affecting the quarterback's statistics.

QB Rating

Created in 1973, the passer rating, or QB Rating, helps measure how well a quarterback has performed across all levels. It speaks to both his efficiency and productivity as a passer.

Four components are needed to calculate a QB Rating, each based on a specific statistical category:

- Completion percentage
- Yards per attempt
- Touchdowns per attempt
- Interceptions per attempt

After calculating each component, the four totals are added together, divided by 6, and multiplied by 100.

The best possible NFL QB Rating is 158.3—a score few quarterbacks have registered in a single game. If a quarterback scores a rating of better than 100.0 for a season, he's had a great year. No quarterback has a career rating above 100.0, although several players, like San Francisco's Steve Young, are close.

Rushing Statistics

Any player who handles the football on a rushing down is eligible to accumulate rushing statistics.

Attempts

Whenever a player is handed the ball from the quarterback on a play that does not involve a pass, it counts as one rushing attempt, or carry. Quarterbacks accumulate rushing attempts for carrying the football as well.

A team's lead running back may carry the ball 15 to 20 times each game. Anything more than 30 attempts in a game is considered a heavy workload. Usually only about 10 NFL running backs carry the ball more than 300 times in a season.

Rushing Yards

Every yard a running back gains counts toward his game, season, and career totals. Of course, it works both ways. If a running back is tackled behind the line of scrimmage for a loss on the play, those yards are deducted from his total.

If a running back gains 100 or more yards in a game, it's noteworthy. It used to be that 1,000 yards was the total all backs were measured against each season, but it's become too common. Now the elite backs gain 1,200 or more yards.

Yards Per Carry

To calculate yards per carry, simply take the total yards a rusher has accumulated and divide it by the total number of attempts he has.

This statistic is sometimes a better indicator of talent and success than total rushing yards. Not every rusher on a team is given the same number of attempts, so the yards per carry tells the coaching staff and the fans which players are doing more with the attempts they have to work with. But to grade a player fairly, he must have a minimum number of carries to fit into the discussion.

A steady NFL back averages no fewer than 4 yards per carry; a back averaging 4½ yards or better usually ranks among the league's best.

Touchdowns

When any offensive player carries the ball over the goal line on a running play, he is awarded a rushing touchdown.

Running backs score touchdowns in bunches, often scoring a few in one game and then going a few weeks without one. The elite running backs score between 12 and 15 rushing touchdowns in a season, averaging roughly 1 per game.

 FUN FACT

Playing against the cross-town rival Chicago Bears, Chicago Cardinals halfback Ernie Nevers scored 6 rushing touchdowns in a November 1929 contest. Nevers also kicked 4 extra points that day, scoring all of the Cardinals points in the 40–6 win.

Fumbles

What interceptions are to quarterbacks, fumbles are to running backs and wide receivers. A fumble occurs after someone delivered the ball successfully to the player, but he failed to keep control of it. Quarterbacks also are credited with fumbles when possessing the ball, and some of the NFL's biggest fumblers played the quarterback position.

Teams keep track of two kinds of fumble statistics:

- Fumbles
- Fumbles lost

A player can register a fumble without losing the ball if he or one of his teammates gain back possession of it. That statistic is far less irritating for coaches than fumbles lost to the defense.

Great backs rarely fumble the ball. Those who fumble a handful or more times in a season end up in their coach's doghouse.

Receiving Statistics

When the ball goes in the air, receiving statistics are up for grabs. The receiving categories differ only slightly from those used for running backs.

Receptions

The wide receiver's primary task is to catch the football. Everything else—long gains, touchdowns, end zone dances—is gravy. A receiver earns one reception, or catch, each time he secures a pass from the quarterback, regardless of how far he travels with the ball afterward.

Not long ago, 100-reception seasons were rare. Now at least a handful of NFL receivers approach that mark each year. For running backs and tight ends, 50 receptions constitutes a good season, but players at both positions have challenged wide receivers atop the leader board.

FUN FACT

Denver Broncos wide receiver Brandon Marshall caught 21 passes in a game against the Indianapolis Colts in 2009.

Receiving Yards

As with rushing yards, a receiver accumulates yards and can lose yards on a negative play, or by running backward after making a reception.

A 1,200-yard season indicates an elite receiver in the NFL, while 1,000 yards is good enough to lead two thirds of the teams in the league.

Yards Per Catch

As noted in Chapter 9, there are different types of receivers. Some excel at making big plays, while others catch short passes and help move the ball a few yards at a time.

The yards-per-catch category distinguishes one from the other. The big-play guy may have a yards-per-catch average of 15.0 or better. Few players average more than 20 yards per catch, but it does happen.

Yards After the Catch

Different from yards per catch, yards after the catch (YAC) shows how many yards a receiver gains on his own. If a receiver catches a pass 20 yards downfield, for example, and runs for an additional 30 yards, he'll be credited for 50 yards on the play. But his YAC on the play is equal to the 30 yards he gained after the catch.

YAC demonstrates a receiver's ability to break tackles or make defenders miss. Whatever the reason for it, teams and fans love it because a receiver with a good YAC rating is someone who makes good things happen when he has the football.

Running backs have a similar category to keep track of the yards they gain after first contact with a defender (yards after touch, or contact), but it's rarely found on the stat sheet.

Touchdowns

When a player catches a forward pass in the end zone, or catches it in the field of play and runs with it across the goal line, he is awarded a receiving touchdown.

History tells us that only roughly a half-dozen NFL receivers catch 10 or more touchdowns each season. Anything more than 15 is a special year.

Dropped Passes

If a ball is deemed catchable but the receiver fails to secure the football for a reception, it is considered a drop. For a wide receiver, a drop is as disheartening as an interception or a fumble, only a drop does not always result in a turnover.

There are a number of reasons why a receiver drops a pass—the sun is in his eyes, the ball was thrown too hard, a defender distracted him, etc.—but coaches care little for excuses and won't tolerate a receiver dropping more than one pass in a game. After that, a receiver may end up on the sideline.

Targets

A statistical category that's becoming more widely used in recent years is the target, which indicates when a player is the intended receiver on that play. Even if a receiver doesn't catch the ball, but it is thrown to him, it counts as one target.

This statistic tells fans how many opportunities each receiver is given during a game or a season. By comparing all the target totals for a given team, you also can see which receivers the team's quarterback favors.

The Pancake Block

Linemen are the cheated ones on offense, because all the statistics belong to the skill players. But the recent addition of the pancake block has given linemen something to cling to (and it's named after a breakfast entrée most linemen appreciate!).

When a defender is left lying flat on the ground, it counts as one pancake block for the offensive lineman. The league does not keep official statistics for pancake blocks.

FUN FACT

It is believed the term *pancake block* was first used by University of Pittsburgh media relations staff to label Bill Fralic's severe blocks in games during the 1980s. It was then popularized when Ohio State media and fans began to use it to describe Orlando Pace's dominance a decade later.

Team Statistics

There are statistics to track team success as well, although some of them aren't as visible as the statistics used to track individuals. In many ways, though, coaches care more about what the offense does as a unit than what any of its individual parts do on their own.

Time of Possession

One indicator of offensive success is how long it holds the football. If a team averages more than 30 minutes per game, it means it held the ball more than its opponents.

Sometimes, though, this statistic can be misleading. Some teams score quickly, and sometimes opponents rack up tons of clock time without putting many points on the board.

Still, when given a choice, every coach would rather have the ball, and thus own the clock, than have his opponent have control of it.

First Downs

The standard measurement of every team is the first down. No matter what type of offense the team uses—relying on long plays or short—every team needs first downs to win games. The great offenses average 20 or more first downs each game.

Penalties and Turnovers

The fewer penalties the offense commits, and the fewer turnovers it gives up, the more likely it is to have success. Don't believe this? Just check the leader board for both columns and then check the standings in the newspaper—the same teams are usually sitting atop both groups.

Every penalty counts as one, but statisticians also track penalty yards to gauge how badly a team has shot itself in the foot thanks to penalties. For turnovers, every lost fumble and interception counts as one.

QUICK HIT

Television analysts usually make mention of one statistic at the end of the half and the game—points off turnovers. Whenever one team loses possession of the ball due to a fumble or interception and the other team scores, either on that play or the subsequent series, it counts toward this statistic for the scoring team. Often, this can be viewed as a factor in the outcome of games.

Sacks Allowed

As a unit, the offensive line can take pride in giving up few team sacks. This category is used to judge the best and worst lines in the league, although sometimes the quarterback, not his blockers, can be responsible for the sack.

Allowing a sack or two a game isn't too bad. Any more than that can be problematic.

Third- and Fourth-Down Conversion Percentage

To win games, more specifically close games, teams need to be efficient on third and fourth down. These statistics show how often a team has gained a first down on a third- or fourth-down attempt (punts excluded).

A 40 percent success rate is about average for NFL teams on third-down attempts; 50 percent is average on fourth down.

Red Zone Success

As mentioned in Chapter 5, the red zone is where points become very likely. Of course, coaches know better. Keeping track of a team's success when it gets within 20 yards of its end zone can tell the coach or his players how well the team finishes those drives.

Red zone success measures points scored against total trips. This helps award more weight to a team that finished its red zone visits with touchdowns versus field goals.

Yards Per Game

You can often hear coaches say, "We moved the ball well; we just didn't score." A team's average number of yards per game may be an indicator of this.

This statistic can also be broken into subcategories, such as rushing or passing yards per game. To calculate it, add the total number of yards gained, subtract the total number of yards lost, and divide that by the number of games played.

Points Per Game

An offense can gauge its true worth by how many points it averages per game. Score a lot, and the offense is doing its job. Hold an average below the rest of the league, and it's time to pick up the pace.

Most NFL offenses average 20 or more points a game; only a few average more than 30 points.

The Least You Need to Know

- Statistics help coaches and players identify strengths and weaknesses and give fans something to recite around the water cooler.
- The QB Rating factors a number of a quarterback's most important statistics together to give him an overall rating to rank against all other passers.
- Running backs are often rated by how many yards they gain and how many touchdowns they score. The best way to judge a back, however, might be to check how many yards he averages per attempt.
- Receivers care most about scoring touchdowns, but racking up receptions and yards is what earns the paycheck.

They Got the Ball

Understanding defense boils down to understanding what makes the men who play it. Save the glory for the offense; the defense doesn't need it. This side of the ball has its own set of rewards—the absence of fear, the thrill of the chase, and the pleasure that comes from denying the other team its objectives.

Part 3 covers all the positions, strategies, penalties, and statistics that pertain to the defensive side of the ball.

Defensive Linemen Are Unyielding

In This Chapter

- The difference between ends and tackles
- Why linemen make everyone else on the defense look good
- Techniques linemen use to rush the quarterback

The offensive line has its beef, so the defense also needs a little beef to balance things out. That's where the defensive linemen come in. Many weigh close to what the offensive linemen weigh—330+ pounds. But size is only a number; the best linemen use leverage and technique, not bulk, to beat blockers.

To play defensive line, a player must also be able to hold his own ground, never relenting to an offensive lineman trying to take him in one direction or another. Whereas the offense knows where the ball is going on every play, the defense must play with its eyes as much as its muscle, observing and interpreting where the play is headed.

Defensive linemen must also be unselfish. These players do not record gaudy numbers, and often their contributions aren't able to be classified or recorded. But make no mistake: coaches and teammates are well aware of the important role the big guys up front play on defense.

What They Do for the Team

The defensive line's job is to limit the boundaries within which the offense has to operate. Defensive linemen try to tighten up running lanes so running backs have little room to work. And they do their best to surround and pester the quarterback with the hope of affecting his ability to make decisions and execute plays. Defensive linemen try to bat down passes and strip the ball carrier of the ball, and occasionally a loose football plops into their hands.

The best linemen never stop working, never give in to the offense, and chase after the ball no matter how far away they are from it. A relentless defensive lineman is like an angry bull—eventually the bull is going to strike and the victim is going to feel its horns.

Much as is the case with their counterparts, defensive linemen exert a lot of energy without usually having to travel a great distance. They work in the trenches, but they're occasionally sent outside their comfort zone when the defense is trying to disguise its alignment.

If the defensive line holds its ground up front, other defenders (i.e., linebackers and defensive backs) are free to step forward and make the play. When the defensive line gets pushed around like a rag doll, the offense has its way.

QUICK HIT

Offensive linemen usually line up in the same spot on every play. Not defensive linemen. They like to test out different places to line up to find a weakness they can exploit.

The Ends

The linemen positioned on either side of the defensive line are appropriately named the ends. Different types of ends suit different types of defensive schemes. For teams that prefer to use three defensive linemen instead of four or five, the ends must be better run-stoppers than pass-rushers. A three-man line needs more bulk, so the preferred ends are larger and rely on their size, much like a defensive tackle does.

In a front, or *scheme*, that features four or five defensive linemen, the ends don't necessarily need to be as large because there are more big bodies along those lines. In such cases, coaches can use ends who are quick and athletic. Often shorter and smaller than the offensive tackles they're lined up against, a speed-rushing end can beat a tackle, thanks to his quickness.

> **GRIDIRON GAB**
>
> A **scheme** is an arrangement of players a particular defense is committed to using. A 3–4 scheme, for example, uses three defensive linemen and four linebackers. Each scheme caters to different sets of personnel. (See Chapter 18 for more information.)

Whatever size an end is, or whatever type of scheme he's a part of, his primary duty is containment, or to seal off the outer edges of his side of the field, forcing the quarterback or ball carrier to roam the middle of the field, where more defenders are positioned. To accomplish this, ends often line up just outside of the offensive tackle or tight end and aim for that player's outside shoulder after the ball is snapped.

The Tackles and Nose Guard

The linemen positioned inside the two ends can all be classified as interior linemen, same as the guards and center on offense. If a defense places someone directly over the nose of the football, he's called a nose tackle or nose guard. Linemen positioned across from the offensive guards or tackles, but on the inside of a defensive end, are called defensive tackles.

> **FUN FACT**
>
> It's believed that William Perry weighed close to 400 pounds at one point during his days with the Chicago Bears in the 1980s. The defensive tackle was so big, he was nicknamed The Refrigerator, which helped Perry become a celebrity off the field.

In football speak, the interior defensive linemen eat up bodies—the more the better—and the bigger the defensive lineman, the more likely the offense will use more men to block him. A defensive tackle or nose guard does not need to make the play; if he can draw two or more offensive blockers, that frees up another defender to make the tackle. It's simple arithmetic.

Sometimes linemen are effective just by positioning themselves in a place where the offense *hopes* to move the football. When linemen fall into openings in the offensive line—this is called clogging the hole—the offense has to change its course and the ball carrier has to take a detour.

Interior linemen make very few tackles and get very little notoriety. The only way to judge these players is through the performances of those around them. When linebackers are making plays at the line of scrimmage and defensive ends are drawing one-on-one matchups on the outside, it likely means the interior linemen are doing their jobs.

PENALTY!

When the quarterback is giving the cadence and preparing the offense for the snap of the ball, no defender is permitted to interfere with or mimic the cadence in an attempt to draw the offense offside.

Penetrate Enemy Lines

If you think of the football field as a battlefield, then the defense's primary task is to advance beyond the line of scrimmage, where the offensive line is stationed to stop them. The defensive line is the first group able to do so.

The rule in the middle of the line is that the low man wins—as long as he can keep his footing. When two linemen collide, the lower one has more leverage and can drive his opponent backward.

When linemen start to make their way into the offensive backfield, good things happen for the defense. The quarterback begins to panic, running backs run out of room, and offensive linemen resort to holding a defender rather than allowing him a free opportunity to hurt the quarterback or another player. And whenever a defensive lineman draws a holding call, he's won the battle.

When a defensive lineman is able to penetrate the offensive line too easily, it could be because the offense is setting up a screen pass. If the defensive lineman senses this, he'll retreat to the line of scrimmage in search of a wall of linemen. That's where he'll find the ball is being thrown.

Close Down the Room to Run

It's been said that football teams that run well, and also defend against the run well, win championships—and that's true. An offense's primary goal is to establish a running game—it's safe and it eats up time, keeping the opposing team's offense off the field. A defense's primary goal is to stop the run. When these two objectives collide, the winner of the battle usually wins the war.

Although the defensive line does not make the majority of tackles on running plays (that job is saved for the linebackers), it does play an integral role in limiting the other team's ability to run. Defensive linemen slide into holes to close lanes where backs can run, and they tie up two and sometimes three blockers—basically doing everything they can to make life miserable for the offense trying to advance the ball on the ground.

Each lineman's goal is to push the blocker he's paired with deep into the offensive backfield, tightening the area where the handoff is made and creating a congested space with few exits for the back to run through.

Chase After the Quarterback

Playing tug-of-war with the offensive line is only so much fun. What all defensive linemen desire is a chance to hit the quarterback, preferably while he has the ball so they can cause a fumble or collect a sack.

Of course, the best-equipped linemen to do this are the ends, who deal with far less congestion and are usually quicker and more agile. Defensive tackles can pursue the quarterback, too, but today's preferred tackles are thicker-bodied and can eat up space more than chase down quarterbacks.

For any defender, the key to getting to the quarterback starts with getting a good jump on the snap of the ball. Defensive linemen often try to anticipate the snap by observing a quarterback's tendencies—how he changes the volume or pace of his voice when giving the cadence, for example—and by observing the offensive line. The standard approach, however, is to simply watch the ball. When the center snaps it back between his legs, the defensive lineman must explode from his stance into the blocker in front of him and then maneuver his way past that individual en route to the passer.

Pass rushers, both ends and interior linemen, use a number of techniques to advance past the person blocking them. Here are a few of the more common ones:

- The swim
- The rip
- The bull rush

To swim an opponent, the lineman winds the arm closest to the opponent facing him over top of his head—much like a pitcher in baseball would, or someone performing the front stroke (hence, the swim)—bringing the arm down to the backside of his opponent. He then uses his momentum to push through the blocker. This can be particularly effective for defensive players who are taller than the offensive player they're going against.

A rip is very much the opposite of the swim. Instead of winding the arm over top of the other player, the defender makes an upper cut–like motion, looking to position his swinging arm underneath his opponent's armpit. The rip gives the defender leverage to lift his blocker up out of his stance, thus weakening that player's strong base. When the offensive player is off-balance, the defender again steps forward and uses momentum to get beyond his blocker.

A bull rush is a head-on technique that works well when the oncoming defender has a few steps to build momentum and can catch the offensive lineman off-guard. By plowing into his blocker square, with all his force, the defender knocks that player backward, sometimes flat, and runs through the blocker on his way to the quarterback.

Every lineman aims to record a sack on every pass play, but even the great ones do so only once every game or so. In many cases, though, falling short of a sack is almost as effective as finishing the job. When a quarterback feels pressure, he'll begin to panic, which forces him to speed up his decision-making process. This is when passers miss open targets or throw errant balls the defense intercepts. A defensive back's best friend is a reliable pass rush.

QUICK HIT

Defensive end Reggie White had a move called the club. While charging at an offensive tackle, White would get that player leaning one way or the other and would then use one arm to toss the off-balance blocker to the ground. It was the perfect display of power and leverage, leaving players on both sides of the ball awestruck.

Names to Know and Performances to Remember

No line was as troublesome for opposing offenses as the Los Angeles Rams' Fearsome Foursome was during the 1960s. The combination of Lamar Lundy, Rosey Grier, and Hall of Famers Deacon Jones and Merlin Olsen paralyzed opponents.

Football carried on the tradition of naming outstanding defensive line groups in the 1970s. Pittsburgh had the Steel Curtain, the Vikings had the Purple People Eaters, and Dallas had its Doomsday Defense. All those defenses led their teams to the Super Bowl on more than one occasion.

Super Bowl voters couldn't decide which Dallas Cowboys defensive lineman had a better performance in Super Bowl XII, so they let end Harvey Martin and tackle Randy White share the honor—the only time that's happened in Super Bowl history.

The most dominant pass rusher of all time was probably defensive end Reggie White. Dubbed the Minister of Defense because he was an ordained evangelical minister, White was anything but kind to those who came upon him on the football field. No lineman could block him, and no quarterback could escape him.

White's 1987 season may have been the greatest ever by a pass rusher. Because of a player strike at the start of that season, the Philadelphia Eagles' star defender played in only 12 games but amassed 21 sacks. No other pass rusher since has come close to his season average of 1.75 sacks per game.

The only pro football player with more career sacks than White is Bruce Smith, who collected 200 sacks during his 19-year career, most of it with the Buffalo Bills.

Want to know the definition of toughness? Los Angeles Rams Hall of Fame defensive end Jack Youngblood played on a fractured left fibula throughout the 1979 playoffs. Ultimately, his Los Angeles Rams lost to the Steelers in Super Bowl XIV.

New York Jets defensive end Mark Gastineau was one of the first players to gain notoriety for celebrating plays made on defense. Gastineau danced after each time he sacked an opposing quarterback, often infuriating the opposing team. In 1984, he sacked 22 quarterbacks, which stood as a record for many years.

Two of the best defensive linemen in the game today play for the Minnesota Vikings. Jared Allen has tremendous quickness as a speed-rushing end, while Kevin Williams is one of the few tackles in the league able to both clog up holes and apply pressure to the quarterback.

The Least You Need to Know

- Defensive linemen are the biggest of the defenders. They line up along the line of scrimmage, across from the offensive linemen.
- The interior defensive linemen help by taking up space. They don't accumulate many of the desirable stats, but their presence helps others around them make plays.
- The ends serve as the team's primary pass rushers and help prevent ball carriers from taking the play to the outside edges of the field.
- The most dominant defensive line belonged to the Los Angeles Rams of the 1960s; the game's all-time greatest defensive lineman was Reggie White.

Linebackers Are Football Creatures

In This Chapter

- Inside versus outside linebackers
- The many ways linebackers lead the defense
- Why linebackers are a crazed, motivated breed

Think of football in its rawest form—muscle, discipline, sacrifice—and the purest football player on the field may be the linebacker. He asks for little recognition, only the satisfaction of getting to wrap his arms around the guy carrying the football. Taking that player to the ground—that's a linebacker's payday.

Linebackers are the roamers of the defense. They cover every inch of ground in the middle of the field, sideline to sideline, and don't stop hunting until the whistle blows the play dead. Their single focus is the player holding the football.

It's a glorious position designed for men who'd be pouring concrete or pounding nails if not pursuing ball carriers. Linebackers are the meanest, baddest men of the gridiron.

What They Do for the Team

Linebackers do everything defenders can do. They engage with much bigger offensive linemen, chase after quarterbacks and ball carriers, and do their best to keep up with receivers. Linebackers force fumbles, grab interceptions out of the air, and tackle everything that steps inside their territory.

Often, the linebacker serves as the defense's vocal leader and cheerleader, barking out instructions on the field and keeping the rest of the unit fired up on the sideline.

It's a busy job that requires a never-stopping motor.

The Outside and Inside

The one quality all linebackers share is the killer instinct. Beyond that, the roles of linebackers vary, depending on where they line up and in what alignment they play. In a 4–3 alignment, for example, the two outside linebackers have drastically different roles than they would in a 3–4 setup. (See Chapter 18 for more on the 4–3 and 3–4 defenses.)

The most recognizable of all linebackers is the traditional middle linebacker of the 4–3 defense. He's the cowboy, the undisputed leader of the unit. Middle linebackers are the guys who have become football immortals. (I introduce you to many of them at the end of this chapter.)

The middle linebacker lines up over the football, a few yards behind the defensive line. Before the snap, his eyes watch the adjustments the offense makes while his ears listen to every word of the quarterback's cadence. When the ball is snapped, he reads the flow of the action of the play, trying to interpret where the ball is heading—pass or run, right side or left. When he figures it out, he attacks.

The middle linebacker is a run-stopper more than a pass-defender, but on passing downs, he must still manage his area of the field, especially if he hopes to pluck a pass out of the air.

For teams that use a 3–4 defense with two inside linebackers versus one middle linebacker, the roles of the two are much the same. They focus on defending against the run first and occasionally take turns blitzing the quarterback through the middle of the line.

No matter the scheme, the inside linebackers are almost always the players who accumulate the most tackles over the course of the season. And at the end of most plays, whether they're credited with a tackle or not, they can be found where the action is.

The outside linebackers in a three-linebacker scheme are defined by which side of the line they're positioned on: the strong or the weak.

The strong side linebacker usually lines up just inside of the tight end, a few yards off the line of scrimmage. Because a high percentage of plays are run to the strong side, this linebacker sees a lot of action and must keep an eye on the tight end on passing downs, doing his best at the line of scrimmage to knock the tight end off-course.

The weak side linebacker is positioned across from the offensive tackle lined up opposite the tight end. This player tends to be the most athletic of all the linebackers, but he's also the smallest and least physical. He aids the defensive backfield on passing plays and rushes the passer on select downs.

QUICK HIT

Defensive coaches use other terms to label each linebacker. The middle linebacker is often called the "Mike" linebacker, the strong called the "Sam," and the weak called the "Will."

In schemes that use four linebackers, the role of the outside linebackers is quite different. On many downs, they act more like defensive ends and are used regularly to rush the quarterback from one side or the other.

Outside linebackers in the 3–4 are the stars, just as the middle linebacker is the star of the 4–3. Usually this type of linebacker has good height and bulk to wrestle with offensive tackles, and he also possesses the explosiveness needed to get to the quarterback. Because a number of pro teams have converted to the 3–4, the demand for playmaking outside linebackers outweighs the supply.

The Do-It-All Captain of the Defense

Each team designates one linebacker to lead the defense in the same way the quarterback leads the offense—usually the middle linebacker, or in a 3–4, one of the inside linebackers. All the discussion flows through him, and his teammates rely on him for adjustments in the seconds before the ball is snapped. For example, when the offense motions a player from one spot to another, the middle linebacker points this out and alerts the defender who must follow the player going in motion.

This linebacker also takes direction from the sideline before each play and relays it to the defense, telling the linemen when they should use *stunts*, instructing a player to blitz, and informing the team what pass coverage it's to use on that particular down. All this information is delivered through a series of codes, same as what the offense uses to instruct each of its players of their given assignment for the play.

Chase Down Ball Carriers

The linebacker is the running back's counterpart on defense. The two are a perfect match, albeit opposites. Running backs are sometimes too quick for defensive linemen to catch and too strong for defensive backs (particularly cornerbacks) to hold on to. But the linebacker is the perfect predator for the task.

At the start of each play, the linebacker watches the running back's eyes and observes his first step. Defensive lineman desire sacks; defensive backs crave interceptions; linebackers want tackles—lots of them—and running backs serve as the primary feast.

WORDS OF WISDOM

Dick Butkus was like Moby Dick in a goldfish bowl.

—NFL Films president Steve Sabol

But first, to get to the ball carrier, a linebacker must break away from, or shed, the blockers he has in front of him. Linebackers are the second-level targets of the offensive line. In some cases, a guard or a tackle will leave his man to go get a linebacker. It's the linebacker's job to be sure the lineman either misses or fails to stay on his assignment.

A linebacker never wishes to get tangled up in the line. He's always attacking the blocker with the intent of disposing of that player to get to the prize behind him. To do this, he must always keep the blocker at an arm's length, never allowing the bigger player to get in tight, where the linebacker can get smothered.

To make the tackle, the linebacker must take the proper pursuit angle. His goal is to meet the ball carrier as soon as possible, but he must also take into account the difference in speed between the two players. The correct angle can help a slower player catch up to a quicker player. Linebackers are masters of knowing which angle to take.

Cover Secondary Receivers

On passing downs, linebackers are usually assigned to cover either a tight end or a running back. In certain coverages, a linebacker is paired with one of the offense's wide receivers.

Most of the time the linebacker is mismatched, not fast enough to run with the speediest of receivers or quick enough to stay with a running back coming out of the backfield. Even tight ends are a chore, as today's model is built more like a wide receiver than a lineman. But linebackers make do. They have to.

A linebacker primarily covers receivers in the middle of the field, leaving the cornerbacks and safeties to cover the outside edges of the field. In zone coverage, linebackers are also often responsible for covering the flats.

Linebackers use their size to their advantage within the first 5 yards of the route, bumping and pushing the receiver to get him off his assigned pattern. After that, the linebacker must do his best to stay with the man he's covering or manage the zone he is responsible for.

One thing linebackers have in their favor on passing downs is fear. Receivers know that if they cross the middle of the field to catch a pass, a linebacker will be waiting to clobber them.

Intensity in Spades

That player you see yelling on the sidelines with a glazed look in his eyes? Chances are he's a linebacker. Linebackers were bred to seek and destroy, and to be a good one requires a level of intensity rare for even football players.

Linebackers must always be up, always thinking about the next play, the next obstacle, the next mission. They can never quit—on a play or in a game—and the players who follow their lead can feed off that energy.

Perhaps no linebacker was more intense than Chicago Bears middle linebacker Mike Singletary. Standing just feet from the offense, Singletary's eyes glared into the backfield, looking for any hint that might tip him to where the play was headed. It gave Singletary the look of an alert madman and distinguished him from his peers on the great Bears defenses of the 1980s.

But offensive players also took notice, always talking about Singletary's wide eyes and his intense demeanor. When a running back or quarterback starts to think about a defender, it plays into the defense's hand.

Names to Know and Performances to Remember

Lawrence Taylor, or L. T., was one of the game's most energetic characters, and one of the few defenders—at any position—capable of taking control of the game from the defensive side of the football. He was instrumental in the New York Giants' Super Bowl wins following the 1986 and 1990 seasons. Taylor had a rare combination of size and speed, and offenses were forced to look for where he was lined up on every play.

 FUN FACT

Lawrence Taylor is the only player to win the NFL's Defensive Player of the Year award three times. He is also the only defender to win it as a rookie.

The vision of the throwback linebacker is that of Dick Butkus, a standout at the University of Illinois and later with the Chicago Bears. Butkus growled and snarled, and opposing ball carriers usually felt the fear of Butkus before they felt the power of his tackle.

Butkus's rival in the 1960s was Green Bay Packers middle linebacker Ray Nitschke. Bald and wearing black-rimmed glasses, Nitschke looked nothing like a football player is supposed to. But he delivered and tolerated pain like few others, and his fine all-around play during his 15-year career earned him a spot in the Hall of Fame.

Chuck Bednarik was the last of the game's 60-minute men, having played every down for Philadelphia on offense as the team's center and then on defense as a linebacker. Bednarik was tough—tougher than the guys of today—and when he hit someone, they felt it. In a 1960 playoff game, Bednarik hit New York Giants running back Frank Gifford so hard, players and fans were genuinely concerned for Gifford's life. He was out cold.

In just his second year in the league, Kansas City Chiefs linebacker Derrick Thomas recorded an NFL-record seven sacks in a single game. Unfortunately for Thomas, on the final play of the game, Seattle Seahawks quarterback Dave Krieg escaped what would have been Thomas's eighth sack and threw the game-winning touchdown.

Who's the greatest linebacker of recent years? Easy, it's Baltimore Ravens inside linebacker Ray Lewis, who is sure to earn a spot in the Hall of Fame soon. Many scouts considered Lewis, a standout at the University of Miami–Florida, too small to play linebacker in the NFL. Lewis proved them all wrong, earning trips to the Pro Bowl in 7 of his first 10 years in the league and winning the Most Valuable Player award in Super Bowl XXXV.

The Least You Need to Know

- Linebackers do it all: chase after ball carries, rush the quarterback, and cover receivers on passing downs. Mostly, though, they're expected to make tackles.
- A linebacker is usually assigned to be the captain of the defense, relaying instructions from the coaching staff to the other defenders prior to the start of each play.
- Linebackers usually are assigned to cover a tight end or a running back on passing downs.
- Lawrence Taylor changed the thinking about what a defensive player was capable of.

Defensive Backs Are the Athletes

In This Chapter

- Cornerbacks and safeties: the last line of defense
- Strong versus free safeties
- Defensive backs and the mental aspect of the game

The brawn of the defense is in its front seven. The finesse and most of the athleticism lies in the defensive backfield, or the secondary. In fact, in many cases, the best athletes on the entire team are the defensive backs—the cornerbacks or safeties—the men able to run stride for stride with receivers, stop on a dime to change direction, and steal interceptions away from the quarterback.

Why "waste" these players on defense when they could be scoring touchdowns on offense? In some cases it's because a defensive back doesn't catch well, or doesn't hold on to the football when he's getting tackled. Defensive backs tend to be a tad smaller than most running backs and shorter than most receivers. The best answer, though, is that having a reliable cornerback or safety is often more valuable to a team than having a standout receiver or running back. A defensive back can negate the other team's best player, offering proof to the theory that sometimes the best offense is a good defense.

What They Do for the Team

Cornerbacks and safeties are a defense's best weapons to counter the offense's passing game. They are well trained to read where the ball is going to be thrown and react, the objective being to knock down the pass, intercept it, or at worst tackle the receiver immediately after he makes a reception.

The defensive backs must also be equipped to assist in defending against the run. Cornerbacks are often considered a team's worst tacklers, but on many downs, they don't need to take down a 220-pound running back, just simply get in his way or take out the back's lead blocker and enable another defender to make the tackle.

The most important role the defensive backs play is to act as the final wall between the offense and the end zone. The defensive backs must take good pursuit angles when chasing after ball carriers and never let a tackle slip through their fingers. Otherwise, it's 6 points for the other guys.

The Cornerback

It's been said that Ginger Rogers could do everything Fred Astaire could do, only she could do it backward and in heels. Well, that's how cornerbacks think of themselves compared to wide receivers—without the heels, of course.

At the snap of the ball, the cornerback must read whether the play is a run or a pass, all the while staying locked in on his assigned receiver. On running downs, the cornerback must shed the receiver trying to block him to get into a position to make a tackle. Often, because the cornerback is positioned at the outer edges of the defense, he's asked to contain the ball carrier back to the middle of the field where more defenders are able to help. If the cornerback fails to do this, the ball carrier can get to the sideline, where he has few defenders between him and the end zone.

A defense usually lines up its cornerbacks on each end of the field, far from the linemen and linebackers, where the cornerbacks are said to be "on an island" all by their lonesome. This means the cornerback must succeed at defending his receiver because no one else is in the immediate vicinity to assist.

Sometimes a cornerback is assigned to a particular receiver and follows, or shadows, that player wherever he goes before the snap of the ball. This helps keep a defense's best cornerback on the offense's best receiver to neutralize that player.

In most cases, however, cornerbacks keep to their side of the field.

QUICK HIT

NFL scouts evaluate prospects on a number of things, including speed, agility, leaping ability, strength, etc. One thing scouts look for in cornerback prospects are flexible hips. A cornerback with flexible, or fluid, hips can change direction on the field with ease—something necessary when trying to cover the game's quickest receivers.

Fans often judge a cornerback by his number of interceptions, but this can be a mistake. Often, the best cornerbacks have few, if any, interceptions because opposing quarterbacks opt not to throw the ball to the receiver that cornerback is covering. Likewise, cornerbacks who collect a lot of interceptions are often those who get beat routinely. No one statistic aptly measures a cornerback's skill.

The Safety

Whereas the cornerbacks are cast as poor tacklers, the safeties must be sure tacklers—some of the team's best. Most teams employ two safeties, a strong and a free. Each has a distinct role and does his part to help manage the defensive backfield and communicate with the cornerbacks.

A team's strong safety can act as an extra linebacker on likely running downs or as a pass defender. He's called the strong safety because he lines up across from the strong side of the offense (usually designated by a tight end). The ideal strong safety possesses both size and speed and acts as one of the defense's lead playmakers. He may line up near the line of scrimmage or down the field, depending on the play situation. On passing downs, he's responsible for defending the tight end or a back most of the time.

In terms of size, the free safety is usually a bit smaller than the strong safety, designed to help defend the pass first and the run second. Positioned the farthest back from the line of scrimmage of all the defensive players—around 15 yards back and usually in the middle of the field—a free safety must read the play at the snap and then respond to where help is needed. On a running down, this means he charges to the ball to help make the tackle. On passing downs, the free safety must identify where the quarterback is going to throw the ball and then assist the defender (usually a cornerback) whose receiver is the intended target.

 FUN FACT

No safety has instilled more fear in receivers than perhaps the Oakland Raiders' Jack Tatum, whose vicious tackles in the 1970s forced receivers to keep one eye on the ball and one eye on where Tatum was at all times. His hits were so deadly, players and fans started referring to him as The Assassin.

Safeties also need good timing. On passing downs, the safety often comes upon the intended receiver at the same time the ball arrives. If he makes contact before the receiver has an opportunity to make a play for the ball, the safety will be called for pass interference. If he times it right, though, the ball will come flying out of the receiver's grasp and the receiver will finish the play lying flat on his back, stinging from the hit.

The Last Line of Defense

Few positions on a football field carry as much pressure as the defensive backs. As the last tier of a team's defense, the defensive backs are usually the ones guarding the goal line on passing downs or long running plays. If they fail to knock down a pass, or miss tackling a wide receiver or running back in the open field, the offense is sure to score.

Therefore, defensive backs are taught to keep the person they're defending in front of them whenever possible. If the receiver begins to sprint down the field, the defensive back must know when to turn out of his backpedal and begin to run elbow-to-elbow with the receiver.

The safety, particularly the free safety, is the absolute last line of the defense. Even when the rest of the defense is crowding around the line of scrimmage for a suspected short-yardage play, the free safety must offer a deep presence on the off chance the offense chooses to take a shot down the field.

QUICK HIT

Offenses use play-action to bring the safeties closer to the line of scrimmage, convincing them it's a running play before dropping back to pass. If the free safety bites too hard on the fake, it may allow a receiver to get behind him on the pass play.

Taking the Quarterback by Surprise

Like linebackers, defensive backs get to do a multitude of things on the field. Defenses send a cornerback or safety on a blitz to apply pressure to (or sack) the quarterback on what can be considered an obvious passing situation. The defense usually tries to mask the blitz by having the player sneak toward the line of scrimmage during the quarterback's cadence. At the snap of the ball, the defensive back blitzes, and unless he's picked up and blocked by a lineman or a back, he has a free lane to the quarterback.

Safeties usually blitz through the middle of the line, whereas cornerbacks blitz from one side or the other. When a safety or a cornerback blitzes, the defense usually designates another player—either a lineman or a linebacker—to fall back into coverage to fill the hole the blitzing defensive back left. Savvy quarterbacks recognize the blitz and throw the ball to the spot where the blitzing player came from … that is, if they have enough time to throw.

> **FUN FACT**
>
> St. Louis Cardinals defensive back Larry Wilson is credited with being the first player used on a safety blitz. It was so effective, other teams quickly began copying the formula. Now almost every team at every level of play uses the safety blitz.

The Absence of Memory

Even the greatest defensive backs get beaten badly, or *burned*, every now and then. It's part of the game. Sometimes players slip, or sometimes defensive backs go for the interception and miss, leaving no one behind them to stop the wide receiver from making a big play.

> **GRIDIRON GAB**
>
> When a defender gets **burned,** the offensive player has beaten him so badly that the defensive player is virtually nowhere in sight when the offensive player makes the play. Usually a defender is only said to get burned on scoring plays or plays that gain a lot of yards for the offense.

Every defensive back must have a short memory—or the absence of short-term memory. After getting beat, that player must be able to pick himself up, shake off what just happened, and prepare for the next play. Because in football, there's always another play, and a player who gets beat is often the target of the offense's next attack. Those cornerbacks or safeties who allow bad memories to linger will only continue to make more mistakes. Those able to put the bad plays behind them are those capable of having lasting careers.

Names to Know and Performances to Remember

No cornerback struck fear into the hearts of opposing quarterbacks as much as Deion Sanders, who defined the term *shutdown corner* during his time in pro football. Sanders was quick with good instincts, and on the rare occasions a wide receiver did lose him for a step or two, Sanders recovered better than any cornerback in the history of the game.

> **GRIDIRON GAB**
>
> A **shutdown corner** is a term teams or fans use to describe a cornerback who can cover the opposing team's best wide receiver and make him a nonfactor in the game, thus shutting down the player. It's a term reserved for only the elite cornerbacks in the game.

From 1989 through 2005, Sanders collected 53 interceptions. He could have recorded more than that, but teams outright refused to throw the ball in his direction. Most consider Sanders the greatest to ever play the position.

One of the most memorable images from Super Bowl history is that of Oakland Raiders cornerback Willie Brown returning an errant Fran Tarkenton pass 75 yards for a touchdown. That play put Oakland ahead for good in Super Bowl XI and helped preserve Brown's legacy as one of the game's great cornerbacks of the 1960s and 1970s.

Few players in the history of football were as fast as cornerback Darrell Green, who played 20 seasons for the Washington Redskins. Green's speed allowed him to stay foot-to-foot with the receivers he covered and made him one of the game's premier cornerbacks of his era.

Ronnie Lott was one of the most accomplished safeties ever to play the game; he was also one of the toughest. Lott once smashed his left pinky finger so hard on the helmet of a ball carrier that he later had to ask a doctor to amputate it—but not before he played a playoff game with it heavily bandaged.

The first superstar defensive back may have been Dick "Night Train" Lane, who joined the Los Angeles Rams off the street in 1952. During that first season, Lane earned a reputation for his hard hitting and for his knack for intercepting the football. Not only were his 14 interceptions a record for rookies, but for all players, and it's a record that stands today.

The game's best two cornerbacks today are Oakland's Nnamdi Asomugha and the Denver Broncos' Champ Bailey, both of whom have earned multiple selections to the NFL's All-Pro team.

The Least You Need to Know

- Defensive backs stand as the last obstacle between the offense and the end zone.
- Cornerbacks and safeties blitz the same as linebackers do, only not as often.
- The free safety lines up the farthest from the line of scrimmage and assists on passes deep down the field; the strong safety is usually the bigger of the two and plays closer to the line of scrimmage.
- The great cornerbacks sometimes record very few interceptions because quarterbacks refuse to throw the ball in their direction.
- Deion Sanders is often considered the greatest cornerback to have ever played the game. He defined the term *shutdown corner*.

Traditional Defensive Alignments

In This Chapter

- Three-, four-, and five-man defensive alignments
- Common pass coverage packages
- Why coaches use the prevent defense … and why some fans hate it

There's no limit to the number of combinations a defense can use to make life miserable for the offense. Anytime a coach takes just one player away from one tier and adds a player to another, it's a different combination—and a different defense entirely.

Most teams use a base defense on most downs. By using the same general alignment, or scheme, it helps defenders become comfortable playing within that arrangement, and it gives the defense some sort of identity.

In the NFL, almost every team puts seven men "in the box," using either three men at the line of scrimmage with four linebackers or vice versa. The differences between having three men at the front of the attack versus four (or, at some levels, five) are subtle yet important.

The Three-Man Front

Popularized in the 1970s, the 3–4 all but disappeared in the NFL until the early 2000s, when teams started to favor it for its versatility and strong pass-rushing presence. That's how football works—everything goes in cycles. When offenses change, defenses change to counter them, or vice versa. Eventually, what is old becomes new again.

The three-man line must be large and able to hold up against double teams from offensive blockers. The alignment places a nose tackle over the ball and uses two ends, lined up either directly across from an offensive tackle or in between the tackle and guard.

The nose tackle is the key to making the 3–4 work. Without a solid player at this position, without that single-person roadblock, the offense will have little trouble pushing through the defensive line and gaining ground. The nose tackle must be able to take on two blockers on every play and stand as an obstacle for teams trying to run the ball through the middle of the line.

The ends must defend both B gaps (the holes between the guards and tackles; see Chapter 19), leaving the outside for the outside linebackers to manage. Defensive ends in the 3–4 are bigger bodies than the ends used in a 4–3 and must be able to play the run while still offering a consistent pass rush.

The outside linebackers in many versions of the 3–4 act as *tweeners*, playing the role of a pass-rushing defensive end on many downs and dropping back into coverage on some passing downs as a typical outside linebacker would in a 4–3 scheme. The outside linebackers produce the bulk of the sacks in a 3–4 alignment, leaving the two inside linebackers most of the tackles on running plays.

GRIDIRON GAB

A **tweener** is a label given to any player who straddles two positions but doesn't perfectly fit into either one. It's most commonly used to describe players who have the shared qualities of a defensive end and an outside linebacker.

Whereas a 4–3 NFL team may invest most of its money in its defensive ends, a 3–4 team's highest-priced talent is probably invested at the nose tackle and outside linebacker spots.

The Pittsburgh Steelers are one of the few teams to have used the 3–4 defense consistently over time, beginning in the early 1980s. To stay with the alignment, a defense must always have a well-stocked cupboard of linebackers, particularly those fit to play in this alignment.

The Four-Man Front

By placing four men, instead of three, along the line of scrimmage at the start of the play, a line can put more bodies at the point of attack and tie up more offensive linemen.

The original version of the 4–3, and still the most commonly used version, places the defensive tackles directly across from the offensive guards and the defensive ends across from the offensive tackles. The middle linebacker is 5 yards away from the line of scrimmage, directly across from the center, with outside linebackers on both sides of him.

In a 4–3, the defensive backfield has the same assignment as it does in the 3–4 defense, using a pair of cornerbacks and a free and a strong safety. Some high school and even college teams add a fourth linebacker, leaving just a pair of cornerbacks and a safety in the secondary. In this alignment, one of the linebackers is usually asked to drop into coverage on probable passing downs.

When a team flexes its linemen, as the Dallas Cowboys defense did so effectively in the 1970s, it shifts them away from their natural spot, even if slightly. In some cases, a defensive end will slide down a spot and line up over the tight end, and defensive tackles can slide down toward the tackle or closer to the center, converting to a nose guard.

Defensive coaches have played with many combinations using a four-man front, changing where the linebackers and defensive backs are positioned to get different effects.

The Bear defense, or the 46, is one such variety of the four-man front. Popularized by Chicago Bears defensive coordinator Buddy Ryan in the 1980s, the defense relies on a talented front four to do their job upfront. Both outside linebackers are positioned near the line of scrimmage next to one another. The free safety is the only player to protect the deep portion of the field, while the other defenders are all used in a variety of blitz packages and coverages.

Offenses can never be sure which players will blitz and which will drop, or sink, into coverage. It's one of the more aggressive-style defenses ever used in pro football, and other than Ryan, few coaches have used it with success. The 1985 Bears finished with a 15–1 record and won the Super Bowl, thanks to a defense that shut out four opponents, including two during the playoffs.

FUN FACT

Buddy Ryan was given so much credit for the Bears' success in 1985 that after the team won Super Bowl XX, the players carried both him and head coach Mike Ditka off the field. It was one of the few occurrences in pro football history when an assistant coach received that treatment.

The Five-Man Front

Usually only high school and college teams use the five-man front; rarely is it seen in the NFL on a regular basis. Teams that use a five-man line do so to help bulk up to defend against the run. They simply replace one of the three linebackers with another interior lineman, placing one over the nose of the ball, two across from the guards or tackles, and two ends flexed outside the tight ends or tackles.

If a school has a schedule that features a lot of power running offenses, it may choose a five-man line to defend against those opponents. Teams that run the wishbone or use any power backfield rarely pass the football, so it becomes a game of stacking one wall of big bodies across from another—old-school football.

Of course, the greatest weakness of a five-man front is that it leaves fewer bodies to defend against the pass, especially true when a team uses a 5–3 alignment. The two linebackers in a 5–2 alignment tend to have the design of a traditional middle linebacker from a 4–3 defense, meaning they're built to stop the run more than defend against the pass. Five-man fronts put a lot of pressure on the two cornerbacks to make plays as well as on the safety to help cover the middle of the field.

The Goal Line Defense

Whenever the offense needs to gain just a few yards (or a few feet), it loads up with big bodies to block along the offensive line. To counter this, the defense does the same, making one defender responsible for each hole, or gap, along the line. This is called a *goal line defense*. Because teams run the ball in these situations more often than not, the defense's mind-set is to get low and eliminate any openings for the running back to slide through.

The remaining few defenders are positioned behind the linemen, ready to crash at the point of attack or defend if the offense chooses to pass the football.

The team that gets the better push at the snap of the ball almost always wins the battle in these short-yardage plays. For the defense, it can be a great challenge, not knowing where the ball is going. But when the defense does prevent the offense from getting the short distance it needs for a first down or a touchdown, it offers a huge shot of adrenaline for its team—"We just stopped the other guys from getting a single yard!"

The Nickel

Most teams use a base defense with seven or more defenders near the line of scrimmage. In certain situations, however, the defense replaces a linebacker with an extra defensive back. This weakens a team's ability to stop the run, but it makes it more difficult for the opponent to find open space to pass the ball.

With five defensive backs, the nickel package offers added protection on obvious passing downs and against teams that regularly employ four-receiver formations. A combination of four linemen and two linebackers helps manage the line of scrimmage.

QUICK HIT

Some teams use three linemen and three linebackers in combination with five defensive backs as a base defense. Because this alignment is more permanent and not used in certain situations, it's often labeled a *3–3–5* defense instead of the nickel.

The Dime

One coin worth more than a nickel is a dime, so when a defense adds one more defensive back to its nickel coverage, it becomes a dime package. Makes sense, right?

The sixth defensive back is called the *dime back* (just as the fifth defensive back is called the *nickel back*). Although not as important as a starting defensive back, a team's nickel and dime backs are different from most other backups because at some point, in most games, the team will need to call on them. There are no such guarantees for other backups.

The Prevent Defense

One thing fans usually hate to hear is that their team has dropped back into a prevent defense. Usually used to "prevent" a team from getting a late score before a half or the end of regulation, it employs a bend-but-don't-break mentality.

The defense puts three or four men along the line of scrimmage to offer some semblance of a pass rush and uses at least seven defensive backs in deep coverage.

Prevent defenses give up yards for the sake of keeping the offense in front of the defenders at all times. The only goal of the prevent defense is to avoid giving up a big play. The most effective plays against this alignment are medium-range passes near the sideline so the receiver can get out of bounds to stop the clock. The defense prefers to give up the middle of the field, where it can make tackles to keep the clock running.

It becomes a race: the offense tries to get as many small chunks as it can to advance down the field, while the defense hopes the clock runs out before the offense gets into scoring range.

WORDS OF WISDOM

The only thing the prevent defense does is prevent you from winning.

—Legendary NFL coach and television analyst John Madden

The Least You Need to Know

- Each team has its own preferred alignment. Most NFL teams have seven men in the box, with either three or four on the line.
- The Chicago Bears' 46 defense was one of the most innovative and aggressive alignments ever featured in pro football. Few coaches use it today.
- Teams use the goal line defense only when the opponent needs just a few yards for a score or a first down.
- The nickel and dime defenses offer added help to defend against the pass.
- The goal of the prevent defense is to limit long plays and keep time ticking off the clock.

Defensive Strategic Tools

In This Chapter

- How the defense labels the holes throughout the offensive line
- The blitz—it can be a valuable tool
- The different types of pass coverages

Since the birth of football, the offense has held most of the cards. It knows where it's going and how it intends to get there. The defense is left to guess.

Over the years, the defense has developed a few tricks to help balance out things. It can send extra players to rush the quarterback, mix and match where its linemen line up, and change up the coverage assignments of its defensive backs on passing downs.

It becomes a game of second-guessing. The offense tries to predict how the defense will line up and then plans accordingly, and the defense tries to think how the offense might game plan and makes adjustments to take them by surprise. It goes back and forth, and sometimes coaches out-think themselves.

Labeling the Gaps

Just like the offense has a system to help instruct its players where to go and why, the defense has a series of gaps, identified by letter, so its players know where to line up and where to blitz. In both cases, the formula is simple enough for a kindergartner to understand.

The defense recognizes each hole, or gap, in the offensive line as a potential place for the play to flow through.

Here's a layout of the offensive line (using two tight ends for full effect) and the gap named to each hole:

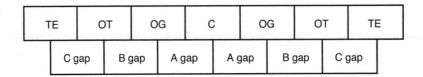

TE	OT	OG	C	OG	OT	TE
	C gap	B gap	A gap	A gap	B gap	C gap	

Blitz Packages

Getting to the quarterback has its advantages. It forces the offense to act quickly—sometimes quicker than it cares to!—and can lead to a sack or turnover. One effective way to apply pressure to the quarterback is in the form of a blitz.

On a blitz, the defense sends a linebacker or defensive back (and sometimes more than one defender) sprinting through a gap or off one side of the line into the offensive backfield. If the blitzing player isn't picked up and blocked by an offensive player (usually a running back), he has an open lane to the quarterback, and good things are bound to happen for the defense.

FUN FACT

One of the more memorable safety blitzes occurred during a 2001 college game between rivals Oklahoma and Texas. Oklahoma safety Roy Williams blitzed when the Longhorns had the ball at their own 3-yard line. Williams dove over a Texas running back and crashed into quarterback Chris Simms, causing the ball to fly into the air before falling into the hands of Oklahoma linebacker Teddy Lehman, who jogged into the end zone. The blitz call, and Williams's efforts, helped seal the win for the Sooners.

The most generic form of the blitz is when a linebacker shoots through one of the gaps. If the blitzing player is a safety or a cornerback, the type of blitz is appropriately called a safety blitz or corner blitz.

Defenses do their best to disguise the blitz, having that person sometimes sneak up on the line during the quarterback's cadence so he doesn't see him coming. If a quarterback knows where the blitz is coming from, his best defense is to throw the ball to a receiver positioned in the area of attack (a spot that's been vacated by the blitzing player). But if the quarterback doesn't recognize where the blitz is coming from, well, it's bon voyage for him.

The zone blitz, popularized by the Pittsburgh Steelers thanks to their innovative defensive coach, Dick LeBeau, helps confuse the offense by replacing the blitzing player with someone else to fill his spot. Sometimes a lineman drops back into coverage as a linebacker or defensive back blitzes on his side of the ball.

Offenses have a much more difficult time beating a zone blitz with the pass because they have to recognize both where the blitz is coming from and where the weakness is in the coverage. That can be a difficult thing to do when a passer has a 250+-pound defender sprinting straight for him.

WORDS OF WISDOM

Find out what the other team wants to do. Then take it away from them.

—Chicago Bears coach George Halas

Defensive Stunts

When the offense comes to the line of scrimmage, its linemen eye up the defensive linemen they plan to block. Some offenses target the best pass-rusher or run-stopper and put an extra body on him at all times.

To get around this, defensive linemen use stunts. At the snap of the ball, two linemen trade places, one stepping in front of the other to take on his point of attack. Sometimes ends trade with tackles, nose guards trade with tackles, and so on.

If a defense has a sense for which lineman is being targeted, where an offensive lineman is going to pull to, or where the ball is going, a stunt can be an effective tool for throwing a wrench into the offense's plans.

Coverage Styles

The defense has two primary ways to defend against the pass:

- Man-to-man coverage
- Zone coverage

Each style has its pros and cons, and most teams use each variety depending on the game situation and the personnel on the field.

Man-to-Man Coverage

Man-to-man coverage is what it sounds like. Every defender in the pass coverage is responsible for one eligible receiver. Each defensive back is locked on an assigned receiver. The cornerbacks handle the best receivers and the safeties take a receiver or a tight end, while the linebackers take any remaining backs or tight ends who release into a passing route.

Man-to-man coverage makes things simple for the defenders to understand and easy for the coaching staff to determine who got beat on a given play. But it follows the weakest link philosophy—if the offense identifies just one weak defender, it can exploit that individual on every pass play without having to worry about the rest of the field.

Zone Coverage

In zone coverages, instead of defending a man, each defender in the pass coverage is assigned to an area. Anything that comes into that area is that defender's responsibility.

Zone coverage is more efficient than man-to-man coverage because defenders don't have to manage too much field on any one play. It can also help a defense account for every inch of the field. But it can also lead to confusion, when defenders dispute just where their territory ends and another defender's territory begins.

Coverage Calls

Now let's look at the different coverage packages, as dictated by what the defensive coaches expect will work best against the opposing offensive formation.

Cover 0

Cover 0 indicates man-to-man coverage. The 0 suggests that no safeties are available to watch over any open areas of the field.

Cover 1

In a cover 1 defense, every player is assigned to a man. Well, all but one, that is—the free safety. He is free to roam the secondary and help out wherever he's most needed.

Cover 2

In a cover 2 defense, each cornerback and safety is responsible for protecting a specific region of the field.

The safeties split the field down the middle through the goal post, each one taking one side to cover. The safeties protect an area that begins roughly 10 yards beyond the line of scrimmage and stretches through the end zone they're defending.

Each cornerback defends the flat on his side of the field—essentially the space from the line of scrimmage to where the safety's territory on their side begins. Linebackers also protect the zones covering the middle of the field.

In a cover 2 scheme, a defense is most vulnerable down the middle of the field and near the sideline at the point where the cornerback's territory stops and the safety's territory begins. This is where the defense's linebackers are asked to help in coverage. If the offense can connect on passes to those spots, it can succeed. If not, the cover 2 is a defense that's tough to beat.

QUICK HIT

The Tampa 2 defense has only a few modifications from the traditional cover 2. Popularized by the Tampa Bay Buccaneers teams of the 1990s under the guidance of head coach Tony Dungy and defensive coordinator Monte Kiffin, the Tampa 2 was actually patterned after the great Pittsburgh Steelers defenses that helped win four Super Bowls in the 1970s.

Cover 3

In a cover 3 zone defense, three players each are responsible for covering one third of the width of the field. Typically each cornerback and the free safety take one third, positioned deep down the field, while the strong safety assists the front seven defenders closer to the line of scrimmage. (He may also assist the linebackers in covering the flats.)

Cover 3 is an effective way for the defense to add an eighth man to the box without becoming vulnerable to a deep pass.

Cover 4

As with cover 3, in cover 4, four defenders each take an equal zone of the field to defend. The linebackers and extra defensive backs help defend the short and intermediate routes, either in zone or man-to-man coverage.

Bump and Run

Cornerbacks and other pass defenders use a technique known as bump and run to try to slow down a receiver after the snap of the ball. As the receiver comes out of his stance, the defender locks up with him, trying to get a good *jam* that puts the receiver at a standstill. If the two get in a tussle and trade blows, the defender has already won. His only goal is to slow down the receiver and keep him off his route.

> **GRIDIRON GAB**
>
> A **jam** is when a defender has control of a receiver, without illegally holding him, and prevents that player from advancing to where he wants to go. One of the best places to jam a receiver is under his shoulder pads, applying force to his chest and armpit area, if possible.

All this must take place within the first 5 yards of the line of scrimmage. After that, the receiver is off limits. The longer the defender can keep the receiver boxed inside that 5-yard zone, the more likely he will eliminate the receiver as a viable option on the pass play.

Because the quarterback expects his receiver to arrive at a certain spot at a certain time on every pass play, bump and run can be effective in affecting the timing of the route. If a receiver is not where he's supposed to be when the quarterback looks for him, the quarterback will move on to another one of his targets.

Most wide receivers don't care for bump and run. It can be frustrating and a nuisance. Receivers do what they can to swim past or slide around the defensive player to avoid contact and get back to their pass route.

The Least You Need to Know

- Each gap in the offensive line is assigned a letter. This system helps defenders communicate.

- Linebackers and defensive backs are sent on blitzes to help apply pressure to the quarterback.

- Teams can defend against the pass using man-to-man or zone coverage. Throughout each game, teams use a bit of both, depending on the circumstance.

- Bump and run is a popular technique defenders use to slow down and frustrate receivers.

Rulings That Affect the Defense

In This Chapter

- Signals game officials make for defensive rulings
- Rulings that govern how a defender can tackle or engage with an offensive player, and the penalties for each
- Why pass interference calls get made, and how they can prove costly

Defensive players are forced to follow a lot of rules. Let's see: no biting, no punching, no eye-gouging, no kicking or tripping, and no using the helmet as a weapon.

But for as many things as defensive players get flagged for, they still test their limits, bending the rules just a bit. Defensive backs make contact with receivers when they shouldn't, just like defensive linemen try to sneak in every lick they can get on a quarterback. Sometimes they get flagged; sometimes they get away with it. It's a game within a game.

Many of the rulings covered in this chapter also apply to offensive players (see Chapter 13) and special teams (see Chapter 24).

General Signals

Most of the time when a game official is making a signal pertaining to the defense, it's a bad thing: interference, unnecessary roughness, taunting.

Occasionally, though, game officials make general signals that indicate non-penalty-related calls—many of them positive.

Change of Possession

Whenever the defense takes control of a fumble, catches an interception, or prevents the offense from getting the necessary yardage on fourth down, the game official shows a change of possession by facing and using one arm to point in the direction in which the defense is also facing.

Safety

When a defender tackles the offensive player with the ball inside that player's own end zone, the game official signals a safety by pressing both of his hands together directly above his head. The defense is awarded 2 points, and the team that sacrificed the safety is forced to kick the ball from its 20-yard line (either by kicking or punting).

The defense can also earn a safety if the game officials rule that the opposing quarterback has committed intentional grounding while in his own end zone, when the offense is called for holding in the end zone, or when the offense fumbles the ball out of its end zone.

Uncatchable Pass

When the game official waves one hand palm down over his head, it signals that the last pass thrown was not a catchable ball for its intended receiver.

A defender cannot be guilty of pass interference on a ball ruled uncatchable; however, the defender may still be called for illegal contact or holding on such a play.

Player Ejection

On rare occasions, game officials feel the need to remove a player from the game, either due to too much violent behavior or for poor conduct. When this happens, the official forms a hitchhiking thumb and makes an ejectionlike motion with his arm. The player is then asked to leave the field of play and enter the locker room.

Penalty Declined

Either team can opt not to accept a penalty, often because the result of the penalty isn't as favorable as the result of the play it occurred on. When a team declines a penalty, the official indicates this by waving both arms in front of his body.

Declining a penalty is common practice for the defense because a penalty often moves the offense back a number of yards but also presents them with a chance to replay the previous down. The defense would rather it be fourth and 5 yards to go than accept a penalty that would make it third down and 15 yards to go.

Defensive Penalties

The rules are much more severe for penalties committed by defensive players, in large part because the defense is capable of causing more harm to an offensive player.

The game of football is constantly evolving, and the rulebook changes with it. Rule changes in recent years have almost all favored the offense, limiting a defender's ability to do his job.

Let's review some of the old and new penalties that get defensive coaches screaming and extend the offense's possession.

Offside

If a defender crosses over the line of scrimmage and doesn't get back to his side of the ball prior to the snap, he's guilty of being offside (indicated by the official putting both hands on his hips). As long as no contact has been made by the defense, the action continues as a *free play* for the offense. After the play expires, the offense is given a choice to accept a 5-yard penalty from the spot of the original line of scrimmage and replay the down, or accept the result of the play.

GRIDIRON GAB

Whenever the defense has a penalty pending and the play is still live, it can be called a **free play** for the offense. No matter if the outcome is negative—interception or fumble—the offense retains possession of the ball with penalty yards tacked on. Free plays are an opportunity for the offense to try a high-risk play in the hope it will yield a lot of yards or a score.

Defenders can also be called for neutral zone infractions, meaning simply that they lined up in the neutral zone prior to the ball snap. This carries the same penalty and is treated the same as an offside call.

Encroachment

This is similar to offside (the signal is the same), except the play is blown dead before the snap, disallowing the offense from having a free play. Officials rule an encroachment if either contact has been made between a defender and an offensive player before the snap, or if a defender crossing the line is ruled to be unabated to the quarterback, meaning the quarterback is at risk of danger on a dead ball. This results in a 5-yard penalty.

Hands to the Face

Due to the increase in the number of concussions players suffer on the field, defenders are penalized for making contact with any part of an offensive player's helmet, either when trying to tackle or in this case, just jamming a hand or a fist into the player's helmet or facemask. The official signals this by putting an open fist under his chin. All defenders can be flagged for hands to the face. It carries a 5-yard penalty and an automatic first down.

Spearing

No player may use the crown, or top, of his helmet as a weapon when tackling another player. This is called spearing, and it carries a 15-yard penalty and an automatic first down. The official signals this with a personal foul call.

Horse Collar

If a defender reaches inside a player's shoulder pad area and uses it as a handle to bring down the player from behind, it's ruled a horse collar tackle, and the offense is awarded 15 yards. The official grabs the inside of his shirt to illustrate this call.

Delay of Game

Defenders can draw a delay of game penalty if the game official determines the defender's intent is to kill time on the clock and slow down the offense. It carries a 5-yard penalty. The official signals this by folding his arms in front of his body. Sometimes laying on a tackled ball carrier while the clock is running draws this call, or if a defender kicks, spikes, or throws the football unnecessarily.

Tripping

Defenders tend to resort to tripping when they fail to get into the right position to make a tackle on the ball carrier, or when a smaller defender is out-manned by a larger offensive player. This results in a 10-yard penalty from the end of the run and an automatic first down. To signal this, the official stands on one leg while using the other to illustrate a tripping motion.

Holding

As is true of offensive players, defensive players aren't allowed to hold. If a game official rules that a defender was trying to prevent an offensive player without the ball from advancing by grabbing hold of that player, a 5-yard holding call and an automatic first down result.

The most common variety of defensive holding is when defenders hold receivers on passing plays to prevent them from catching the football, but defensive linemen can even be guilty of holding offensive linemen on their way to make a block downfield. The official holds one arm with a closed fist against his body with the arm grasping the wrist.

Illegal Contact

This is most commonly called on defenders trying to cover a receiver on a passing play. NFL rules state that a defender can make reasonable contact with the offensive player within the first 5 yards beyond the line of scrimmage, but after that, no contact is permitted, whether that player is the intended receiver or not. Same as defensive holding, this carries a 5-yard penalty and an automatic first down. The official shows this by pushing one palm out in front of his body.

 FUN FACT

Prior to 1978, defenders could be much more physical with receivers on passing downs, which made throwing the ball difficult for the offense. When the league instituted its 5-yard rule, preventing contact beyond that point, offenses began to throw the ball more regularly with success.

Pass Interference

This can be a devastating call for the defense, especially at the professional level where the ball is placed at the spot the interference took place. This means that the penalty has almost no limit as to the number of yards the offense can gain. At the high school and college levels, the penalty is far less severe (15 yards).

Game officials flag a defender when they feel he has interfered with the offensive player's ability to catch the ball. The primary difference between pass interference and defensive holding or illegal contact is that an interference call is made only after the ball is in the air. If the call is made before the pass is thrown, the ruling is one of the other two varieties. The signal for this is one fans dread seeing: the official pushes both palms out away from his body.

Even though pass interference calls often can play a role in the outcome of a game, they're not eligible for review by instant replay because they are deemed *judgment calls.*

> **GRIDIRON GAB**
>
> A **judgment call** is any ruling a game official makes that relies on his interpretation of the action. Think of judgment calls as matters of gray while other calls are more black and white.

Unsportsmanlike Conduct

By holding both arms out to each side of his body, parallel to the ground, the game official has signaled that a defender has committed an unsportsmanlike act. This call is often reserved for noncontact acts, such as arguing with an official or doing a celebratory dance the league has deemed inappropriate. For this, the defense is flagged 15 yards and the offense is awarded an automatic first down.

Taunting

Taunting is a form of unsportsmanlike conduct when a defender in some way demoralizes an offensive player, either verbally or through an act (usually after delivering a vicious hit), or otherwise embarrassing the offensive player in some way. The NFL has put an emphasis on eliminating unnecessary showboating from its players. Officials use the unsportsmanlike conduct signal for this call.

Personal Foul

Every personal foul the defense commits gives the offense an additional 15 yards and an automatic first down. The official shows this by holding one arm out, head high, and striking it with a chopping motion using the other arm. Usually these are penalties of frustration or poor judgment. Regardless, personal foul calls are killers for the defense.

A game official first signals that a personal foul has occurred and then offers details as to the type of infraction.

The penalties in the following sections are all considered personal fouls.

Facemask

Anytime a player grabs hold of an opponent's facemask, a 15-yard penalty results. NFL game officials used to have two varieties of facemask penalties—those severe enough to warrant a 15-yard penalty and incidental face masks that carried only a 5-yard penalty. Now every facemask violation is worth 15 yards. The official makes a motion of grasping his invisible facemask to illustrate this call.

Unnecessary Roughness

A number of actions could draw an unnecessary roughness call, but usually defenders get flagged for making contact after the play stops. When a ball carrier is hit after he has already stepped out of bounds, an official may feel the defender had an opportunity to pull up but hit the ball carrier late anyway. Officials use the personal foul signal to illustrate this call.

Roughing the Passer

This call is another variety of unnecessary roughness. Football rules have been changed in recent years to better protect the quarterback. If the game official watching the quarterback believes a defender has hit the passer unnecessarily anytime after the passer has thrown the ball, he'll flag the defender for roughing. After giving the personal foul signal, the official makes a slashing motion with one hand in front of his body to signal this call.

The Least You Need to Know

- Defenders may not make contact with an offensive player's helmet or facemask or use their own helmet as a weapon.
- At the NFL level, pass interference calls on the defense give the offense the ball at the spot of the foul, often greater than 15 yards. These calls cannot be reviewed by instant replay.
- Any personal foul called against the defense results in a 15-yard penalty and an automatic first down for the offense.
- If a defender hits a player out of bounds or after the play has been stopped, he'll be flagged for unnecessary roughness.

Defensive Statistics

In This Chapter

- The most important defensive statistic: the tackle
- The sack and the hurry—two friends of quarterback chasers
- The categories defenders collect on passing downs
- The statistics used to compare team defenses

In most sports, the numbers are reserved for the offensive side. They're the ones who move the ball and score the majority of points, and usually that's where the excitement is. But football has a real need to track the success of its defensive players as well, and does so over a number of categories, each designed to gauge a defender's skill and performance.

Defensive statistics may not be as colorful or as plentiful as the statistics kept for the offense, but it matters little to defenders; these statistics are all their own.

The Categories of Pursuit

As a team's defense surrounds the ball carrier, its fans start yelling things like "Get him!" and the excitement of the chase isn't capped until the end of the play. When a defender secures (or applies pressure to) the offensive player carrying the football, the statistics start being tallied.

Tackles

If the yard is the fundamental offensive statistic, then the tackle is the fundamental defensive statistic. On almost every snap of the game, a defensive player registers a tackle. Linebackers usually collect more tackles than any other position, but defensive backs and defensive linemen rack up a fair number, too.

Every defender is judged by how many tackles he makes; it often serves as an indicator for the coach as to which players swarm to the ball and which ones are late to arrive.

A tackle is awarded anytime a defender is responsible for bringing the ball carrier to a stop on the play. He can make just enough contact with the ball carrier so he falls, or wrap up and drive that player into the ground. Textbook tackles, ugly ones, and everything in between all count for one tackle.

When two or more defenders are credited with bringing the ball carrier to the ground, each receives an assisted tackle. Here's the odd thing about this statistic: when all the tackles are added up—solo tackles and assists—they all count as one. So if a player has 18 solo tackles and 5 assists, he has 23 tackles. Doesn't seem right, but that's how it works.

Usually, a team's leading tackler has 100 or more total tackles for the season. The very best in the NFL collect more than 150 tackles in a 16-game season.

 FUN FACT

As a rookie in 2007, San Francisco 49ers linebacker Patrick Willis led the league with 174 tackles. No other NFL player had more than 150 that season.

Sacks

Whenever a defender tackles the quarterback behind the line of scrimmage while he still has possession of the football, it's ruled a sack. Half-sacks are awarded when two players are credited with bringing down the quarterback at the same time. Statisticians also keep track of the number of sack yards for each play, calculated by subtracting how many yards away from the line of scrimmage the sack took place.

The elite players in the NFL record a sack or more per game. Few defenders have collected more than 100 sacks in a career, and only one (defensive end Bruce Smith) has reached the 200-sack plateau.

The quarterback sack didn't become an official NFL statistic until 1982. Private researchers have used play-by-play sheets from past years in an attempt to determine how many sacks players had in seasons prior to 1982. Unofficially, Detroit Lions rookie Al "Bubba" Baker had 23 sacks in 1978, a record for a single season.

Quarterback Hurries

If a defender fails to sack the quarterback but forces him to get rid of the ball or scramble from the pocket, the defender is credited with a *quarterback hurry*.

> **GRIDIRON GAB**
>
> **Quarterback hurries** are also often referred to as *quarterback pressures*. The two terms are interchangeable.

This is a relatively new statistical category, and one not always seen credited in box scores or in a player's stat line. It is, however, a good indicator of a defender's pass-rushing prowess. Quarterback hurries can result in poor decisions or turnovers.

Pass-Defense Categories

On passing plays, defenders have an opportunity to collect a number of statistics for making a play on the ball thrown. A team's defensive backs claim the lion's share of these statistics.

Interceptions

Anytime a defender catches a forward-moving live ball before it touches the ground, it's credited as an interception. Sometimes interceptions are due to a poorly thrown ball or a mistake on the intended receiver's part; sometimes the defender just makes a nice play and steps in front of the pass.

In most NFL seasons, 8 or 9 interceptions are good enough to lead the league; 11 or 12 are even better. Defensive backs usually dominate the leader board, and linebackers get a few, too. When a defensive lineman collects an interception, it's usually the result of a deflected pass or a quarterback's inability to throw the ball cleanly. It's rare, and defensive linemen look like a fish out of water when it happens.

FUN FACT

No player in the history of the game has recorded more interceptions than Washington Redskins and Minnesota Vikings defensive back Paul Krause, who notched 81 interceptions during his 16-year career.

Passes Defended

Anytime a defender makes a play to prevent the receiver he's defending from catching the ball, it's considered a defended pass. Although not cited as often as interceptions, defending a pass is nonetheless an indicator of how well a defender performs in coverage.

Some of the finest cornerbacks in the game claim very few interceptions or passes defended because quarterbacks refuse to pass the ball in their direction.

Fumbles

Whenever a defender is credited with causing a ball carrier to lose possession of the football, the defender is awarded one forced fumble. The player who gains possession of the loose ball after it's been fumbled is credited with one fumble recovery. Often, the same player who forces the fumble recovers it, earning him a mark in both statistical categories.

Forced fumbles and fumble recoveries are both rare—a half dozen in a given season usually leads the league. Excluding offensive players, who are given credit for recovering their own or a teammate's fumble, few defenders in the history of the league have recovered more than a couple dozen fumbles over the course of their career.

FUN FACT

As a rookie in 1965, Chicago Bears linebacker Dick Butkus recovered seven fumbles and intercepted five passes to post one of the best stat lines of any first-year defender.

Safeties

The rarest of all defensive statistics is the safety. The two players who share the career record for safeties (Ted Hendricks and Doug English) each own just four. A number of players have recorded two safeties in the same season, but never more than that (see Chapter 20).

Whenever the offense senses that it's pinned up against its own goal line, it usually tries a safe running play to pick up a little breathing room. Because offenses are so conservative and so alert when threatened with the possibility of allowing a safety, it makes them hard to come by for the defense.

 FUN FACT

Los Angeles Rams defensive lineman Fred Dryer recorded two safeties in a single game against Green Bay in 1973—a feat no other player has duplicated since.

Team Categories

When fans compare team play, they usually rely on the categories that rank the league's best pass, run, and total defenses. All are based on the number of yards the team has allowed, which often isn't a telling statistic of that team's performance.

To more accurately evaluate a defense, or even one aspect of it, a fan must dig a little deeper into the statistics.

Pass Defense

The league's top-ranked pass defenses allow the fewest number of yards passing per game. This isn't necessarily an indicator of the best pass defense, only the stingiest.

Other indicators of a strong pass defense are the combined numbers of sacks and interceptions the unit has created, and the average number of yards gained by the opposition per passing attempt.

Another way to judge a pass defense is to look at the average rating of the quarterbacks it has faced throughout the season.

Run Defense

Same as with pass defense, a run defense is judged by the number of rushing yards it allows per game.

A more important team statistic, though, may be the average yards a run defense allows per rushing attempt. That illustrates the defense's strength per play, whereas any average per game may be skewed by an opponent's insistence on doing one thing, whether successful or not. For example, if a team runs the ball 47 times in a game for 132 yards, the total yards gained may adversely affect the defense's run defense ranking even though the offense gained a paltry 2.8 yards per attempt.

The NFL's best run defenses allow fewer than 100 yards rushing per game and fewer than 4 yards per attempt.

Total Defense

A team's total defense ranking is determined by the average number of total yards it has allowed each week over the course of the regular season. To calculate it, a team adds its total passing and rushing yards allowed and then divides by the number of games played.

Strong defenses are well balanced, ranking among the top 10 in the league in both pass and run defense.

Scoring Defense

Arguably the most important team statistic for a defense, scoring defense is calculated by adding the number of points the defense has allowed and dividing it by the number of games played. When opponents score touchdowns on special teams or by returning a turnover committed by the offense for a touchdown, that's not added into the points the defense has allowed.

One thing that can help a team's scoring defense immensely is a shutout (when one team holds the other scoreless). Shutouts were more common in the NFL before rule changes made life easier on the offense.

 FUN FACT

On their way to an NFL title, the 1932 Chicago Bears allowed just 44 points in 14 games. Opponents scored a total of just six touchdowns against the Bears that year.

The Least You Need to Know

- Statisticians award partial counts for sacks and tackles.
- The safety is one of the most desirable defensive statistics for a player to obtain; it's also one of the most uncommon.
- Many of the numbers used to judge unit play, or a total team defensive effort, are not accurate indicators of how strong the unit really is.

The "Other" Third of the Team

Every family has at least one outsider. Special teams are the "black sheep" of the football family. They're the units that receive very little attention or respect but nonetheless can play a large role in helping determine the outcome of each football game.

Part 4 showcases the stars of the special teams—the kicker, punter, return men, and coverage teams—and the ways coaches use them to gain a competitive advantage.

Meet the Special Teams

In This Chapter

- The different special teams units
- The role of a team's kicker and punter
- Why it's important to have a reliable long-snapper and placeholder

The word *special* in "special teams" is there for a reason. When a team's return or kicking games are successful, special things happen for that team. Plays made by the special teams can offer a positive start for a drive, change the momentum of a contest, and lead to touchdowns. And when the game is on the line, a specialist is often asked to come in and try to win the contest for his team.

Like the other two facets of the game, it takes time to develop all the special teams units. For example, a kicker must feel comfortable with his placeholder and long-snapper, just as the long-snapper must learn to deliver the ball with the right velocity and to the spot where the punter expects it.

Coaches often cringe at the thought of special teams plays because they feel they have so little control over them. Linebackers and running backs can be molded, quarterbacks can be nurtured, but a kicker or a punter? Those guys are pretty much left alone until the team needs them and then everyone expects them to perform perfectly.

Why Are Special Teams So Important?

When coaches suggest that special teams make up one third of the game, along with offense and defense, they're not overselling their point. Teams with special teams units that perform well tend to do well in all facets. Good kickoff and punting units give the defense more field to defend, while good return teams give the offense a shorter distance to travel to score points.

That's the real contribution special teams make—they're a leading component in a team's battle for field position. And the game of football is all about which team has the fewest yards to travel for a score.

The Kickoff Unit

When kicking off, all the members of the team assemble in a horizontal line stretching from sideline to sideline, just behind the team's own 30-yard line where the ball is positioned on a kicking tee (at the high school level, the kickoff occurs from the 40-yard line). After receiving the official's go-ahead to start the play, the kicker begins his approach toward the ball with all 10 of the other men following his lead.

The kicker's goal is to reach the ball at top speed, kick it with maximum force, and send it sailing high and deep down the field.

PENALTY!

One official is assigned to watch the line of scrimmage on every kickoff to ensure no players go over the line before the ball is kicked. Kickoff teams practice to be sure no man on the unit gets ahead of the kicker.

The Kicking Unit

For field goals and extra-point attempts, teams have a special group of 11 that comes onto the field for the attempt:

- A front wall of eight blockers, many of them part of the starting offensive line
- A *long-snapper*
- A *placeholder*
- A kicker (short for placekicker)

GRIDIRON GAB

A team's **long-snapper** acts like a center, only instead of handing the ball back between his legs, he launches it to the recipient (either the team's placeholder or punter). The **placeholder** kneels down 7 yards directly behind from where the ball is spotted at the beginning of the play, catches the snap, and places it on the ground for the kicker.

The long-snapper, placeholder, and kicker act as a three-man team. They often work together during practice, trying to get the ball snapped to the right spot and put down on the block where the kicker wants it—at the same speed and location every time.

For the eight men blocking, the mission is clear: buy just enough time for the holder to get the ball down and the kicker to get it into the air. This is a matter of less than two seconds, but it can feel like an eternity when you're trying to hold off a charge of bodies pushing their way through the middle of the line.

The line stands foot to foot, as tightly together as it can, and at the snap of the ball, the men huddle together to build an impenetrable wall. Few blockers get through the middle; when a defender does block a kick, it's usually because someone was able to fly around one end and reach the kicker before he sent the ball sailing, or from a defender leaping into the air to deflect a ball that's been kicked too low to the ground.

QUICK HIT

When a field goal is blocked, it becomes a live ball, so the defense can return it to the opposing team's goal for a touchdown. When an extra point is blocked, it's ruled a dead ball because it was on a point after attempt, not a live play.

The Punting Unit

When faced with an unfavorable fourth-down situation, a team often chooses to punt the ball to the opponent versus giving them the ball at its current location. Punting is an integral part of the game, often an aspect that indirectly leads to wins and losses.

Some teams receiving the punt bypass going after the block and focus instead on setting up for a return, in large part because blocks are rare occurrences. But that doesn't mean the punting team can avoid preparing for it on every punt snap.

To defend against the block, the punting team has its linemen all tightly together, with two or three blockers positioned a foot behind the line of scrimmage to stop any players who make their way through the line or around one of the sides.

Other than the gunners (more on them later in this chapter), the punting team cannot chase after the ball until after the punter has sent it flying into the air. If anyone other than the gunners advances down the field before the punt, the game officials will flag the punting team for an offside call.

> **QUICK HIT**
>
> Some teams use a rugby-style punt, in which the punter takes his approach toward the sideline of his punting leg instead of straight forward toward the line.

The Return Teams

The kick and punt return units are set up to offer their returner—the guy who ends up fielding the kick—the best opportunity to run as far as he possibly can. They do this using a series of blocking strategies (more on these in Chapter 23).

The punt-return team lines up five men along the line of scrimmage to keep the punting team honest. These men come after the punter to try to get a block, but as soon as the ball is in the air, they must sprint back down the field to help set up the return.

Two men are positioned behind the line. Their job is to watch for fake plays and block the first lineman who releases from the line of scrimmage. The punt-return team also positions men in front of the punting team's gunners, trying to prevent them from getting downfield. That leaves the two remaining men to field the punt, one who fields the ball and the other who acts as an immediate blocker for him.

Kick-return units are a bit more complex. Again, a front wall of blockers is lined up along the 40-yard line, 10 yards away from where the kicking team kicks the ball (or at the 50-yard line in high school games). Other blockers are lined up in waves deeper down the field, and two return men, one on each half of the field, are positioned down near their own goal line to field the kick.

If the ball is kicked into the end zone, the returner has the option of kneeling with the ball and having his team start at the 20-yard line, or running it out of the end zone to try to gain yards. Most returners opt for the second choice, and most often they get the ball beyond the 20-yard line.

The Kicker

No player on a team receives as little respect as the kicker. Teammates make fun of him, and both fans and coaches have suggested that kickers aren't "real players" because they neither hit nor get hit. But kickers face a pressure no player, other than perhaps the quarterback, can understand.

When the game is on the line, the kicker is often the player called upon to come in and be the deciding factor. Make the field goal and the team wins the game; miss it and every fan demands the kicker's head on a platter. A kicker is either the scapegoat or the hero, and rarely something in between.

For kickers, it's all about understanding the conditions and having a good feel for one's limitations. This is called range. A kicker must know how far he can kick in domed stadiums versus outdoors and how the wind or a frozen surface might affect him. He tells the coaching staff all this, and they use this data to help make decisions as to when to kick a field goal versus punt the ball.

At the end of a game, though, whether a kick is within the kicker's range or not, everyone expects him to make it.

Most of today's kickers use a sweeping soccer-style kick to propel the ball through the uprights. In the early days of football, the straight-on kick was more common.

To kick soccer-style, the kicker takes a few steps back from the placeholder and then a few steps off to the side. As the ball is snapped, the kicker makes an arced motion toward the holder, kicking with the inside of his dominant foot.

With the straight-on approach, the kicker lines up directly behind where the holder puts down the ball and kicks with the toe of his foot.

One famous straight-on kicker was Tom Dempsey, who had no toes on his kicking foot. Dempsey kicked a 63-yard field goal in a 1970 game that stood as an NFL record for many years until the Denver Broncos' Jason Elam matched its distance in 1998.

 FUN FACT

Only one placekicker has been inducted into the NFL Hall of Fame: Jan Stenerud. The Norwegian-born Stenerud kicked for 19 seasons. His best year, however, was one of his last. In 1981, at the age of 39, Stenerud made 22 of 24 field goal attempts, giving him a career best 91.7 percent success rate.

The Punter

Think, for a second, about standing 13 yards away from an angry mob of padded warriors, all of whom would love nothing more than to bowl you over. That's what a punter faces every time he stands behind his long-snapper and awaits the snap. But he mustn't flinch; his job is to receive the ball and immediately send it sailing high and deep down the field.

The punter has very little time to get the ball off after catching the snap. His routine must be the same every time, without disruption. The slightest pause could open the door for the opposing team to block the punt. When that happens, they take possession of the ball wherever it's spotted at the end of the play.

A punter is focused on accomplishing two things with his punt: height and distance. Having good height, or hang time, on the punt allows time for the coverage unit to get down the field and prepare to tackle the returner. The longer a punt travels, obviously, the better for the team punting it.

But one without the other is no good. A punt that goes straight up into the air without traveling far doesn't gain any yards for the punting team, while a line-drive-style punt driven deep provides the receiving team plenty of time to set up a return.

Most punters acknowledge that one of the most important actions during the punting process is the drop of the ball. If the punter drops the ball properly before punting it, he'll strike it on the right part of his foot, giving the ball maximum distance and the proper spin. If he fails to execute the drop, the ball can come off the foot in any direction, sometimes sailing out of bounds not far from the original line of scrimmage.

The punter must also act as the last defender in between a returner and the end zone. The punter is taught to either push the returner out of bounds or flush him back toward the middle of the field where others may be able to tackle him. Above all, the punter is to put his body in harm's way for the sake of saving a touchdown.

The Return Men

Each team needs a few players to return punts and kicks. Sometimes, although rarely in the NFL, the same player handles both tasks.

To field a kick or punt, the returner creates a basket with his arms in front of his body for the ball to drop into. After securing the ball, the returner explodes up the field, running to his blockers and searching for holes, or creases, to run through. Most of the time he doesn't get far. Kick returners usually get tackled somewhere between the 20- and 30-yard lines, while punt returners usually make it 8 to 10 yards away from where they catch the ball. On those rare occasions when the returner does find an open hole to run through, it can change the outcome of the game.

Often a team's return men consist of backup running backs, wide receivers, or defensive backs. These players keep their roster spot largely based on their ability to make plays as returners, but if the offense or defense is in a pinch, they can step in as a fourth receiver, emergency back, or extra defender. A few of the best return men were leaders for the offense or defense. Deion Sanders was one such example. The league's best cornerback of his time, Sanders was also one of its best punt returners, capable of taking the ball back for a touchdown on any play.

If a returner chooses, he can call for a fair catch before fielding the punt. Punt returners do this when they feel threatened by the opposing team's oncoming tacklers; a successful fair catch eliminates the risk of a violent collision and fumble. To do this, he must wave one arm high over his head before catching the ball. No player can make contact with him after he has fielded the punt, but he may also not advance the ball. The offense takes over from that very spot.

QUICK HIT

If a returner calls for a fair catch and bobbles the ball when trying to field it, it becomes a live football. The returner is then fair game for all the coverage men who have gathered around him.

On kickoffs, returners also have the option of downing the ball if it lands in the end zone. By kneeling down on one knee, the player has chosen not to take his chances on the return. His team automatically gets the ball at the 20-yard line. When the ball is kicked deep into the end zone, sometimes the returner is best off taking those 20 yards instead of testing the open field, where every yard must be earned.

The Other Specialists

Kickers and punters aren't the only spaces reserved on a special teams roster. Each team carries several such players, all with a very distinct role on the team.

The Long-Snapper

The long-snapper is nothing like a center, other than the fact that both line up over the football. The long-snapper keeps his head down on the snap and sends the ball spinning back to the placeholder or punter. After that, he must engage with the rest of the linemen as a blocker.

Every snap needs to be in the same place, where the holder or punter expects it. If not, chaos can occur.

A long-snapper is an extremely valuable position for each team to fill, even though that player may only see the field on a dozen or so snaps each game. Some NFL teams spend large amounts of money to sign a premier long-snapper.

The Placeholder

Situated 7 yards behind the line of scrimmage, usually on one knee, the placeholder's job is to call for the long-snapper to snap the football, catch it, and place it just right for the kicker. In the middle of all this, the placeholder must also be sure the ball's laces are away from where the kicker will strike. That means the holder must sometimes spin the ball ever so slightly before placing it.

It's a thankless job, often reserved for a team's backup quarterback or another skill-position player with reliable hands.

 FUN FACT

The placeholder is almost never recognized for doing something right, but he's immediately identified when he fails to do his job. In a 2007 playoff game against the Seattle Seahawks, Dallas Cowboys quarterback and placeholder Tony Romo fumbled a snap and failed to run to the goal line before getting tackled. The play ended the season for the Cowboys.

The Kickoff Specialist

Some teams carry two kickers on their active roster, one to kick field goals and extra points, and another to handle kickoff duties. This can be a wise move if the kickoff specialist kicks the ball deep into the end zone with regularity, limiting other teams from returning the ball.

Teams hate to use roster spots on specialists, but sometimes it's worth it if it means having a reliable field goal kicker and someone who aids the team in its fight for field position.

The Upback

When a team is in punt formation, the upback is often put in charge of getting the play started. Positioned a few yards behind the line and just off to one side of the long-snapper, he calls out the cadence, alerting the center when to snap the ball.

The upback is also responsible for pointing out anything the punter should be aware of and giving the signal for a fake.

And it's the upback who often gets to run or pass the ball on fake plays.

The Gunners

These players lined up out wide, away from the linemen, on punting downs act as heat-seeking missiles, heading directly for the intended return man at the snap of the ball. The receiving team often puts two men across from a gunner to block him, pushing the gunner out of bounds and trying to break him down before he reaches the returner.

The elite gunners can beat any jam and make sure-handed tackles at the point of attack. They don't make contact with the returner before he's able to field the ball or step into his safe zone when he calls for a fair catch. They limit the opposing team's ability to gain return yards and, on occasion, make a bone-crushing hit that energizes the sideline and the fans.

Names to Know and Performances to Remember

For years, the NFL's leader in points scored was George Blanda, who played in 26 seasons—some of them as a quarterback, but most as his team's placekicker. In 1975, at the age of 48, Blanda finished his career with 2,002 points.

That record stood until Morten Andersen and Gary Anderson started to chase after it 20 years later, each one holding the record at various times, trading it back and forth. Both began their careers in 1982, and when each had stopped playing, Morten Andersen was atop of the record books with 2,544 points, having made 565 of 709 field goal attempts. Gary Anderson finished his career with 2,434 points.

The Morten Andersen of returners is former Washington Redskins great Brian Mitchell, who accumulated almost 20,000 total yards as a kick and punt returner. Only one other returner, Allen Rossum, is within 6,000 yards of Mitchell's career mark.

In the New England Patriots' record-setting 2007 season, second-year kicker Stephen Gostkowski set a record for the most extra points attempted in one season with 74. Before that, only roughly a dozen kickers had attempted more than 60 extra points in a year.

The kicker whom Gostkowski replaced for the Patriots, Adam Vinatieri, is the most clutch kicker of all time. He's known for delivering in the big moments—making game-winning kicks in the final seconds. During his team's playoff run in 2001, Vinatieri made two late kicks in the snow to beat the Oakland Raiders—and then made a 48-yard game-winning kick in the final seconds of Super Bowl XXXVI to beat the St. Louis Rams. Two years later, in Super Bowl XXXVIII, a 41-yard Vinatieri field goal gave the Patriots another title.

Most experts agree that the greatest punter who ever played—at any level—was Ray Guy, who starred at the University of Southern Mississippi before enjoying a 14-year career with the Raiders. Guy was the only punter ever selected in the first round of the NFL Draft, and each year the best punter in college football receives an award named in Guy's honor.

FUN FACT

Only one returner, Desmond Howard, has been named the Most Valuable Player of a Super Bowl. In Super Bowl XXXI, Howard gained 244 yards for the Green Bay Packers on his punt and kickoff returns, including a 99-yard score in the third quarter that gave the Packers a commanding lead.

The Least You Need to Know

- Special teams play accounts for one third of a team's efforts to win a game.

- Kickers and punters are both under a great deal of pressure to perform, although many of their peers don't consider them "true" football players.

- The long-snapper and placeholder work as a unit, much like a pitcher and catcher in baseball. Every snap and every hold is expected to be perfect.

- No NFL player has scored more points than kicker Morten Andersen, while Ray Guy was the greatest punter who ever played the game.

Special Teams Strategic Tools

In This Chapter

- Onside kicks, and when teams are most likely to use them
- The different blocking methods return teams use
- Special teams fake plays

Game-changing plays happen in every quarter of every football game, and the team with the highest number of them usually wins the game. On every kick or return, there's a good chance of a shift in momentum, and teams practice these plays—even the trick ones—to be sure that when the time is right, they're ready to execute them properly.

Special teams units use fake plays, try reverses, and go for blocks—everything that can be drawn on a chalkboard. When things work, everyone is happy and the coach is credited for his brilliance. When things fall apart, fans and media start to point fingers. But for coaches, the risk is worth the reward. Special teams is all about making the big play, and coaches search for every tool and possible advantage they can find to make that happen.

The Free Kick

After a team has suffered a safety, it's forced to perform a free kick from its own 20-yard line. This is a unique special teams play because the kicking team has the option of either drop-kicking the ball or punting it. Most teams opt to punt.

The receiving team must line up 10 yards away from the kick, same as with a kickoff. When the kicking team has kicked the ball, the play is treated the same as a kickoff, with the kicking team pursuing the returner down the field.

For the punter, this is one of the least nerve-racking plays he takes part in because he's free to punt the ball without worrying about someone crashing into him at top speed to block it.

The Onside Kick

When time is running short, and the team trailing on the scoreboard is starting to get desperate, it may be time for an onside kick. Rules state that the kicking team can recover its own kick as long as it travels at least 10 yards from the point of kickoff. If the return team touches the ball before it travels 10 yards, it becomes a live ball and can be recovered by either team.

Statistics suggest that the kicking team has much less than a 50 percent chance of recovering the kick, but teams in need of the ball have no choice but to try for it. Some coaches also gamble and try an onside kick at other points of the game when they suspect their opponent won't be prepared for it.

Some kickers kick the ball so it dribbles along the ground, while others try to *pooch* the ball a short distance into a zone where there are few, if any, receiving players. The most common onside kick is one that rolls on the ground for a few yards, end over end, before shooting straight into the air. When this happens, the ball is up for grabs to the first player, offense or defense, able to catch it.

GRIDIRON GAB

A type of punt or kick that travels only a short distance, much like a chip shot in golf, is called a **pooch.** It's designed to limit the return team's ability to have a long return.

The kicking team sends its men after the ball, some of them assigned to take on blockers and others assigned to go for the ball. If successful, the kicking team keeps the ball where it is downed. If the kick goes out of bounds or the other team recovers, the receiving team will have the ball with favorable field position.

PENALTY!

If a member of the kicking team touches the ball before it travels 10 yards—and before a defender touches it first—it's a penalty, and the ball is given to the receiving team.

The Hands Team

Every kick-return unit needs a special hands team to be ready for times when the opponent is likely to try an onside kick. The hands team is made of a number of specialty players: those better equipped to handle the football and those fit to take on a flood of oncoming defenders. Backup receivers, running backs, tight ends, and defensive backs are all likely candidates to fill in on the hands teams.

Usually, the receiving team builds a front wall of blockers to defend against the oncoming charge and follows that with a row of a few players to field the ball. The goal of the front wall is to keep every defender off the fielding player so he gets a clean opportunity.

Positioning to Block a Kick or Punt

Next to a return for a touchdown, no special teams play has the potential to make as big of a difference in a game as a blocked punt or kick. Blocked punts give the receiving team favorable field position, while a blocked field goal negates points for the kicking team. In either instance, the blocking team may also advance the blocked ball for additional yards or even a score.

On field goal attempts, blocks usually come in one of two ways:

- Someone leaps into the middle of the line hoping to deflect a low-flying ball.

- A player runs around the outside of the line and is able to reach the kicker before he sends the ball into the air.

Punt-blocking units usually try to overload one side of the line, forcing teams to choose which players to block and which to let pass by.

The person able to get through, on either a kick or a punt, is coached to take a good angle and aim for where the ball will meet the kicker's or punter's foot. If the blocker misses, he doesn't want for his momentum to carry him into the kicker. Otherwise, it will draw a stiff penalty from the officials.

PENALTY!

When trying to block a kick, members of the blocking team aren't allowed to step on another player—either from their team or the opposing team—in an attempt to reach higher into the air.

The Coverage Teams

The teams assigned to cover on a kickoff or punt have roughly the same duties—to cover the entire field and limit the number of yards gained by the returner.

In both cases, the men in the coverage unit each have assigned lanes they run in. They are coached not to go outside their lanes until they reach the depth of the returner, at which point they can begin to converge. By staying in their lanes, the coverage unit can cover each section of the field, limiting the size of the holes for the returner to run through.

One player on each end of the line is responsible for not letting the returner get outside of him, while the kicker or punter is one of the last to get down the field and acts as a safety net if the returner gets by the rest of the players on his unit.

The Wedge

One of the most battle-tested strategies for returning the ball on a kick or punt is the wedge, or a line of blockers that stands between would-be tacklers and the returner.

To form a wedge, players come together in the middle of the field and join hands. From there they create a V, much like a flock a geese, and begin to run up the field. The returner runs behind the wedge, using it to shield him from oncoming tacklers. As he runs, the returner looks for one hole he can run through for a long return. When he finds it, he breaks from the wedge and sprints full steam ahead.

The coverage team's job is to break apart the wedge—and the sooner the better.

The Wall

Teams that don't use a wedge, or middle return, often use a wall instead. The object of this return is to create an alley, on either side of the field, through which the returner can run hassle-free between his blockers and the sideline.

After the punt or kick, the front wall of the receiving team runs down one side of the field until each person in the wall reaches his designated spot. From there, the men form a line running parallel to the sideline that they use to shield off any pursuing tacklers in the middle of the field. If the returner can get to the wall, he has a good shot of shooting down the sideline for lots of yards.

The Reverse

On a reverse play, after a punt- or kick-return team fields the ball, the ball carrier begins running horizontally toward one side of the field. Another player, usually the other returner on the play, begins running toward the ball carrier. When they meet, the person with the ball hands it to the person heading in the opposite direction.

If the coverage team isn't disciplined in its lanes, the person running the reverse is able to get to the outside of the coverage and race down the sideline for a score.

To keep the coverage team guessing, sometimes the returning team fakes the reverse and the original ball carrier keeps it.

Schoolyard kids love to run the reverse; pro and college coaches do, too.

The Fake Punt

Nothing says a team has to punt the ball on fourth down just because the punting unit is on the field. To catch an opponent off-guard and retain possession of the football, a team may choose to fake the punt if it believes it can gain the necessary yardage for a first down.

Teams snap the ball to the punter, who can then run or pass the ball for a first down, or to the upback, who has the same options. The person barking the cadence to start the play usually uses a code word that tells the long-snapper who to snap the ball to.

> **QUICK HIT**
>
> To fool the defense, sometimes the punter pretends the snap has gone over his head or through his hands. While the defense focuses on the punter's acting performance, the upback is well on his way to a first down.

Teams rarely fake a punt. They either choose to keep the offense on the field on fourth down or punt to the opponent. If a coach sees a potential weakness in the return team, however, such as not enough men defending the middle of the field or an absence of defenders on one side of the line, he may call for a fake.

The Fake Field Goal

Six points are better than three, and sometimes even when a team shows it has conceded the touchdown to attempt a field goal, it really plans to go for the six anyway.

Most fake field goals are focused around the placeholder's ability to make a play. Because that player is usually a quarterback or skill player, he tends to be a good athlete capable of throwing or running with the ball.

Teams usually run fake field goals to one side of the field or the other, away from the middle, where the vast majority of defenders are stacked trying to block the kick.

Sometimes the fake really isn't a fake at all, but rather the result of a botched hold or a poor snap. If the placeholder feels the kicker won't be able to get off a good kick, he'll tuck the ball and call out the team's signal for the fake. The placeholder can run, pitch the ball to the kicker, pass, or do anything that gains a first down or gets the ball to the goal line. Usually these situations end badly for the kicking team and look more like chaos than an organized play.

> **FUN FACT**
>
> In a 2007 game, Louisiana State University placeholder Matt Flynn caught the snap and then flipped the ball blindly over his shoulder to the team's sprinting kicker, Colt David, who raced 15 yards for a score to give the Tigers a 21–7 lead over South Carolina. The next week, college and high school kicking units everywhere were trying to perfect that fake in practice.

Icing the Kicker

In situations when the kicking team can make a field goal to help change the outcome of the game, the opposing coach may try to ice the kicker. Just as the kicking team is about to snap the ball, the opposing coach calls a time-out to stop the action in hopes of fazing the kicker in some fashion. No matter how many time-outs a team has left, the coach may only do this once before the kicker is allowed his attempt.

Sometimes the strategy is effective and the kicker misses on the live kick. Most of the time, however, it makes no difference at all.

The Least You Need to Know

- An onside kick must travel 10 yards before the kicking team can recover it legally.
- A coach calls on his hands team when he suspects the other team will kick an onside.
- Return teams use the wedge or wall as blocking schemes to help them gain big yards.
- Opposing coaches sometimes call a time-out before a field goal attempt to try to ice the kicker.

Special Teams Statistics and Rulings

In This Chapter

- The statistics used to measure kickers, punters, and returners
- Statistics that measure the performance of special teams units
- The penalties officials call during special teams play

Statisticians keep track of numbers for special teams players and units just as they do for offense and defense. The numbers that track kickers, punters, and returners are as recited as those kept for defense and can be used by the opposition as another way to identify a team's areas of weakness.

As for penalties, special teams players are called for many of the same things offensive and defensive players are, with a few exceptions. One thing to know is that calls made on a special teams play can sometimes prove to be the difference in the outcome of a game. Nothing can infuriate a coach more than a penalty during a special teams play that negates a large return or successful punt or field goal.

Kicking Categories

More than a dozen statistics are kept on kickers, and they all serve to judge the kicker's reliability and leg strength.

The two that matter most, though, are the number of points he scores and the accuracy with which he kicks.

Points Scored

Kickers accumulate points for every field goal and extra point they make. Every point counts, and kickers view scoring the same way position players do.

The kickers who score the most points tend to play for teams with strong offenses but ones that sputter in the red zone. These types of teams allow for more field goal opportunities.

For NFL kickers, the benchmark is 120 points in a season—an average of just fewer than 8 points per game.

FUN FACT

The record for most points scored by a kicker in a season is 164, set by Minnesota Vikings kicker Gary Anderson during the 1998 season. Anderson didn't miss a single kick all year—until the playoffs, that is, when he missed a 38-yard attempt that would have likely sent his team to the Super Bowl. Instead, the Vikings lost that game in overtime.

Field Goals Made

Every field goal attempt that sails through the uprights on a legal play is considered a completed, or made, field goal.

Only one player in NFL history has ever made 40 field goals in a season. That was Arizona Cardinals kicker Neil Rackers in 2005. For most players, making 25 or more kicks in a season equates to a good year.

Field Goals Attempted

Anytime a kicker sends a field goal sailing on a live play, it counts as an attempt, no matter where the kick ends up.

The average number of attempts a starting kicker sees in a full season is 30, or roughly 2 field goal attempts per game.

Field Goal Accuracy

Making good on every opportunity is what separates the great kickers from the merely good ones. How many field goals a kicker attempts, or makes, is as indicative of how good his offense is as it is an endorsement for the kicker. But field goal accuracy is all on the kicker. No matter if a kicker gets 8 attempts or 40, has 100 points or few points at all, his accuracy is the best indicator of his ability.

To calculate a kicker's accuracy, divide the number of field goals made by the number of field goals attempted. A percentage of 80 or better is good enough to keep a job in the NFL; a percentage of 90 or better puts a kicker at the elite level.

Field Goal Categories of Length

Other important data a team tracks includes a kicker's accuracy from various ranges on the field. For example, a team needs to know how many kicks a kicker has made from between 30 and 39 yards, 40 and 49 yards, and from beyond 50 yards. These help show how accurate a kicker's leg is in relationship to distance.

Statisticians also reserve a category for length, both for the longest kick made and attempted for the year. This statistic shows the extent of a kicker's range and also from how far his coaches are willing to let him attempt a kick.

Extra-Point Statistics

Teams keep track of a kicker's extra-point attempts, attempts made, and accuracy.

Most of the time it's a moot point, though. At the pro level, extra-point attempts are rarely missed.

QUICK HIT

Teams also keep track of touchbacks for kickoffs. Kickers with a large percentage of touchbacks are valued weapons for a team because they allow very little opportunity for the returning team to make a big play. For kickers, touchbacks are a good thing. For punters, touchbacks are not a good thing.

Punting Categories

The important thing to know about punting categories is that no one category gives a fair representation of a punter's abilities. All the statistics used to grade or measure punters are skewed by many factors beyond the punter's control.

Average Yards Per Punt

To calculate a punter's average, simply divide the total number of yards all his punts have traveled by the number of punts. A good average is 45 or more yards per punt.

One factor that can affect any punting statistic is the location where the player punts from. Good offenses may take the ball down the field, asking the punter to regularly kick from near midfield. This limits the distance the punt can travel, thus weakening the punter's average. Poor offenses that don't move the ball far give their punter the entire field to kick to, offering no limits on how far a punt can travel.

Average Net Yards Per Punt

This statistic factors in the return yards gained by the opposing team for each punt. For example, if the punt travels 50 yards but is returned 15 yards, the punter is given credit for a net punt of 35 yards. A good net average is anything above 40 yards.

This category can be affected by the quality of a punter's coverage unit. If the players covering the punt are ineffective, the other team will gain good yardage on each return. Likewise, if the coverage team does its job, the return yards will be minimal, helping the punter improve his net average.

Punts Placed Inside the 20-Yard Line

Ideally, a team hopes to have its opponent start a drive inside its own 20-yard line. Punters can do this in a number of ways, including pinning the ball or creating a good hang time that forces the return man to fair catch the ball inside the 20.

Punters who regularly pin the ball inside the opponent's 20-yard line are good weapons to have on your team.

QUICK HIT

Teams also track the number of fair catches a punter helps create, although that statistic isn't as popular as some of the others.

Touchbacks

When a punter has too many touchbacks compared to his number of punts, it illustrates his lack of control. Teams want punters who can get the ball to go out of bounds near the goal line, called the *coffin corner*, or position it in such a place that the coverage unit can down the ball before it reaches the end zone. This requires punters to have good touch and placement.

> **GRIDIRON GAB**
>
> **Coffin corner** is a term used to describe the corners of the field where the sideline intersects with the goal line. When a punter is able to punt the ball out of bounds into this region without it traveling into or over the top of the goal line, he is said to have hit the coffin corner. Few punters use this method anymore. Most kick straight down the middle of the field, hoping the ball is downed by a member of the coverage unit before it crosses over the goal line.

When the opponent gets a touchback, there's a sense that the opponent has won the battle—and that it could have been much worse.

Return Categories

There's more separation between the elite and everybody else in punt- and kick-returner statistical categories than perhaps any other. The best return men make large gains with regularity, while the average ones pick up a predictable number of yards on each return.

Of course, each return man's blockers cannot be discounted from the equation. A good front wall of blockers can make an average return man great, just like a weak bunch of blockers can make a great return man look subpar.

Number of Returns

A kick or punt returner's number of returns says very little about his ability. If anything, it says something about his team's defense. If a kick returner has a large number of returns, it means the defense has surrendered a lot of touchdowns. If a punt returner has a large number of returns, it means the defense has done its job and ended a lot of its opponents' drives short.

Most NFL kick returners log 30 or more each year. For punt returners, that number is closer to 20.

Average Per Return

This is how return men are judged. Those kick returners who average 25 or more yards per kick are in high demand. The same is true of punt returners who average better than 10 yards per return.

In the case of punt returners, an average can be impacted by factors beyond their control. Where they field the punt is just as critical as how well the blockers block for them. If a punt returner is constantly pinned back toward his own goal line, his chance for success is far less than if he's fielding punts near midfield, where he has more open space to work with.

Long Returns

As with kicking and punting, teams keep track of a returner's longest return of the year. It shows what he's capable of. If a return man hasn't recorded a return of 50 or more yards on a kick (30 or more on a punt), he may not have a job for long.

Teams like to know the guy they have assigned to return the ball at least has the ability to take a return in for a score.

Touchdowns

Though few and far between, even for the very best return men, the sexiest statistical category of all for returners is that of touchdowns.

In most years, only a few players will have more than one kick or punt return for a touchdown. Occasionally, an elite player has several in one season, but it's rare.

 FUN FACT

As a rookie in 1951, Detroit Lions punt returner Jack Christiansen returned four punts for touchdowns, including two in one game against the Los Angeles Rams.

Team Categories

Most of the kick-related statistics for special teams are contained in the individual categories for punters and kickers. A team's net punting average or field goal success is the same as that of its kicker, unless a team employs more than one, which is not usually the case.

The only categories that really measure team play are the ones for the return and coverage units.

Return Averages

Unlike with its kicker and punter, teams often use more than one return man throughout the course of a season. The combined average of all of a team's kick or punt returners helps show how well the blockers are performing for those players.

Opposing Team Return Averages

How well a team covers a kickoff or a punt is reflected in the average yards it yields to returners on opposing teams. The fewer the yards, the better the unit that races down the field to make the tackle.

Elite NFL coverage units hold opponents to fewer than 20 yards per kick return and fewer than 6 yards per punt.

Rulings That Affect Special Teams

Several varieties of calls can be killers for a team trying to block a kick or make a big play on a return.

Here are some of the more common calls made during special teams play.

Roughing the Kicker or Snapper

No player can collide with the kicker or punter after he has successfully kicked the football. If a player makes significant contact without getting a piece of the ball in the process, the official will make a kicking motion with his leg and flag the player for roughing.

Players are also not allowed to abuse the person snapping to the punter or the placeholder until the snapper has raised his head and is in a position in which he can defend himself.

Like with any roughing call, it's 15 yards and an automatic first down.

Running Into the Kicker

When the contact an opposing player makes with the kicker or punter is minor (both nonviolent and unintentional), the game official may rule it to be running into the kicker versus roughing. To signal running into the kicker versus roughing, the only difference is that the penalty is not preceded by the roughing signal. This carries a 5-yard penalty and is not an automatic first down.

Illegal Block in the Back

Anytime a player blocks another player in the back, he's guilty of an illegal block, which carries a 10-yard penalty from the spot of the foul.

This is often seen on kick and punt returns as players come back to help the returner and fail to get a proper angle to block an opponent. Officials rarely miss this call because it's obvious when someone's been blocked from behind. The signal is the left hand out with the right hand grasping the left wrist.

Clipping

When the block is made behind and below an opponent's waist in pursuit of the kick or punt returner, the game official will throw a 15-yard flag for clipping, signaling it by striking the back of his lower leg.

Interfering with the Returner

If a member from the coverage team makes contact with a punt returner after he has called for a fair catch, or before he fields the ball, the player will be flagged 15 yards for interfering with the returner's ability to field the punt. To signal this, the official pushes both palms out away from his body.

Football is serious about this ruling because a punt returner is considered a defense-less player while he's waiting for the punt.

FUN FACT

During a 2009 game, Carolina Panthers player Dante Wesley hit Tampa Bay Buccaneers punt returner Clifton Smith before he could field the punt. The hit was so vicious, it caused an on-field fight between the two teams. Game officials both penalized Wesley and ejected him from the game.

Illegal Touching of a Kick

If a team kicking an onside kick touches the ball before it reaches the mandatory 10 yards it must travel, it will be flagged for illegal touching. The official touches both shoulders with the tips of his fingers.

The Least You Need to Know

- Kickers are measured by the number of points they score and their success rate on field goals.

- No common statistical category fairly measures how good a punter is.

- If the opposing team collides with the kicker or punter without making contact with the ball, it's a stiff penalty and an automatic first down.

A Spectacle at Every Level

Part

5

If football was only a game, there would be no point to your reading this book. Thankfully, football is much more. College and professional football enable millions of fans to connect with the game every Saturday and Sunday in their living rooms, while youth and high school football provide local access.

Part 5 dissects the many levels of football and the ways in which fans can interact with it.

The NFL

In This Chapter

- The business end of professional football
- How the teams are organized
- How teams qualify for the playoffs and, ultimately, the Super Bowl
- The great teams in NFL history

There is football, and there is the National Football League (NFL)—the pinnacle of the sport, the level all players hope to reach one day. The NFL offers its players wealth, fame, and the possibility of immortality—but at a cost. NFL players are full-time athletes ... and full-time entertainers.

Everything in the NFL is first class—how teams fly, the stadiums they play in, and how the league office conducts business. The teams work together for the good of the league (or in the best interests of every team's bottom line) and to protect its image. The league represents the teams collectively and negotiates television contracts and licensing deals. The players work together as a union to accomplish similar goals.

Modern-day football isn't what it was at its start, or what it was even 30 years ago. Pro football players today are celebrities, akin to movie stars. Their private lives are as much news as how many yards they gain or tackles they make on Sunday.

Somehow, amidst all the revenue and headlines, the league still manages to produce a first-class product, making the NFL the envy of all other sports leagues.

A Business First (Then a Game)

Football players grow up playing the game on sandlots and schoolyard fields, just for the thrill of it. In high school, it gains them attention, and in college, it can pay for tuition. But in the NFL, football is no longer only a game but a way for each player to support his family. Likewise, for the team owners, it's an opportunity to turn a profit.

> **WORDS OF WISDOM**
>
> Pro football is like nuclear warfare. There are no winners, only survivors.
>
> —NFL Hall of Fame running back Frank Gifford

If a team is losing on the field, there's a good chance it's not doing very well on the balance sheet either. If a team is winning, everyone is happy. The pressure to perform is intense, and the thrill of winning is replaced by the need to win.

When an NFL team cuts a popular player, or when a player chooses to sign with a rival team, the fans often take it personally; the players, coaches, and management know better. There are no *personal* moves, only *personnel* moves, and everything is a business decision.

A Historical Timeline

Over its almost 100-year existence, the NFL has grown from a small Midwestern league of hard-nosed squads into a multimillion-dollar industry with global fanfare.

Here are a few of the important points along the way:

- In 1920, the American Professional Football Conference is born in Ohio. Football legend Jim Thorpe serves as its first president and one of its star players.

- The 1958 sudden-death overtime championship game between the New York Giants and Baltimore Colts draws a large television audience.

- The first Super Bowl game is played in January 1967.

- The NFL merges with the American Football League in 1970, doubling the number of pro teams.

- On Monday, September 21, 1970, the first *Monday Night Football* game is televised. The Cleveland Browns beat the New York Jets 31–21.

- For the 1978 season, the league extends the regular season from 14 to 16 games and changes a number of rules to open the passing game.

- Under the terms of the collective bargaining agreement between the league and its players union, unrestricted free agency is introduced in 1993.

- In one of the most exciting Super Bowl games ever, the Pittsburgh Steelers claim their sixth Super Bowl title in 2009—the most by any franchise.

Divisions and Conferences

Like all other professional sports leagues, the NFL separates its teams into sets to make it easy to arrange a schedule and construct a system for postseason play.

The NFL's 32 franchises are separated into 2 conferences, the National Football Conference (NFC) and the American Football Conference (AFC), each made of 16 teams. Within each conference are four divisions of four teams. (The league used to have only three divisions in each conference before it expanded its number of teams.) Generally speaking, the goal has been to position teams located in the same geographic region. This creates for better natural rivalries and limits the travel for intra-divisional contests.

National Football Conference	American Football Conference
NFC North	**AFC North**
Chicago Bears	Baltimore Ravens
Detroit Lions	Cincinnati Bengals
Green Bay Packers	Cleveland Browns
Minnesota Vikings	Pittsburgh Steelers
NFC East	**AFC East**
Dallas Cowboys	Buffalo Bills
New York Giants	Miami Dolphins
Philadelphia Eagles	New England Patriots
Washington Redskins	New York Jets

continues

continued

National Football Conference	American Football Conference
NFC South	**AFC South**
Atlanta Falcons	Houston Texans
Carolina Panthers	Indianapolis Colts
New Orleans Saints	Jacksonville Jaguars
Tampa Bay Buccaneers	Tennessee Titans
NFC West	**AFC West**
Arizona Cardinals	Denver Broncos
San Francisco 49ers	Kansas City Chiefs
Seattle Seahawks	Oakland Raiders
St. Louis Rams	San Diego Chargers

Scheduling

There are three types of games fans should make note of:

- *Preseason games* do not count in the final won-loss record. These games, usually played in August, are used to help determine which players a team will keep on its final regular season roster and as a tune-up for players to prepare for the regular season.

- *Regular season games* do count, and how well a team performs during the regular season determines whether it will qualify for the postseason.

- *Postseason, or playoff, games* occur during January and February. (More on this in a bit.)

Each year, NFL teams play 4 preseason games before beginning on a 16-game regular season schedule. The league's regular season is actually 17 weeks, so each team has 1 week off.

 FUN FACT

The NFL has held a number of games in foreign markets over the past few decades in an attempt to expand the game's appeal globally. From 1986 to 2005, the league brought two of its teams to countries such as Mexico and Japan for the annual American Bowl.

Most of the games are played on Sunday, but a few are scheduled for Monday, Thursday, and occasionally Saturday.

Each team's regular season schedule looks like a random collection of contests, but the league follows a very simple formula:

Each team plays the other three teams in its division twice each year, once at home and once at the other team's field.

Each division plays all the teams of one selected division within its conference. This rotates from year to year. For example, if the teams of the NFC North play the teams from the NFC West this year, next year they might play the teams of the NFC East and then the teams of the NFC South the year after that. Then the cycle starts all over again.

Each division plays all the teams of one select division outside its conference. For example, the teams of the NFC North might play the teams of the AFC South. This is also cyclical so every four years teams have a chance to play every other team in the league.

The remaining two games of the schedule are predetermined based on the previous year's finish. For example, if the Chicago Bears finished third in the NFC North, they will play every other third-place finisher in the NFC. Because the Bears are already playing all the teams from one select NFC division, it leaves two other third-place finishers for their schedule.

QUICK HIT

Television networks carry the NFL regular season schedule based on conference. One network televises all the NFC games, while another televises the AFC games (*Sunday* and *Monday Night Football* games belong to different networks). For interconference games, the visiting team's network gets to televise the game.

Other than the final two games mentioned, a fan can pretty much figure out well in advance who his team will play each year. The fun part of the schedule, though, is the where and when. The league announces its final schedule, with primetime assignments and locations, in the spring each year.

Primetime Football

Since 1970, *Monday Night Football* has been a weekly happening for football fans, regardless of which teams are scheduled for that given week. The strategic move was a success largely because the NFL only plays once a week, so the demand for more televised games was greater than what the league was supplying to its fan base. No other professional sport has been able to duplicate this feat.

The league later capitalized on the success it was having on Monday night and added Sunday evening games. It later added games periodically on Thursdays midway through the season.

Another football tradition is the scheduling of games on Thanksgiving Day. The Detroit Lions and Dallas Cowboys always host an opponent that day, one playing an NFC foe, the other an AFC opponent. Detroit has been playing on Thanksgiving for several decades, while the Cowboys first were scheduled during the 1966 season. In 2006, the NFL added a third game to Thanksgiving, rotating different teams each year.

The Playoffs

After the regular season has wrapped up, the league's best teams continue to play in the postseason. Of the 16 teams in each conference, 6 qualify (so 12 teams total): each of the 4 division winners along with the next two best records of any team in the conference. Those teams are the wild cards.

The league then *seeds* each conference, giving the best record the top, or number-1 seed, and the lowest-ranking team the number-6 seed. Division winners are always seeded higher than the wild card teams, regardless of record.

In the first round of the playoffs, the top two teams in each conference are given a *bye*. The remaining four teams play, with the number-3 seed playing the number-6 seed, and numbers 4 and 5 playing. The next week, the lowest-remaining seed plays the number-1 seed, and the highest-remaining seed plays the number-2 seed. The winners of those contests face off in the conference championship game, which decides the conference's representative for the Super Bowl.

The higher seed always gets to host the playoff game, giving that team a decided home field advantage.

> **GRIDIRON GAB**
>
> In the NFL, two teams in each conference receive a week off, or **bye,** during the first round of the playoffs for having secured the top two records among division winners. Every team gets a bye during the 17-week regular season. Heading into the playoff season, the league must **seed** the six teams that qualify for each conference. The four division winners all are seeded, or labeled, one through four, regardless if the two other teams to qualify have a better win-loss record. Those division winners are seeded based on record first and then by a series of tiebreakers when needed. The fifth and sixth seeds go to the wild cards, the two remaining conference teams with the best records not to have won their division.

Unlike other sports that have a series of games for each round (best of five games, or best of seven games), in the NFL it's a one-time deal. You either win, or you go home. This is why the adage "any given Sunday" is so dear to football fans. They know that on any one day, a lesser team can rise to the occasion and upset the favored team.

The Super Bowl

There's no bigger game—no bigger singular world sporting event—than the Super Bowl, which pits the winner of the AFC against the winner of the NFC in February. The winner of the game is crowned champion of the world, and each team member is later presented with a custom-made ring that's a tad smaller than a golf ball.

The game began as a way to showcase the winners of the NFL and AFL and has grown into a must-see event. Game tickets go for hundreds (in some cases, thousands) of dollars, and millions of people watch it across the globe. Along with New Year's Eve, it's one of the most common excuses for adults to throw a party.

Some "fans" watch the Super Bowl just to see the commercials, usually some of the most inventive advertisements of the year. If anything, the commercials are expensive; a 30-second commercial during the game costs advertisers as much as $3 million.

The Super Bowl also is full of side entertainment, with hours upon hours of analysis leading up to the game. The NFL hosts a pregame concert and usually a big-name band or musical artist performs during an extended halftime. This all adds to the pageantry of the event.

Beyond all this, the Super Bowl is a 60-minute football game like any other, only with more television time-outs.

The Pro Bowl

Each year, the best AFC and NFC players are selected to take part in pro football's all-star game known as the Pro Bowl. The two conferences field a full roster and have a week's worth of practice before the game is played.

In the past, the Pro Bowl was always played the weekend after the Super Bowl, most of those years in Honolulu, Hawaii. In January 2010, the Pro Bowl was moved to the weekend *before* the Super Bowl and played in the Miami, Florida. The NFL made the change in hopes the game would draw more fan attention. No players from either of the two Super Bowl teams were required (or allowed) to take part.

The game is toned down some, as players from neither side wish to be injured in a relatively meaningless game.

The NFL Draft

Each April, representatives from all 32 teams gather in New York City to select players who have recently completed, or decided to end prematurely, their collegiate football careers. To be eligible for the NFL Draft, a player must be at least three years removed from his graduation date of high school. For example, a player who graduates high school in 2010 is eligible for the 2013 NFL Draft.

Scouts evaluate players all year, of course, but in the months separating the playoffs and the Super Bowl, teams begin to invest even more time in evaluating players they might select. The NFL holds the *Combine* each February in Indianapolis, where a large number of the eligible prospects are invited to run drills, get measured, and answer questions for team executives. Teams scrutinize every detail before deciding to invest millions of dollars in a player they hope can make their team better.

GRIDIRON GAB

The finest eligible prospects are invited to the **Combine** in February where they are subjected to body testing, a number of drills, and interviews with NFL team representatives. The event was first held in Tampa, Florida, in 1982, and has been located in Indianapolis each year since 1987.

At the Draft, teams take turn picking players over a series of seven rounds. The team that finished the previous year with the worst record in the NFL is given the highest draft pick in each round, followed by the second-worst record, and so on, leaving the

Super Bowl winner with the final pick of each round. Teams are allowed to trade picks for players, or for other picks, and are given only so much time to make a selection.

The greatest teams in league history were built through the draft, and some of the game's all-time greatest players were selected in the late rounds. Here are a few examples:

Eight quarterbacks were selected before Green Bay picked Bart Starr in the seventeenth round of the 1956 Draft. Starr later helped the Packers win five titles, and finished his career with the best playoff winning percentage of any quarterback (9–1 record).

Two other legendary quarterbacks were also bargain picks: the San Francisco 49ers grabbed Joe Montana in the third round of the 1979 Draft, while the New England Patriots were able to wait until round six of the 2000 Draft to pick Tom Brady. Montana won four Super Bowls; through the 2009 season, Brady has won three.

If the Pittsburgh Steelers of the 1970s are the greatest team of any decade, it can be said they owe much of their success to the 1974 Draft, which produced four Hall of Fame players—wide receivers Lynn Swann and John Stallworth, linebacker Jack Lambert, and center Mike Webster.

In 1998, 20 picks came and went before the Vikings finally gave wide receiver Randy Moss a home. All the teams that passed on Moss later paid for it on the field.

The Chicago Bears were fortunate to have two top-five picks in the 1965 Draft, but unlike the teams drafting around them, the Bears used those picks wisely. They picked linebacker Dick Butkus and running back Gale Sayers—both Hall of Famers helped define the franchise for the next decade.

Likewise, over the years many teams have been burned by so-called bust picks—players who came into the NFL with high expectations and provided little to nothing to the teams that drafted them. Here are a few of the greatest busts in Draft history:

Tony Mandarich was labeled a sure thing, and many expected the offensive tackle would become a dominant player for the next 10 years. Green Bay certainly thought so in 1989 when they picked Mandarich with the second pick that year—one spot in front of Hall of Fame running back Barry Sanders. Mandarich held out of training camp and never lived up to his potential.

After the Colts selected Peyton Manning in 1998, the Chargers picked another quarterback with the next pick—Ryan Leaf. While Manning threw touchdowns, Leaf threw temper tantrums. In 21 career starts at quarterback, Leaf's teams won just 4 games.

Lawrence Phillips is an example of how attitude can derail talent. The running back was picked in the first round of the 1996 Draft by the St. Louis Rams, but couldn't keep himself out of trouble off the field long enough to build his NFL career.

The Jets picked Blair Thomas with the second pick in the 1990 Draft. During his six-year career, he gained little more than 2,000 yards rushing. The next running back picked in the first round that year? Emmitt Smith, who gained more than 18,000 yards over his 15-year career.

The NFL has used a draft to help place fresh talent on team rosters since the early years of the league, but in the 1980s, television helped make it a spectacle for fans. People flock to New York to sit in and watch their favorite teams pick the players of tomorrow, and millions of people watch in their living rooms as teams debate who to take next.

The "Off-Season"

Fans and the league consider the months between the playoffs and the start of training camp the off-season, but for today's players, it's hardly time off.

Before football became a multimillion-dollar industry, players would spend the off-season working another job for extra cash. Today, players make so much money they don't need to work in the off-season, but the sizable investment the teams make in them forces players to keep their bodies in top condition 365 days a year. Thus, the off-season has become a series of "voluntary" mini-camps and workout programs.

Contracts, Agents, and Free Agency

Football is a sport of dollars as much as it's a sport of yards. Teams must sign players to contracts, some for one year, and some for multiple years.

Unlike in professional baseball and basketball, very little money is guaranteed in a football contract. At any point, a team can cut a player and terminate the deal. For this reason, players ask for large signing bonuses whenever they sign a new deal with their team.

In the "old days," many players handled their own negotiations and signed the contract when everything was agreed to. Today, athletes rely on their agent to handle all the finer points of the contract. Agents are a big part of the game, and some have become celebrities in their own right. In addition to landing their clients a fat contract, some agents act as their client's publicist and manage damage control in times of controversy.

Drew Rosenhaus, for example, became highly visible for representing troubled wide receiver Terrell Owens and for helping running back Willis McGahee get picked in the first round of the 2003 NFL Draft despite having a badly injured knee.

The arrival of Plan-B free agency in 1989 helped players gain control over their playing futures, albeit at a limited scale. Players designated as Plan B free agents had to give their current team an opportunity to sign them, and any competing team willing to sign a Plan B free agent had to compensate the team they were signing him away from. Following an anti-trust lawsuit, the league changed its policy, and in 1993 began to allow veteran players who had fulfilled their contracts to seek offers from the rest of the teams in the league.

A player can now be classified as either a restricted or an unrestricted free agent. Unrestricted free agents can sign with any team they choose, with no compensation due to the team they're leaving unless that team places its *franchise tag* on the individual. Restricted free agents have spent less time in the league (eligible after their third season), and therefore have less freedom to sign with another club.

GRIDIRON GAB

Each NFL team gets to use a **franchise tag** once each off-season, usually for a free-agent player. If another team makes an offer to sign that player, the team holding his rights has the option to match. If it declines, the new team is forced to give up compensation in the form of draft picks. However, for the team using the franchise tag to retain the player, it must either sign him to a new contract or offer him a one-year deal that would pay him money equivalent to the average of the top five paid players at his respective position, or 120 percent of his previous year's salary, whichever is greater.

The Salary Cap

To keep the playing field level in the NFL—i.e., to protect small-market teams from the deep pockets of larger cities like New York and Chicago—the league uses a *salary cap* so all teams have the same amount of money to spend on their 53-man roster each year. It's much more complex than that, but for the sake of simplicity, all you really need to know is that it leads to league parity.

Each team has more than $100 million to spend on its players and must manage that money the same way an investment banker would, spreading it around and working on cycles to maximize its purchasing power. Teams try to balance out when they need to make money available to sign their star players, and sometimes are forced to cut ties with good players just for the sake of saving cap money.

In rare cases, star players already under contract restructure their agreements so the team can make room to sign someone else.

If a team goes over its spending cap, it receives a punishment from the league office, usually in the form of lost draft picks—something no team dares to risk.

The Hall of Fame

Golf has the green jacket of the Masters. For football, there's no finer colored jacket than the yellow one presented to newly inducted members of the Hall of Fame.

A panel of distinguished football writers picks a handful or so of new Hall of Famers each year, and in August, the living inductees are given an opportunity to give their acceptance speech on the steps of the Hall of Fame.

It's an elite club; even great players don't get enough votes to gain entrance. Being a member of the Hall of Fame means a player was one of the elite, the best of the best—and for many players, it's the last piece of their legacy.

The Hall of Fame was established in Canton, Ohio, in 1963 in large part because the city served as the home to the first league office in 1920. The 83,000-square-foot facility has expanded several times since its first construction.

FUN FACT

Of the 17 members of the inaugural class of the Hall of Fame, several were responsible for helping shape the league. One was Joe Carr, who helped guide the NFL in its infancy and served as its commissioner from 1921 until his death in 1939.

NFL Charities and Other Programs

One of the many things the NFL does better than other professional leagues is use its popularity to bring goodwill to communities across the country. For many years the league has enjoyed a relationship with the United Way, and its athletes have come to the aid of those in need in times of crises like Hurricane Katrina.

Fans have the ability to take part as well. The Join the Team program encourages volunteer participation on a number of regional projects.

The NFL also participates in cancer awareness programs. Each October it encourages coaches and players to help bring awareness to breast cancer. Players are allowed to wear pink accessories on their uniforms during games, and many coaches and league representatives wear a pink ribbon. The league also has been active in the fight against prostate cancer.

One campaign the league has pushed heavily in recent years has been the NFL Play 60 Challenge, which encourages all grade-school kids to get a minimum of 60 minutes of physical activity each day. The league has a program that works with local classrooms to help build a physical fitness plan.

The Great Teams and Dynasties

No NFL franchise has dominated through the annals of NFL history quite like the Green Bay Packers. The Packers won a title in the 1920s, four in the 1930s, one in the 1940s, five in the 1960s, and one in the 1990s. At the start of pro football, many of the franchises were positioned in small Midwestern towns. Today, the Packers stand as the smallest-market team in professional sports, but the franchise is also one with a rich tradition of winning.

In the 1950s, the Detroit Lions and Cleveland Browns ruled the game, much thanks to their respective quarterbacks, Bobby Layne and Otto Graham.

The 1968 New York Jets were not the greatest team of their era, but they're also one of the most important teams in league history. After quarterback Joe Namath guaranteed it would happen, his Jets defeated the heavily favored Baltimore Colts in Super Bowl III. It was the first time an AFL team had defeated an NFL team in the title game, and the game helped give football's "other" league tremendous credibility.

The 1970s may have been the greatest era in pro football history, as two of its great dynasties—the Pittsburgh Steelers and Dallas Cowboys—dominated their respective conferences like no other teams have done throughout a decade. Dallas earned its way to five Super Bowls during the 1970s, winning two of them. Pittsburgh's success was even greater; during a six-year period, the Steelers won four championships, including two Super Bowl wins over Dallas. Both of those meetings are considered among the greatest games ever played.

What made San Francisco special in the 1980s? Well, besides its well-educated head coach Bill Walsh and his perfect offensive system, the 49ers won three titles with three mostly different rosters, following the 1981, 1984, and 1988 seasons. San Francisco's dynasty actually extended into the 1990s under the guidance of Walsh's replacement, George Seifert. From 1989 through 1996, the 49ers never won fewer than 10 games in any one season under Seifert, and they claimed two more Super Bowl titles.

As great as the 49ers were in the 1990s, the Cowboys were even better. The team's trio of Hall of Famers, Troy Aikman, Emmitt Smith, and Michael Irvin, along with a supporting cast of superstars, helped Dallas win three Super Bowls in a four-year period—something no other team had accomplished before them.

The New England Patriots matched Dallas's feat by winning three titles between 2001 and 2004. In 2007, the Patriots became just the second team in league history to win all its regular season games, but that club fell to the New York Giants in Super Bowl XLII.

FUN FACT

The greatest team of all time? Some would say that title belongs to one of those Packer teams of the 1960s or Steeler teams of the 1970s. The 1985 Bears won 15 regular season games and dominated in the playoffs with one of the all-time great defenses. But it's hard to argue against Don Shula's 1972 Miami Dolphins, which won all its contests in the NFL's only perfect season.

The Least You Need to Know

- The 32 NFL teams are divided into 2 conferences, each separated into 4 divisions.
- Teams play a 16-game schedule that helps determine which teams qualify for the playoffs. From there, it's win each week, or go home.
- The Super Bowl is one of the biggest spectacles of the year, sports or otherwise. The game's commercials and side attractions sometimes draw as much attention as the game does.
- The Green Bay Packers have won more NFL titles (12) than any other franchise; the 1972 Miami Dolphins are the only team to finish a season with a perfect record.

College Football

In This Chapter

- Why football is important to a college campus
- How teams use the recruiting process to get better
- College football's most prestigious prize, the Heisman
- The great teams and rivalries in college football history

A large number of college football loyalists prefer their game over the NFL—better tailgate parties, more tradition, and a purer form of football, they argue. These folks believe football is meant to be played on Saturdays, not Sundays. It's up for debate. What cannot be debated is the scope of the college game: hundreds of teams, thousands of student-athletes, and millions of crazed fans.

College football is governed by the National Collegiate Athletic Association (NCAA), which helps evaluate rules and opportunities for growth in collegiate athletics. The NCAA's primary objective is to protect the integrity of its student-athletics and preserve college football's amateur status. But college football is also a big business, just like the NFL, earning millions for its member schools each year.

Football Drives the Cart on Campus

Some people think football is a distraction to a school's academic platform, but this does not factor in the potential impact the sport can have on a university.

Football is a money-maker, and in some cases, a well-performing football program can bring millions of dollars to a university—that's money other athletic programs can use or that can help pay for the construction of new facilities.

So when the football team wins, the university wins, too.

A Historical Timeline

The history of college football follows the same track as the history of the game because the college game was the *only* game in the early years. College football, like the NFL, has grown to unimaginable heights over the last half-century.

Here are a few of the important points, from the birth of the game to the growth of its bowl season:

In 1869, Rutgers and Princeton meet to play a game blended from soccer and rugby. The rules have yet to take form.

In 1902, Michigan beats Stanford 49–0 in the Rose Bowl—college football's first-ever bowl game.

The game's growing reputation for violence draws the attention of President Theodore Roosevelt, who demands change or threatens to ban the game. The forward pass becomes legal.

Knute Rockne's plane crashes on March 31, 1931, ending the greatest run ever by a college football program. In 13 seasons, Rockne's Notre Dame teams win 105 games and 6 national championships—and lay the foundation for what is to become the most followed team in college sports.

The University of Chicago's Jay Berwanger becomes the first-ever player to win the Heisman Trophy in 1935.

Within a 30-year period, the number of bowl games almost doubles, from 8 in 1950 to 15 in 1980. After another 30 years, the bowls double again, increasing to 34 in 2010.

In 1998, the NCAA introduces the Bowl Championship Series (BCS), which aims to end the debate over which team deserves to be crowned number 1 at the end of the year. Instead, the BCS intensifies the debate.

Divisions and Conferences

Hundreds of college football programs operate around the United States, all with varying levels of enrollment and athletic budgets. The NCAA uses a number of divisions to sort teams and then further organizes them into conferences designed to keep teams regionally aligned.

The Football Bowl Subdivision (FBS) is the highest level of college football. It contains 120 schools scattered across 11 conferences:

- Atlantic Coast Conference
- Big 12 Conference
- Big East Conference
- Big Ten Conference
- Conference USA
- Mid-American Conference
- Mountain West Conference
- Pacific-10 Conference
- Southeastern Conference
- Sun Belt Conference
- Western Athletic Conference

A few schools, including Notre Dame, are independent of a conference.

The NCAA has three other divisions of football schools:

- The Football Championship Subdivision (FCS), also known as Division 1-AA
- Division II
- Division III

Like the FBS, each division groups teams regionally by conferences. The level of competition does not necessarily decline at each step; a number of Division III programs are just as talented as those competing at the Division II level, for example. The primary difference, though, are the financial incentives. Division III schools cannot award scholarships, while other levels of college football can. For this and other reasons, student-athletes weigh a number of factors when determining which school to attend.

Recruiting

College teams don't draft players, and they aren't allowed to make trades with other schools, so the only way a school can improve its roster is through recruiting high school players to attend the school, often enticing them with scholarship offers.

Teams are given only so many scholarships to hand out to incoming freshmen, so each school must make wise decisions as to which prospects it provides with an offer.

Of course, every team is after the same high school superstars, fostering a competitive chase for the nation's top recruits. Teams that attract a large number of *blue-chip prospects* can feel a level of accomplishment, even if nothing has been accomplished on the field per se.

> **GRIDIRON GAB**
>
> A **blue-chip prospect** is considered one of the country's elite prospects at his respective position. Few college programs, even the very best, are able to recruit more than a handful of blue-chip recruits in any one year.

It's a game for the recruits as much as the school. They get to visit campuses and see the country, all the while deciding the best fit for them. Recruits sometimes offer a verbal commitment to a school. Such a commitment is nonbinding. To make it binding, the recruit signs a letter of intent to attend that university. This is considered a contract to which the player and university are bound. If a player changes his mind (sometimes due to a coaching change), he can ask for a release so he can be free to sign with another school.

National Signing Day, which occurs the first week in February, is the day when everything becomes official. Some high-profile prospects hold out until that day to make their intentions known. In most cases, though, recruits have committed to their school of choice well before then.

Much like the NFL Draft, fans follow the recruiting process closely to learn the potential future stars of their favorite college football team. Analysts grade each team's incoming class and measure it against the other schools in that team's division and/or conference.

Scheduling

College teams usually begin the season with a series of nonconference games that count toward their final win-loss record but play no role in determining where they finish in the conference race. Some schools pick opponents that offer a high chance of success so they can boost their winning percentage, while other schools schedule well-matched opponents to help them prepare for the rest of the season.

Teams then play against the teams of their conference. At the end of the season, the school with the best conference record is crowned that year's league champion. In some conferences, there are two divisions, and the winners of those divisions face off in an end-of-season conference championship game to determine conference supremacy.

QUICK HIT

Nonconference scheduling is often done years in advance and usually with games planned for consecutive years. This way, each program gets to play host to the other.

The Polls

College football is unlike any other sport in that it places a large emphasis on its polls, or rankings. Ultimately, some of those polls help determine which teams will contend for a national championship at the FBS level.

Prior to the start of the season, and following each weekend's action, voters in various polls, such as the Associated Press Poll and the *USA Today* Poll, submit their lists of the top 25 teams in the country. All the lists are tabulated to offer a comprehensive top 25. Mostly, voters base their rankings on a team's record and the strength of the competition it has faced. When a team loses, even to a strong opponent, it can fall far down the poll in a single week.

The difference between being ranked among the top 10 or top 25 teams in the country does not affect a school's wins or losses, but the prestige brings added exposure for the program and helps in areas such as recruiting and end-of-the-year jockeying.

The Bowl Season and the BCS

The FBS is judged subjectively more than any other sport because, in large part, factors not related to game outcomes and the opinions of pollsters help determine where a team plays its bowl game and which teams play for the national title.

After the regular season and conference championship games conclude, a series of more than two dozen bowl games take place in stadiums all across the country during December and January. In most cases, the earlier in the bowl season the game is played, the less prestigious the bowl.

To earn a trip to a bowl game, a team must win at least six games. This allows for roughly half of the 120 FBS schools to become bowl eligible. Considering each school makes a considerable amount of money for earning a bowl bid, it's welcome money to all the participating universities.

Nothing but bragging rights are at stake in any of these bowls except for the national title game, played at the end of the bowl season.

The BCS is the conclusion of the bowl season, pitting the year's finest in its series of bowl games. Think of it as the grand finale at the annual fireworks display on the Fourth of July. The 10 top finishers, as determined by the BCS standings (a compilation of polls and strength of schedule formulas), are assigned one of five BCS bowl games, all played on or after January 1. The top two ranked teams play in the national title game, usually held a week after New Year's Day.

QUICK HIT

The four bowls that make up the BCS include the Orange Bowl, the Rose Bowl, the Fiesta Bowl, and the Sugar Bowl. The sites rotate hosting the BCS National Championship Game (meaning each year one of the sites hosts two games).

Independent surveys have shown that a majority of fans would like to see college football move away from the BCS and incorporate a playoff system, similar to what the NFL uses, to determine its champion. Congress has even tried to explore ways for the sport to determine its winner on the field rather than in the polls.

All-Star Games

One of college football's many traditions is its postseason all-star games, which serve as a reward for those players who have stood out from their peers during the season. (These games also serve as an opportunity for pro football scouts to get another look at the incoming talent.)

The East-West Shrine Game is the oldest such game, dating to 1925. Another popular contest, the Senior Bowl, is played in Mobile, Alabama, usually in the final week of January. The Hula Bowl has been in existence since 1947, while the Aztec Bowl (for the nation's best Division III players) started three years later. Many of the biggest names in pro football participated in one of these bowls upon leaving college.

FUN FACT

From 1934 to 1976, the NFL champions played against an all-star team made up of college players. The college team won several of the early contests played but none after 1963.

All-American Teams

Players aspire to be named to their all-conference squads each November, but a higher honor is to be selected to the All-American squad, which features the finest players from the country in their respective division. (Division II and III have their own All-American squads.)

Started in 1889 by Caspar Whitney and Walter Camp, the latter of whom made it his hobby to tour the country to catch a glimpse of the finest players, the All-American team has become a staple of college athletics, not just football.

Several outlets pick an All-American squad today, consisting mostly of the same group of players, with few exceptions.

 FUN FACT

Playboy magazine selects one of the most popular and well-documented pre-season All-American teams. Players are asked to gather for a photo shoot each spring when the team is picked. When the magazine first began to select its team, some coaches prohibited their players from taking part as a way to show their disapproval for the magazine's content.

The Heisman Trophy

The best player of college football is recognized each December with the Heisman Trophy, named for former college football coach John Heisman. The Heisman, which recognizes individual accomplishment, is perhaps the most prestigious award in all of sports.

Modeled after New York University running back Ed Smith, the bronze statue features a player in a distinct pose that has become synonymous with the award itself.

A select group of writers and former Heisman winners rank the year's top three performers, and five finalists are invited to a ceremony in New York where the winner is announced.

A few interesting notes about the Heisman Trophy:

- Only once since its inception in 1935 has the Heisman Trophy been given to a player on a team with a losing record (Paul Hornung, Notre Dame, 1956).

- In 2007, University of Florida quarterback Tim Tebow became the first sophomore to win the award. No freshman has ever won.

- Ohio State running back Archie Griffin is the only person to win the Heisman twice (1974 and 1975).

- The trophy has a bias for offensive players. Only one defender, University of Michigan defensive back Charles Woodson (1997), has ever won the award.

FUN FACT

In 2009, University of Alabama running back Mark Ingram edged Stanford's Toby Gerhart in the closest Heisman balloting ever. Ingram received 1,304 points to Gerhart's 1,276.

The Hall of Fame

Like the NFL, college football has its Hall of Fame, too. A large number of the game's greatest football players are enshrined in both.

Sponsored by the National Football Foundation (NFF), the facility has been relocated a couple times through the years, from Ohio to South Bend, Indiana; in 2011, the NFF plans to move to Atlanta, Georgia.

The 1951 inaugural class included 54 of the game's early legends and pioneers—men like Knute Rockne, Red Grange, and Bronko Nagurski.

The Great Teams and the Bitter Rivalries

With 11 national titles and 7 Heisman Trophy winners to its credit, few schools can match the level of success reached by Notre Dame. It's a program built on legends upon legends, and that history carries weight in the recruiting process to this day.

Notre Dame has the country's largest fan following and a long-standing television deal with NBC to broadcast Fighting Irish games each Saturday in the fall. In terms of general interest and football dollars and cents, few other programs compare.

One of the country's biggest rivalries features two of college football's most storied programs—Texas and Oklahoma. Called the Red River Rivalry, the game is played in Dallas's Cotton Bowl, which is considered a neutral site. Fans for the two schools share the tickets, and the schools share the profits. After that, it's blood and guts, with the winner not only claiming bragging rights but gaining a large advantage in the race to win the Big 12 Conference title.

Perhaps no college program has transcended time as well as the University of Southern California. From Howard Jones' teams in the 1930s to John McKay's outstanding teams of the 1960s and 1970, to Pete Carroll's teams of the 2000s, USC has been a force on the national scale in every decade.

The rivalry between Ohio State and Michigan may have more bad blood attached to it than any other. For many years, Michigan dominated its Big Ten foe, but Ohio State's program began to grow, and when Woody Hayes arrived in Columbus in 1951, things evened out. Now it doesn't matter which team is ranked and which team has struggled when the two meet in the final regular season game of the year—only the hatred the schools have for one another.

WORDS OF WISDOM

When asked why he would attempt a 2-point conversion with a 36-point lead against rival Michigan in 1968, Ohio State coach Woody Hayes responded, "Because they wouldn't let me go for three."

Alabama had a successful program before Paul "Bear" Bryant arrived in late 1957, but the coach took it to another level of success, winning six national championships during his 25-year tenure. Throughout the 1970s, no school was as successful. In recent years under coach Nick Saban, the Crimson Tide has again risen to national prominence.

No two teams have played one another as often as Wisconsin and Minnesota, which began their rivalry in 1890. Each year the two schools face off to claim Paul Bunyan's Axe, a 6-foot-long trophy celebrating the long-standing rivalry.

The Least You Need to Know

- College football teams are first separated by division and then grouped into conferences.
- The polls have as much say in who is crowned the national champion as the teams do.
- More than a dozen awards are handed to individual players at the end of the year. The one most college players dream about winning is the Heisman Trophy.
- Notre Dame has a rich tradition and a large fan base.
- Rivalries help make college football special.

Youth and High School Football

In This Chapter

- Local football: a positive impact on the community
- The objectives of youth and high school football
- The differences between the high school and pro football rulebooks

Wherever there's a ball and an open field of grass (or dirt), kids will pick sides and play football. From a young age, kids learn to love the game, but as they enter elementary school, they begin to have opportunities to play organized football, perhaps for the first time.

Youth football (ages 8 to 13) and high school football present athletes with an opportunity to develop and compete against other schools in their area. It acts as the breeding ground for future college and pro players, but also enables kids to learn valuable life skills through the game of football.

But what really makes youth and high school football special is the impact it has on those around the game.

Friday Night Lights

The atmosphere at a high school varsity football game on a Friday evening is like no other. Parents, students, teachers, business owners, community leaders, and visiting fans all pack together to watch two local teams duke it out. The closer the two towns are located to one another, the stronger chance they act as rivals, making the towns rivals as well.

One major reason why a large percentage of high schools have a football program is because they understand the potential impact the team can have on the community. Football teams bring fans of all feathers together into one setting, bonding them through the sport they share. It offers something for the barber to talk to the postman about on Monday morning, and something for its residents to do on a Friday evening. High school football is a happening.

Youth games are often played on the weekends, but the camaraderie is much the same. Dads and moms get to share the experience with the parents of their sons' and daughters' classmates.

Sportsmanship and Amateurism Trump All Else

At the youth and even high school level, football is about the game and nothing more. Players are truly student-athletes, not paid professionals or globally known superstars. High schools make an effort to protect their athletes' best interests and keep academics as each athlete's top priority.

QUICK HIT

One way schools encourage sportsmanship is by having all members of both teams form a line to shake hands at the end of a game.

Schools also put a large emphasis on sportsmanship. Game officials tolerate far less from youth and high school athletes and coaches because the focus is less about the outcome of a game and more about the indirect impacts football has on its athletes.

Coaches are mentors and examples for the kids who play for them. If a coach is ejected from a game at the high school level, it's a far bigger "crime" than if the same were to happen at the college or professional level. It could even cost the coach his job. Coaches are assigned to develop young men, to build their work ethic, and to test their character. To do this, the coaches and staff must set a good example.

At the youth level, especially, winning comes second (or third, or fourth). Youth coaches are in place to ensure the kids learn the basics of the game—how to block and tackle properly, how to catch and throw—and have fun. Every kid gets to make the team and play in the game.

The number-1 priority of every youth football league should be to foster an environment that encourages kids to continue in the sport. And kids won't come back next year if they didn't have fun.

> **QUICK HIT**
>
> Most communities work to form a bond throughout the entire football program, from varsity down to the youngest level of play. High school players act as mentors for the younger kids, and varsity coaches work with youth coaches to be sure fundamentals are taught consistently throughout. The stronger the bonds formed within a program, the more likely the program is to have success at the highest levels of competition.

Rule Variations

The rules at the high school and youth levels differ from those at the pro and college level to help better protect the younger players of the game. High school football does all it can to limit the risk of player injuries and to encourage sportsmanlike play.

Here are a few of the rules that are different at the high school level:

- The playing field is the same size, but the hash marks are farther apart. This leads to more wide-side and short-side plays. In the NFL, they are closer to the direct center of the field, keeping things fairly balanced when the ball is placed on either hash mark.

- As is true at the college level, a receiver only needs to have one foot in bounds to establish possession of the ball instead of the two needed in the NFL.

- A pass interference call is worth 15 yards and a first down versus being placed at the spot of the infraction.

- Referees do not allow returners to bring the ball out of the end zone on kicks. It is automatically ruled a touchback.

- High school games consist of four 12-minute quarters; college and professional quarters are 15 minutes.

- Teams kick off the ball from the 40-yard line instead of from the 30-yard line.

Punt, Pass & Kick

For half of a century, the Punt, Pass & Kick (PPK) program has helped young players develop necessary football skills through the fun of competition. Boys and girls between the ages of 8 and 15 gather at events and earn points for the longest and most accurate kicks, punts, and throws.

The NFL now partners with the program and has awards for both genders in each state.

Flag Football

In some towns, organized youth football replaces pads with flags. These leagues teach the same fundamental skills to young players, but in a safer, more controlled environment.

Each player wears a belt containing several flags, each attached by a strip of Velcro. Instead of tackling one another, players are ruled down when one player grabs another player's flag. Usually the dimensions of a flag football field are set smaller than a regulation field, and rules are flexible based on the league.

PENALTY!
Most flag football leagues do not allow players to spin while carrying the football, as it makes it too difficult for defenders to grab their flags.

Many adults also play in flag football leagues, much the same as they would in a softball or sand volleyball league.

Big Schools and Small

One of the great things about high school football is that there are so many different scales of it in every state. Some schools have high school enrollments of just a few hundred kids, while a school a few miles down the road may have an enrollment of a few thousand.

State athletic associations work with high school administrators and athletic directors to group schools of similar size into conferences or districts, each with a half dozen or more schools. These are the schools that make up the bulk of a football team's schedule.

Sometimes schools within a conference or district have to travel great distances by school bus to play an opponent, but the benefit is that every school can play a schedule against its peers, and not over- or undermatched opponents.

No State Quite Like Texas

They say everything's bigger in Texas. It's certainly true of football. Some high school games in the Lone Star State are played in huge, college-size stadiums. Fans in many Texas communities care more about how the local team performs than they do one of the area college programs or the state's professional football teams.

In Texas, the competition level is higher than perhaps anywhere else in the country, and the drive for athletes and their schools to succeed is higher as well. This is why many of the greatest players to have ever played the game came from the state where football is king.

 FUN FACT

The most famous Texas prep football product is probably running back Earl Campbell, nicknamed the Tyler Rose for the incredible high school career he had in Tyler, Texas (and because Tyler is the "rose capital of the world"). Campbell later won a Heisman Trophy while at the University of Texas and had a distinguished career for the NFL's Houston Oilers.

Names to Know and Performances to Remember

Kenneth Hall ran the ball for Sugar Land High School in Sugar Land, Texas, way back in the early 1950s, yet to this day, he remains the most accomplished rusher in the history of high school football. The Texas prep phenom gained more than 3,000 yards rushing in both his sophomore and junior seasons, and more than 4,000 yards as a senior, to finish with 11,232 yards. Hall scored more than 30 points per game in his final season. The Kenneth Hall Trophy is awarded annually to the best high school player in the country, on par with college's Heisman Trophy.

One of the best prospects to come out of the state of Kentucky, quarterback Tim Couch threw 133 touchdowns for Leslie County High School—a national record—and had every college recruiter in the country drooling.

The NFL's all-time leading rusher, Emmitt Smith, was also one of the finest high school running backs ever to play. At Escambia High School in Pensacola, Florida, Smith gained almost 8 yards per carry. Smith set a record by gaining 100 or more yards in 45 of his games.

When quarterback Ben Mauk finished his career at Ohio's Kenton High School, he held the national records for most passing yards in a season and career and had thrown the second-most career touchdown passes (178).

At New York's Onondaga Central High School, running back Mike Hart gained 11,045 rushing yards and set a national record by scoring 204 touchdowns.

The Least You Need to Know

- Local football teams have the ability to bring together residents and leaders from a community.
- High school and youth football put an extra emphasis on sportsmanship.
- A number of rules are different at the high school level. Most notably, the game is shorter.
- Kenneth Hall is the most accomplished high school running back of all time.

Fantasy Football

In This Chapter

- The origin of fantasy football
- The rules for scoring and setting up a league
- Tips for newcomers
- Helpful team-management tools

For the person trying to learn the game of football, there may be no better training ground than a fantasy league. Joining and managing a fantasy team forces one to learn quickly the many rules of the game, the names of the players and the teams, and how the NFL schedule works. Before long, the novice fan will know how long a running back takes to heal from a case of turf toe and be able to recite the number of 300-yard passing games Peyton Manning had for the Indianapolis Colts last season.

But fantasy football is more than an education; it's a phenomenon. According to industry research, more than 20 million Americans play fantasy football each year—that's a large percentage of the football viewing audience.

Curious what the big deal is? Read on and start to play.

A Way for the Fan to "Play"

Fans love to second-guess personnel decisions and play-calling. It's human nature to think, *Hey, I could do better than that guy!* Fantasy football empowers the fan to be the coach and the general manager of his (or her!—lots of ladies manage fantasy leagues, too) own team—to assemble a team of players he likes and manage the starting lineup during the season.

Playing fantasy football is easy. There's little to no investment required, and each fantasy player controls how much time he invests in managing his team. For some, it can be as little as a few minutes each week to make lineup changes. For others, fantasy football can become a full-blown hobby, with countless hours spent evaluating players and communicating on league message boards.

No matter how competitive it is, or how detailed a league chooses to get with its rulebook, the only thing that really matters is that everyone is having fun. It's as close as most couch potatoes will ever come to living out their fantasy of running an NFL franchise.

The History

Believe it or not, fantasy football began within the inner circles of the NFL—more specifically, the Oakland Raiders organization. In 1962, several Raiders minority owners began the Greater Oakland Professional Pigskin Prognosticators League (GOPPPL), considered the first-ever fantasy football league. The men established a set of rules, held a draft, and crowned a league champion just like fantasy players do in every league today.

The difference was that they had some inside help. The leader of that first league was Wilford "Bill" Winkenbach, an Oakland businessman who owned a stake in the Raiders. The eight-team league Winkenbach helped set up occasionally tapped a few of the team's scouts for advice on players from around the league. Often, Winkenbach would seek the knowledge of a young scout named Ron Wolf, who later became one of pro football's most respected general managers.

 FUN FACT

In the first fantasy football draft, George Blanda was selected by two teams; one team claimed him as its quarterback, the other as its kicker. This wouldn't be allowed in most leagues today, but then again, no current NFL player wears those two hats like Blanda once did.

For the men of GOPPPL, fantasy football was fun. None of them had a clue that by the 1990s it would grow to be a multimillion-dollar industry with celebrity spokesmen representing major media company products.

How to Start Your League

Starting a fantasy football league is as easy as getting a card game together or organizing a night out on the town. All one needs is a group of reliable buddies, an agreed-on set of rules, and a meeting area where a draft or auction can be held—and with online technology, even this is optional.

Most fantasy leagues have anywhere from 8 to 12 teams, each managed by an individual owner. Finding the right group is important, but once you have a league, it often lasts for years. Pick 10 people from your bowling league or from the office. It works best when the people in the fantasy league are the same people you interact with on a regular basis; the more you all discuss the league, the more fun everyone will have.

It's recommended for leagues to choose a commissioner—someone to keep track of the rules and act as a centralized voice of reason when disputes arise. The commissioner should be someone everyone in the league trusts, and someone willing to do a little more work than everyone else. People can trade off handling this post from year to year, but not everyone makes for a good commissioner. When you find the right person for the job, try to convince him or her to stay.

The most important thing to know when assembling a league: fantasy football is all-inclusive. People of all cultures and ages play it. Diehard fans and people who watch very little football at all play it. Men and women play it. In fact, females are one of the fastest-growing demographics in fantasy sports.

Basic Rules and Scoring

The greatest thing about fantasy football is that there is no set system for rules or scoring. You can customize everything depending on your and your league's preferred tastes.

However, some rules have evolved over time and become common for most leagues.

Scoring

In most fantasy leagues, the game is dominated by offensive skill players. Quarterbacks, running backs, wide receivers, tight ends, and kickers score the bulk of the points.

Here's the most common scoring system:

- 6 points for all rushing and receiving touchdowns
- 4 points for passing touchdowns
- 3 points for every field goal
- 2 points for a 2-point conversion, whether the player passes, catches, or runs with the ball
- 1 point for every extra point

For yardage, leagues typically award the following:

- 1 point for every 25 yards passing
- 1 point for every 10 yards rushing or receiving

Points per reception (PPR) leagues also award 1 point for every reception a player makes. Some leagues opt to award partial points, such as ½ point for 5 yards receiving, or extra points based on the length of the field goal or touchdown.

For defense, every league is different. Some prefer to use *individual defensive players (IDP)* and score points for tackles, sacks, interceptions, fumbles, and touchdowns, while other leagues use a team defense each week and award it points for mostly the same categories. In general, touchdowns are worth 6 points, with sacks, safeties, and turnovers worth 2 points and tackles worth 1 point.

GRIDIRON GAB

Fantasy leagues that use **individual defensive players** (**IDP**) keep track of player statistics rather than team defensive statistics, as has been more common in fantasy play.

The Roster and Starting Lineup

In most leagues, fantasy players set up a starting lineup consisting of a quarterback, two running backs, two or three wide receivers, a tight end, a kicker, and either a team defense or a collection of defensive players. This lineup can change each week, but once the games start, the lineup is locked until the last game of the week is played.

To allow for backups, a fantasy roster usually reserves two spots for every one player in the starting lineup. For example, in leagues where you start two running backs, each fantasy player can draft four running backs to add to a roster. Again, leagues can add or subtract from these numbers, but generally that's the rule of thumb.

As a fantasy player, you collect players through a draft held before the season. No NFL player can be selected by more than one fantasy player. Each fantasy player takes a turn selecting a player for his team until every roster spot is filled. For many, the draft is one of the highlights of the fantasy season.

QUICK HIT

Fantasy drafts operate much the same as the NFL Draft, with the worst place finisher from the previous year given the option of drafting first and so on. After the first round, most leagues use snake-style drafts, meaning that the last team to pick in round 1 is the first team to select in round 2.

Other leagues use an auction to build team rosters. The players take turns throwing out the name of a player, and the bidding begins, with the highest bidder winning the player. Each fantasy team is given a budget to purchase all its players, so remember to bid wisely.

After the season begins, you can change players through the waiver wire, a collection of players left undrafted. To pick up one of these players, you have to discard one player already on your roster.

Some leagues even allow trading. Just like football cards, you can trade one of your players for a player on someone else's team in the hopes the trade makes your team better.

Determining a League Winner

Some leagues keep a running tally of each team's points, and at the end of the year, the fantasy player with the most points scored is crowned champion.

The other way to play is to mimic real football by creating a weekly schedule and each week, fantasy players pair up. At the end of the week, the player with the most points wins. The league counts wins and losses and has a playoff and a championship game.

Following is a quick rundown of how to manage the season, playoffs, and title game for leagues of any size.

Map out a regular-season schedule, beginning in week 1 and running through week 13 or 14.

Depending on the playoff format, the top four to eight teams will qualify for the playoffs. In a four-team playoff system, the regular season should end after week 14; for six or eight teams, it'll end after week 13.

For a four-team system, the number-1-ranked team faces the number-4 team in round 1, with numbers 2 and 3 facing off as well. The winners of those two games will play in the championship game in week 16 of the NFL season.

For a six-team system, the number-1- and -2-ranked teams will receive a bye for week 13, while number 3 faces number 6 and number 4 faces number 5. The highest-ranked winner of the first round faces the number-2 team in week 14, with number 1 facing the lowest-ranked club. Again, the winners of those games get to play for the title in week 16.

For an eight-team system, number 1 faces number 8 in the first week, and so on. The method continues for the next two weeks, same as with the six-team system.

QUICK HIT

Most fantasy leagues don't run through week 17 of the NFL schedule because NFL teams whose playoff futures are already determined tend to sit star players that week, leaving fantasy players with that player bitter and disappointed.

Dynasty Leagues

NFL teams don't rebuild a roster from scratch each year, so why should fantasy teams? While some leagues throw all the players back into the pot prior to the next season's draft, most leagues allow teams to hold over a few players, or keepers, from the previous year's roster. This is the foundation for a dynasty league.

There's no set rule as to how many players to keep—three, four, eight—and some dynasty leagues even incorporate special designations for players, such as free agents and franchise players, that help make the experience even closer to how NFL teams manage offseason personnel decisions.

Dynasty leagues require little more from the fantasy players, other than a couple extra rules and a little imagination.

Managing a Winning Team

Fantasy football is a game of skill, not chance. This is why it's safe from gambling legislation, but also why not just anyone can stroll into a league and claim first place without much effort. To win at fantasy football requires time researching players and matchups and an understanding for how to make the right decisions. It's lots of homework, just like in grade school, but this time, it's fun!

It all starts with your draft. The players you select on draft day serve as the base you work with throughout the season. Mess up on draft day, and you'll have a miserable year. Do well, and watch your team succeed Sunday after Sunday. Just remember: managing a fantasy football roster requires patience, knowing when to trust your gut over your head, and a whole lot of luck.

Here are some tips for new players:

- Study your league scoring rules and then evaluate which NFL players will produce the most points in this system.

- Most league formats favor running backs more than other positions. Having a pair of good running backs is often vital to having a successful season.

- Evaluate trade offers and waiver wire pickups carefully. Don't add or discard players without first doing your homework.

- Study the matchups each week, looking for the players on your team who will face a weak defense. Big points can be scored in these games. But don't go overboard; rarely should you replace one of your premier players with a backup who has a favorable matchup.

- Play the odds when it comes to star players. Some fantasy players take a player out of the starting lineup the instant he has a bad game. Good players post good numbers over the course of the season. Ride out the averages.

Tools That Can Help

A wealth of resources can help you build and manage your fantasy team. Some resources are free, some cost money, but all aim to make you and your team better.

Dozens of magazines are available on newsstands each summer containing player rankings, capsules for each position, and strategy articles.

Online information sites provide the same services, but they can assist a fantasy player throughout the season. It's essential to know which players are injured or not in top health, which players are facing difficult matchups, and which players have poor histories against their upcoming opponent.

Check online for sites that allow fantasy players to test their drafting skills before they have to partake in the real thing. Mock drafts, as they're called, can give you a sense of potential outcomes so you can get a better feel for which players to draft and when.

Online league management software eliminates the need for fantasy players to keep track of scoring or rely on the designated commissioner to keep track of lineups each week. Some sites allow for customizable scoring and provide news and injury updates in one location. Some sites charge users a fee for this service, while other sites offer it at no charge.

The Least You Need to Know

- It's easy to start a league. All you need are some good friends.
- There's no one set system for scoring and league setup. Fantasy football is meant to be catered to each league's specific preferences.
- Services are available online to help you manage your team and keep track of scoring. For some players, the pen and paper method is still preferred.

Fanfare

In This Chapter

- Finding NFL game tickets
- Football wearables and collectables
- Tailgating tips
- Fantastic football foods

One thing that makes football special is the commitment fans have to the game and the teams they follow. It's not enough for fans to watch football games on Saturdays and Sundays; they want to wear it, collect it, ... *live it*.

Diehards maximize the fan experience in several ways, and some never seem to find a cure for their hunger. Being a fan of a college or NFL team is more than a pastime or a hobby—it's a marriage of sorts. A loyal fan knows he has to show his support, stand up to detractors, and stick by his team in good times and bad.

Ticket Information

Of course, a big part of the fan experience is viewing a football game up close and in person. Attending a game can offer a lifelong memory and serve as a way for parents to bond with kids, or for friends to establish new relationships with each other.

When shopping for tickets, whether in person, over the phone, or online, be sure the vendor is reputable and that the transaction is secure. Every NFL team has a website where fans can go to view a stadium seating chart and get a sense of all the amenities available to view at the stadium. Here are the websites for all 32 NFL teams.

National Football Conference

Chicago Bears	www.chicagobears.com/tickets
Detroit Lions	www.detroitlions.com/tickets
Green Bay Packers	www.packers.com/tickets
Minnesota Vikings	www.vikings.com/tickets
Dallas Cowboys	www.dallascowboys.com/tickets/newStadiumMain.cfm
New York Giants	www.giants.com/tickets
Philadelphia Eagles	www.lincolnfinancialfield.com/tickets
Washington Redskins	www.redskins.com/gen/tickets.jsp
Atlanta Falcons	www.atlantafalcons.com/Venues/Landing.aspx
Carolina Panthers	www.panthers.com/tickets
New Orleans Saints	www.neworleanssaints.com/Tickets%20Suites.aspx
Tampa Bay Buccaneers	www.buccaneers.com/tickets/ticketsmain.aspx
Arizona Cardinals	www.azcardinals.com/tickets/index.html
San Francisco 49ers	www.49ers.com/buy-tickets
Seattle Seahawks	www.seahawks.com/tickets
St. Louis Rams	www.stlouisrams.com/Tickets

American Football Conference

Baltimore Ravens	www.baltimoreravens.com/GamedayTickets.aspx
Cincinnati Bengals	www.bengals.com/tickets
Cleveland Browns	www.clevelandbrowns.com/tickets
Pittsburgh Steelers	news.steelers.com/tickets
Buffalo Bills	www.buffalobills.com/tickets
Miami Dolphins	www.dolphinstadium.com/content/ticketoffice.aspx
New England Patriots	www.patriots.com/stadium/index.cfm?ac=TicketSales
New York Jets	www.newyorkjets.com/tickets
Houston Texans	www.houstontexans.com/tickets
Indianapolis Colts	www.colts.com/tickets
Jacksonville Jaguars	www.jaguars.com/Tickets
Tennessee Titans	www.titansonline.com/tickets
Denver Broncos	www.denverbroncos.com/tickets
Kansas City Chiefs	www.kcchiefs.com/tickets/index.html
Oakland Raiders	www.raiders.com/tickets
San Diego Chargers	www.chargers.com/tickets/index.html

Fan Gear

To be a fan, one has to dress like a fan. There's no shortage of team-related apparel to purchase—only a shortage of closet and dresser space to store it all!

The NFL licenses all the products carrying its franchise logos and team representations, and the NFL Players Association does the same for all products containing images of its players.

QUICK HIT

At the college level, the NCAA and universities work together to manage all apparel. Nothing is sold with player names or images because it's restricted by the NCAA due to its amateur status policy.

It's big business for the NFL, and there's no end to the demand for team hats, shirts, coats, posters, license plate holders, and everything else imaginable. Fans buy everything and wear everything.

In some NFL towns, apparel is unique. Here are a few examples:

- Pittsburgh fans have been waving yellow Terrible Towels for decades. When all the fans in the stadium wave their towel at once, it helps create an intimidating atmosphere for the opposition.

- Many Green Bay Packer fans come to the game wearing a cheesehead—a spongelike hat in the shape of a slice of cheese. Wisconsin is the Dairy State, and so Green Bay fans have combined their love for cheddar with their love for football.

- The Cleveland Browns stadium is home to the Dog Pound, a mob of rowdy fans who support their team wholeheartedly. To be a part of the Dog Pound, though, one must wear the dog mask.

Collectible Items

Football fans know all the players and never miss a snap of the ball game. Football fanatics collect items of their favorite player and dress up their room (or sometimes their whole house!) in the colors of their favorite team. When football becomes a hobby instead of just a game, it can intensify the fan experience. And good news: there's no shortage of items you can collect.

Player Autographs

Getting a player's John Hancock on a ball, photo, or even a piece of paper makes a lifelong keepsake. Now the autograph business is a multimillion-dollar industry, overloaded with both authentic and, unfortunately, counterfeit items.

It's difficult to catch a player before or after a game for an autograph, so fans attend functions where players appear for the sole purpose of selling autographed material.

Some autographs of deceased players and coaches can fetch tens of thousands of dollars if you can find someone willing to pay that much.

Player Gear

Fans used to wear their favorite player's jersey; now they frame it and put it up on their wall. Player uniforms, helmets, and other gear have become very collectible items, especially when the player adds his signature to it.

In some cases, fans are able to buy items worn by the actual player in a real game; these come with a much higher price tag.

Player Trading Cards

Similar to baseball cards, a number of brands produce football cards with the pictures and statistics of players on each card. You can purchase these in packs of five or more cards or as a complete set.

Some collectors choose to purchase vintage, or older cards of players from seasons past. Some of the most collectible cards are rookie cards (the first card issued of a player).

Here's a list of 10 desirable football rookie cards to own (with year, brand, and the card's number in the set) in the order of the year they were released:

- 2007 Topps Finest Adrian Peterson (card #112)
- 1998 SP Authentic Peyton Manning (#14)
- 1991 Topps Stadium Club Brett Favre (#94)
- 1990 Score Update Emmitt Smith (#101T)
- 1986 Topps Jerry Rice (#161)
- 1981 Topps Joe Montana (#216)

- 1976 Topps Walter Payton (#148)
- 1958 Topps Jim Brown (#62)
- 1957 Topps Johnny Unitas (#138)

Football in the Movies

Football and the box office have mixed well together since the early days of film, starting with 1940's *Knute Rockne, All-American*. More recent football movies have tried to catch the action on the field along with the pressures that come with being a football star off the field.

Many of the best films are those based on true stories of gridiron greatness, whatever the level. Here are a few of the finer football movies:

Remember the Titans (2000)   A high school team comes together in the racially divided south of the early 1970s.

North Dallas Forty (1979)   Based on former NFL player Peter Gent's life in pro football, the movie presents the side effects of what the game can do to its athletes.

Friday Night Lights (2004)   Based on a true story of a Texas high school team's run at the state title, the film also became a popular television series.

The Blind Side (2009)   Based on the story of high school kid Michael Oher (who now plays in the NFL), this movie won Sandra Bullock an Oscar for her portrayal of Leigh Anne Tuohy, a mother who takes Oher into her home and helps him get on the right track.

Rudy (1993)   Rudy Ruettiger's dream was to play football at Notre Dame, but his lack of size limited his potential. Ruettiger overcame obstacles and eventually earned his place among the Fighting Irish.

The Junction Boys (2002)   Paul "Bear" Bryant put his first Texas A&M team through a grueling training camp that caused half of the players to quit and almost cost one athlete his life.

Brian's Song (1971)   This is the story of Chicago Bears teammates Gale Sayers and Brian Piccolo and the bond they create when having to deal with one's terminal disease.

The Longest Yard (1974)   A group of inmates, led by a former pro football quarterback, is invited to play a game of football against the prison's guards.

The Art of Tailgating

When going to a football game, at any level, it's essential to get the pregame festivities going early. This includes tailgating, a ritual that's practiced a little differently in every state.

All you need to tailgate is a grill, a little charcoal, a well-stocked cooler, and an imagination. Hours before the start of a game, fans gather outside the stadium on lawn chairs or on the tailgate of their truck or SUV to converse about the game and share food with friends.

It may not involve X's and O's, but tailgating is an important part of the football fan experience.

FUN FACT

Each year, the University of Georgia and the University of Florida play in Jacksonville, Florida, in what's referred to as the World's Largest Outdoor Cocktail Party. The two Southeastern Conference schools host one of football's best tailgatelike events, with thousands of fans flocking to Jacksonville just for the festivities.

Football Food for Game Day

You can't watch a game on an empty stomach! Well, you *can*, but why would you want to? Food complements the viewing experience—and it's usually one of the few times a person's diet permits the types of foods commonly found at football game parties. No matter if a person is eating from a seat at the 50-yard line of an NFL stadium or in a recliner in his living room, food is as much a part of the plan as the game.

Here are a few staples to get your football menu started:

- Chips and dip

- Beverages appropriate for the game and the company you're keeping

- Potato salad (For whatever reason, this seems to be a must-have for any party or tailgating experience.)

- Buffalo wings (These seem to show up no matter what state the game is being played in.)

For some, the main course must fit the geographical region of the game, whether it's a hot dog or chili on the East Coast, a bratwurst in the Midwest, or a rack of ribs for a game down south. In California, who knows?

The key to football food is that it shouldn't detract from the game or the conversation. The best food for football is quick, hearty, and not the least bit healthful.

The Least You Need to Know

- When purchasing tickets, be sure the transaction is secure and the vendor is reputable. The safest way to inquire about tickets is through the team's ticket office.
- Fans collect football apparel and other items of value.
- Tailgating is an essential part of any football stadium visit. All one needs is a grill, food, beverages, and friends.
- Food helps make football watching even better. The sport has its staples, but the best football food is whatever fits the crowd consuming it.

Glossary

46 Defense   An aggressive style of defense popularized by Buddy Ryan and the 1985 Chicago Bears.

agent   Someone who represents the interests of a professional football player.

all-American   A football player recognized as one of the finest at his position in all of college football (and a member of the All-American team picked by football writers).

any given Sunday   A popular adage used to describe the unpredictable outcomes of football games. (Pro teams play on Sundays, but this is used at all levels of play.) Simply, it suggests that any team can be beaten by its opponent if the circumstances are right.

arm tackle   A term for when a defender does not use proper form to bring down a ball carrier, but instead only uses one arm. These tackles are dangerous for the defender and far less successful than a textbook tackle.

artificial turf   A playing surface popularized in the 1970s and 1980s that looks like grass but requires far less maintenance. Many players do not care for it because it can be the cause of serious injuries.

audible   When a quarterback changes the play at the line of scrimmage after having a look at how the defense is lined up.

back judge   The game official who helps monitor action downfield between offensive and defensive players. He also must monitor the play clock.

backfield   The area where the offensive (or defensive) backs line up prior to the start of each play.

barnstorming tour   A phrase used when a team plays a lot of games in a condensed amount of time during a road trip. This is most common for less-strenuous sports such as baseball and basketball, but in football's early era, professional teams went on barnstorming tours as a way to earn extra revenue and gain more exposure.

base defense   The scheme a team uses on defense most of the time. For example, if a team features four linemen and three linebackers on most downs, its base defense is a 4–3.

battle for field position   The object of football. Teams trade possessions hoping to gain a little ground on their opponent, always trying to shrink the field in their favor.

between the tackles   Activity that takes place within the space that separates an offense's left and right tackle.

blindside   A quarterback's area of vulnerability on passing downs. A right-handed quarterback's blindside is the left side of the offensive line, protected by his left-side tackle and guard.

blitzer   Either a linebacker or defensive back who is assigned to rush the quarterback on a given play.

blue-chip prospect   A football player heading on to a higher level of play—either from high school to college or college to the pros—who is considered an elite player at his respective position as compared to his peers.

bomb   A long pass a quarterback throws to one of his receivers.

bowl eligible   When a college team has won enough games during the regular season to qualify for a bowl game assignment.

bull rush   A technique a defensive lineman uses to pursue the quarterback, pushing straight through the lineman trying to block him.

bump and run   A technique defenders use on passing downs to slow down the receiver they're assigned to. The defender tries to make contact with the offensive receiver within the first 5 yards of the line of scrimmage in an attempt to throw him off his pass route.

bye   When a team is given a week off when other teams are playing. In the NFL, every team is given one bye week during the regular season; the best two teams in each conference earn a bye for the first week of the postseason.

cadence   A sequence of colors, numbers, and code words the quarterback says before the snap of the ball.

center   The offensive player who lines up over the football and snaps the ball to the quarterback to start each play.

center-quarterback exchange   The transfer of the ball from the center to the quarterback, either when that player is directly under center or in the shotgun formation.

chain gang   The men who carry the first-down chain and yard marker along the sideline throughout the game.

change of possession   When one team loses control of the football to the other team, often due to a turnover or a failed fourth-down attempt.

cheeseheads   Term used to describe Green Bay Packers fans. It's also the name for the foam cheese hats some Packers fans wear.

chop block   An illegal block that occurs when an offensive lineman hits a defender at or below the knees while that player is already engaged in physical contact with another offensive lineman.

clogging the hole   A phrase used to describe how a defender positions his body into a hole in the offensive line to close off the ball carrier's ability to run there.

coffin corner   The area on the field where the sideline meets the goal line. For many years, punters tried to land the ball in this area so the return team had little chance for a return and started with poor field position. Few punters use this method today.

coin toss   The activity that begins every football game and also occurs at the start of an NFL overtime period. The visiting team is given the honor of calling heads or tails, and the winner of the coin toss is afforded the right to determine which team possesses the ball first.

collapsing pocket   A phrase used to describe what happens when the area of space the quarterback uses on passing downs begins to shrink due to the defense's pass rush.

Combine   An event held in February to which the finest eligible prospects are invited. They are subjected to body testing, a number of drills, and interviews with NFL team representatives. The event was first held in Tampa, Florida, in 1982, and has been located in Indianapolis each year since 1987.

commissioner   The person who represents the NFL owners' interests and serves as a figurehead for professional football.

containment   A term for a defender's responsibility for keeping the action on a play near the middle of the field, not allowing a ball carrier to get to the outside of him.

coordinator   A coach who manages one of the three aspects of the team: offense, defense, or special teams.

corner blitz   When a cornerback is assigned to rush the quarterback on a given play, usually from one edge of the line.

crease   An opening in the defense or special teams coverage unit a ball carrier or return man uses to advance the football.

crossbar   The bottom bar of the goal post that runs parallel to the field over which kickers try to kick field goals and extra points.

decoy   An offensive player used to draw attention away from where the play is designed to go.

defenseless player   A player who is vulnerable to a potentially dangerous hit without an ability to defend himself.

defensive end   A defensive lineman usually placed across from a tackle or tight end. His job is to rush the passer and contain the action on the play to the middle of the field.

defensive tackle   A lineman positioned across from a tackle or guard who helps stop the run and also assists as a pass rusher.

defer   An option given to the team that wins the pregame coin toss. If that team chooses to defer, it will have the option of choosing to receive or defend at the start of the second half.

dime back   A term for the sixth defensive back added to a defense, usually in situations in which the offense is certain to pass the ball often.

down   Another word for an offensive play. The offense gets four of these to advance the ball to (or past) the first-down marker or it must relinquish the ball to the other team.

dual-threat quarterback   A quarterback who is competent both running and passing the ball.

duck   A pass that wobbles out of the quarterback's hand without a tight spiral.

encroachment   A penalty for when the defense makes contact with a member of the offense prior to the snap of the ball.

end around   A play in which a split end carries the ball around one edge of the line heading toward the sideline and then up the field.

end zone   An area at both ends of the field 10 yards deep and the length of the field where the offense hopes to place the football, either by running or passing into it, to score a touchdown.

end zone dance   A performance players offer to the crowd or television viewing audience after scoring a touchdown. The NFL has implemented rules in recent years limiting a player's ability to celebrate.

extra point   The kick that occurs after a touchdown is scored. (It is rarely missed.)

facemask   The mesh on a player's helmet that protects his facial features from potential injury. Grabbing it, inadvertently or on purpose, is considered a serious penalty at all levels of play.

fair catch   A term used to describe when a member of the return team waves his arm high into the air prior to fielding the ball (almost always on a punt). The coverage team is not allowed to make contact with him after he does this, and he can then secure the ball safely.

false start   A 5-yard penalty that occurs when a member of the offense moves from his set position before the snap of the ball.

fantasy sports   A game of skill played by men and women of all ages that bases its scoring system on real game outcomes.

field general   Another name used for a quarterback.

field goal   A kick that occurs on a live offensive down and is worth 3 points.

field judge   The game official who helps watch the action along one sideline and who, along with the back judge, helps determine whether field goal attempts are successful.

field of play   The area in which teams can legally advance the football.

field turf   A playing surface that has the benefits of artificial turf but with the soft and forgiving nature of grass.

first down   A play accomplished when the offense advances the ball 10 or more yards from its original line of scrimmage.

first-down marker   The marker placed on the sideline that indicates the yard line the offense must reach to achieve a first down.

flak jacket   A form of padding some players wear under their uniform to protect their rib cage area.

flats   The area between the edge of the offensive line and the sidelines around the line of scrimmage. This is often a place teams target in the passing game.

flea flicker   A play during which the quarterback hands the ball to the running back, who then pitches the ball back to the quarterback, who then throws the ball to a receiver, usually one deep down the field.

formation   The way in which an offense arranges its players for that particular play.

franchise tag   A protection an NFL team has to keep one player who is eligible to become a free agent from going to another team.

free agency   A way for NFL players who have satisfied all the terms of their most recent contractual agreement to take offers to sign with other teams.

free kick   A punt or kick from the 20-yard line that occurs after the kicking team has surrendered a safety.

free play   A term used to describe a situation when the defense has committed a penalty and play resumes, offering the offense a no-lose-type scenario. On these plays, the offense is most likely to take a risk on a big-gain play.

front   The term for how a defense positions its men near the line of scrimmage.

fullback   The player on offense who most often blocks for the halfback carrying the football. The fullback can also act as a ball carrier, receiver, and pass protector, depending on the offense.

fumble   Occurs when the ball carrier loses control of the football during the course of action.

game official   The men in the black-and-white-striped shirts who help spot the football, manage the game clock, and ensure players follow rules.

game plan   The strategy the coaching staff prepares for the upcoming opponent.

gap   Any one of a number of openings between two linemen where defenses can place one of their guys or send a blitzer.

general manager   An individual responsible for overseeing the personnel and business aspects of a professional football team. Duties vary based on each team and contract arrangement.

getting to the corner   An expression used to describe a ball carrier's desire to get to the outer edges of the field where there's more room to run.

goal line   The white line that stretches from sideline to sideline on both ends of the field, separating the playing field from the end zone.

goal line defense   A specialty defense designed to load up its players along the line of scrimmage to stop short-yardage and goal line plays.

goal post   The forklike structure on both ends of the field through which kickers attempt to kick the football on field goal and extra-point attempts.

Greater Oakland Professional Pigskin Prognosticators League (GOPPPL)   Believed to be the first-ever fantasy football league. It was organized in the 1960s by a few members of the Oakland Raiders ownership group.

gridiron   Another term for the playing field.

guard   Guards are the linemen positioned on either side of the center. These blockers are the most likely to pull on running plays.

gunner   The player who releases at the snap of the ball on a punt and sprints downfield to chase after the other team's punt returner.

H-back   A hybrid offensive player who shares the qualities of a running back and tight end and can be lined up in any number of ways. He's used most often in specialized offensive formations.

Hail Mary   A desperation passing play in which the quarterback waits for his receivers to get downfield before launching a long pass. It's seldom successful.

halfback   The offensive player who more often than not gets to carry the football on rushing downs.

halfback pass   A play in which the halfback accepts the ball from the quarterback, or directly from center, and fakes a run before throwing the ball to a receiver downfield.

hand signals   Motions used by offensive and defensive coaches to help them instruct the players on the field on what to do for each play.

hands team   A special group of players inserted into the game for the kick return unit to safeguard against an onside kick.

hang time   A measurement for how long a punter's kick stays in the air. Teams value a long hang time because it allows the coverage team time to get down the field to tackle the other team's return man.

hard count   A tool a quarterback uses to try to draw the defense offside before the snap of the ball.

hash marks   The short white lines in the middle of the field marked 1 yard from each other and running parallel to the sidelines.

head linesman   The game official who watches to be sure no players move or line up improperly prior to the snap of the ball. He also helps spot the ball after the play.

Heisman Trophy   An award presented annually to the player considered the best in all of college football.

home field advantage   The belief that a team playing on its own field, in front of its home crowd, has a decided advantage over its opponent.

horse collar   A penalty that protects against defenders reaching inside a ball carrier's collar area to pull that player to the ground.

huddle   A gathering used by teams prior to the start of the play so one player, usually the quarterback or defensive captain, can deliver instructions to the others. In most huddles, players gather in a circular arrangement.

ice the kicker   An expression used to describe what coaches do to try to faze the opposing team's kicker prior to an attempt, usually in the form of a last-minute time-out.

in the box   A term to describe the area that contains all the defenders in a space that stretches from one offensive tackle to the other and within 5 yards of the line of scrimmage.

indisputable evidence   A term for what game officials must see while using instant replay to overturn a call made on the field.

infraction   Another term for a football penalty.

inside linebacker   In a 3–4 defense, the two inside linebackers are those lined up across from, or inside, the offensive tackles. These players make the majority of the team's tackles.

instant replay   A device used in pro and college football that allows for game officials to look at the previous play on a video monitor to determine if an error has occurred in the ruling on that particular down.

intended target   The receiver to which the quarterback is throwing the football.

intentional grounding An infraction caused when a quarterback attempts to avoid a sack and throws the ball to an area of the field where no receiver is present. In the NFL, the quarterback must also be within the tackle box and fail to get the ball back to the original line of scrimmage to get flagged for this.

interception This occurs when the defense secures a ball that was thrown forward before it hits the ground or is possessed by a receiver.

jam A technique defenders use in pass coverage to slow down a receiver, making contact with that player within the first 5 yards of the line of scrimmage.

judgment call A ruling a game official makes that's purely subjective, most notably pass interference.

kickoff specialist A player used exclusively on kickoffs, most commonly because the team's regular placekicker has proven ineffective. Some NFL teams hold a roster spot for a player to do only this.

lateral Occurs when the person in possession of the football passes it to another member of his team in a direction moving *away* from that team's goal line.

lead blocker The player who runs in front of the ball carrier and tries to clear a path by blocking oncoming defenders.

letter of intent A document incoming college football players sign upon deciding which school they want to attend.

line judge A game official who helps the head linesman watch for presnap penalties. He is also responsible for ensuring the offense has the correct numbers of players on the field.

line of scrimmage An imaginary line that runs sideline to sideline through the forwardmost tip of the football at the start of each play.

lineup The players who start the game for a team, on either side of the ball.

locker room The location where players prepare before the game and where most pregame and halftime speeches are given.

long-snapper The player who snaps the ball through his legs on kicking and punting situations.

measurement When the game officials cannot determine whether the offense has reached the first-down marker, they'll bring in the chains to take a measurement on the field where the ball is spotted.

middle linebacker   The defender who lines up across from the center and several yards off the line of scrimmage. He often serves as the captain of the defense and collects the most tackles.

motion   Occurs when an offensive player releases from his set position and shifts from one spot on the field to another prior to the snap of the ball. Only one player can go in motion at a time.

National Collegiate Athletic Association (NCAA)   The organization that oversees college athletics and drafts rules pertaining to student-athletes.

National Football League (NFL)   A collection of 32 professional football teams divided into 2 conferences, each with 4 divisions of 4 teams. It's considered the highest level of play.

National Football League Draft   A weekend-long event held in New York City each April during which NFL teams take turns selecting college prospects. The Draft is seven rounds and has become a spectacle millions of fans watch on television.

National Signing Day   The day when high school football players officially announce where they intend to play at the college level.

neutral zone   An area on the field of play the length of the football that runs sideline to sideline before the start of each play. Only the center is allowed to be in this area.

nickel back   A term for the fifth defensive back added to a defense (called a nickel defense).

no-huddle offense   A device an offense uses when it wants to speed up the tempo of the game or limit the defense's ability to substitute. Instead of huddling, the quarterback relays the play to the other 10 offensive players as everyone approaches the line of scrimmage.

nose guard   A defender who lines up across from the center. Also called a nose tackle.

off-season   The months that separate the end of one season and the start of training camp for the following season.

on an island   An expression used to describe when a defense's cornerback is locked into man-to-man coverage without any help from the rest of the defense.

onside kick   A technique used by the kicking team when it hopes to retake control of the football. An onside kick must travel at least 10 yards downfield before a member of the kicking team can recover it legally (unless it touches a member of the defense first and then is recovered by the kicking team).

outside linebacker   In a 3–4 defense, the two outside linebackers are those lined up outside of the offensive tackles. These players serve as added pass rushers.

over   Refers to a player's positioning on the field relative to other players. A defensive lineman, for example, may line up over an offensive lineman, meaning he is directly across from that player.

overpursue   A term used to describe when a defender takes a poor angle to get to the play, overshooting where the ball carrier is going to be, and often misses the tackle.

pancake block   A statistic of sorts for when an offensive lineman knocks the person he's blocking flat to the ground.

penalty   A term for an occurrence when game officials determine a member (or members) of either team has broken a rule.

pick-six   A term that describes when a defensive player intercepts a pass and returns the ball to the end zone for a touchdown.

pigskin   A term that has long been a substitute word for the ball used to play football. It's sometimes used today, even though balls are made of leather, not pigskin.

pitch   A term for when a player, usually the quarterback, tosses the ball to another player underhanded and in a direction away from the line of scrimmage.

placeholder   The player who holds the ball for the kicker on field goal and extra-point attempts. He also calls for the long-snapper to snap the ball.

placekicker   The player who kicks the field goals and extra points. This is also usually the person who kicks the ball downfield on kickoffs.

play-action   The action when the offense fakes a running play and passes the ball on a down the defense would expect to see a run, or following a series of successful running plays.

playbook   The binder or book containing all of a team's offensive or defensive plays and formations. Most NFL playbooks are thicker than a large metropolitan-area phonebook.

playoffs   The games that take place after the regular season has concluded, consisting of the few teams that have qualified. Also called the postseason.

pocket   The imaginary zone where the quarterback sets up to pass the ball. It's as wide as the distance between where his two offensive tackles line up and stretches several yards deep behind the line of scrimmage.

pocket passer   A quarterback who appears most comfortable when he's able to pass within the tackle box, as compared to a scrambling quarterback who makes plays while on the run.

pooch   A type of punt or kick that travels only a short distance, much like a chip shot in golf. It's designed to limit the return team's ability to have a long return.

possession   A set of plays run by one team without interruption. Once that team relinquishes control of the football, or scores, the possession is over.

prep   A high school football player.

prevent defense   A type of defense teams use when they're trying to limit the opposing offense from achieving a scoring play. This defense includes more defensive backs and fewer linemen or linebackers.

primary receiver   This receiver is the quarterback's first option on a particular pattern or play. Usually teams make their best receiver the primary receiver for a large percentage of the passing plays.

pro set   An offensive formation featuring two running backs side by side in the backfield, two wide receivers, and a tight end.

punter   The player who kicks the ball to the opposing team, almost always on a fourth down after his offense has determined it cannot achieve a first down.

pursuit angle   The route a defender takes to get to the ball carrier away from him.

pylons   The orange rectangular-shape bean bags that outline each end zone.

QB Rating   A sophisticated formula used to compare quarterbacks based on a number of relevant statistical categories.

quarterback   The leader of the offense who accepts the snap from the center on each play and either hands the ball to a running back, runs himself, or passes it to the receivers.

quarterback hurry or **quarterback pressure**   A statistical category for when a defensive player has forced the quarterback to get rid of the football sooner than it would appear he would have wanted to.

red flag   The flag coaches use when they want to challenge a play using instant replay.

red zone   The area of the field from the 20-yard line to the goal line where offenses have a high potential for scoring points.

referee   The lone game official wearing a white hat whose primary responsibility is to watch the quarterback on every offensive snap. He's also the official who communicates with the fans and manages instant replay.

release   The way a receiver gets off the line of scrimmage and into his route at the start of a play.

restricted free agent   A classification for an NFL player who can be pursued by other NFL teams, but not without consequences for the team that signs him.

reverse   A misdirection play whereby the ball carrier moves horizontally across the field and then hands the ball to another player heading in the opposite direction.

rip   A technique defenders use to get through the offensive line, relying on an undercut-like motion from one arm.

roll out   Occurs when a quarterback leaves the pocket on a passing play, either running out toward the left or right sideline while searching for open receivers down the field.

rookie   A player who is in his first year of professional football.

roster   A complete listing of a team's players, usually also listing each player's jersey number, height, weight, and years of experience.

route   The steps, moves, and direction in which a receiver runs on a passing down, all designed to take him to a location where the quarterback can throw him the football.

safety   The defenders positioned farthest away from the line of scrimmage most of the time. Most defenses use a free and strong safety.

safety blitz   A technique used by the defense whereby a safety is positioned near the line of scrimmage at the start of the play and rushes the quarterback, often unaccounted for by the offensive line.

safety net   A receiver the quarterback can throw to if his other options in the passing game aren't open.

salary cap   The total amount of money an NFL team is allowed to spend on all of its players for the entire season.

scheme   A description for the way in which a defense arranges its players.

scoop-and-score   A term for when a defensive player picks up a live football (a fumble) and runs it back to his end zone for a touchdown.

scoring sheet   A list of the decisions coaches ought to make when facing a variety of scenarios in a game. More than anything, the sheet suggests when a coach should go for the 2-point conversion or kick an extra point.

scout   A member of a team's support staff who searches for new talent for the team to try to acquire, either through recruiting in college or the draft and free agency in pro football.

scripting plays   A list of the plays the offense will run, in order, some coaches prepare prior to the start of the game in an attempt to stick to the game plan.

season   A predetermined number of games a team plays. The NFL has a preseason (4 games), regular season (16 games), and a postseason (up to 4 games).

seed   Heading into the playoff season, the league must seed, or label, the six teams that qualify for each conference. The four division winners all are seeded one through four, regardless if the two other teams to qualify have a better win-loss record. Those division winners are seeded based on record first and then by a series of tie breakers when needed. The fifth and sixth seeds go to the wild cards, the two remaining conference teams with the best records not to have won their division.

series   A collection of plays run during the course of one possession.

set position   A still, statuelike position for offensive players prior to the snap of the ball. Any movement earns a false start penalty.

shadow   A term for when one defensive player follows one offensive receiver or back at all times, regardless of the offense's formation or the defense's alignment.

shed   A term used to describe when one player pushes away one player to get to another.

short-yardage situation   Reserved for any situation in which the offense has a yard or two to go to achieve a first down or score.

shotgun   A formation in which the quarterback lines up several yards behind the center, forcing the ball to be snapped through the air. This formation gives the quarterback more space and time on passing downs.

shutdown corner   A term for an elite cornerback who doesn't allow the receivers he covers to catch many passes.

shutout   A term for when one team holds its opponent scoreless through all four quarters of a football game.

side judge   The game official whose primary roles are to count defensive players on the field and watch for penalties on passing downs.

skill position player   Any player who relies on athleticism or a specific skill set to perform his football responsibilities. The term is often reserved for receivers, backs, quarterbacks, and defensive backs.

snap count   The number, color, or word on which the center is to snap the ball to the quarterback. Teams use different snap counts to keep the defense from getting a quick jump at the start of each play.

soccer-style kick   A kicking method the placekicker uses. In it, he takes an arched approach to the ball and kicks it using the inside part of his foot.

special teams   One of three facets of the game. The special teams units handle the kicking, punting, and return plays in between each offensive possession.

speed-rushing end   A defensive end who specializes in rushing the quarterback. He's usually someone smaller than typical ends but with great quickness and athleticism.

spiral   A pass achieved when the ball comes out of a quarterback's hand with a perfect rotation.

spot the ball   After every play, the game officials must determine the exact location for where the ball was at the time the ball carrier was ruled down or traveled out of bounds.

stalk block   A block receivers use to help shield a defender from the ball carrier. The receiver positions his body between the defender and his teammate's running lane and makes continual contact with the defender while jogging his feet in place.

standings   A listing of win-loss records for all the teams playing in a specific league, conference, or division.

statistics   The numbers used to track team and player success.

stiff arm   A defense used by the ball carrier to fend off an oncoming tackler. The ball carrier sticks his arm straight out to create a cushion between himself and the defender and tries to push the player away or to the ground.

straight-on kick   A kicking style used by placekickers whereby they line up straight behind the ball and kick with their toes.

strength   The side of the offensive line that has more players, usually easily identified by where the tight end is lined up.

stunt   A tool used by defensive players, most often defensive linemen, to aid in their attempt to penetrate the offensive line.

sudden death overtime   Overtime used at the end of a tie game in the NFL (but not at any other level of football). A coin flip determines possession to start the overtime, and the first team to score wins.

Super Bowl   The NFL's championship game, pitting the winners of the American Football Conference (AFC) and National Football Conference (NFC).

sweep   A type of running play in which the running back takes a pitch from the quarterback and runs toward one sideline, allowing his blockers to get out in front of him.

swim   A technique defenders use to get through the offensive line, relying on an overhand, wind-up-like motion from one arm.

tackle   The offensive lineman positioned to the outside of the guard and sometimes inside of a tight end. Usually these are the tallest and heaviest of all the offensive linemen.

tackle box   The area between the two offensive tackles, setting the outside edges of the quarterback's pocket.

Tampa 2 defense   A coverage scheme that has been linked to the Tampa Bay Buccaneers, similar to a cover 2 defense with a few adjustments.

Terrible Towel   Yellow towel popularized during Pittsburgh's dominant play throughout the 1970s. Pittsburgh Steelers fans still wave these during home games.

Thanksgiving Day   A holiday identified with football. The NFL's Detroit Lions and Dallas Cowboys play every year on this day.

tight end   The player who lines up next to the tackle on offense and acts as both a blocker and extra receiver.

time of possession   The amount of time a given team has possessed the ball in the game. This is usually, but not always, an indicator of which team is dominating the game.

time-out   A tool teams use to stop the game clock or delay the action to take more time to make an important decision. Each team is given three time-outs for each half.

touchdown   A 6-point scoring play achieved anytime a player crosses his goal line while in bounds and in possession of the football. It's worth more points than any other possible football scoring play.

transmitting device   A tool placed inside the helmet of one offensive player, usually the quarterback, and one defensive player, usually a linebacker, through which a member of the coaching staff can communicate plays.

trenches   The area around the line of scrimmage in which offensive and defensive linemen battle one another.

trick play   A play that defies traditional (and conservative) strategy. These plays often produce either fantastic or disastrous results for the team that employs them.

tuck rule   A somewhat controversial rule that allows the quarterback the ability to bring the ball back to his body on a passing play while benefitting from the same no-fumble protection a forward pass provides.

turf toe   A nagging injury athletes suffer to their big toe area during the course of play. It can hold football players out of action for several weeks because it makes running and normal athletic movements extremely painful.

turnover   A term for when the offense loses possession of the football during the course of a play, through either a fumble or interception.

tweener   A player who straddles two positions, not really fitting into either category. The term is most commonly used for players who share the qualities of a defensive lineman and linebacker, and also for players who share the qualities of a tight end and wide receiver.

two-minute warning   The time at which only two minutes remain on the game clock before the end of a half or the game. In the NFL, the clock stops at the two-minute mark, or as soon as a live play is ruled dead.

two-point conversion   An alternative teams have to kicking an extra point. A 2-point conversion places the ball at the same yard marker, but teams are required to pass or run the ball over the goal line instead of kicking it through the uprights. It's worth 2 points.

umpire   The game official who stands behind the linebackers and observes the linemen on both sides of the ball.

unabated to the quarterback   An expression used for when a defensive player is offside and sprinting toward the quarterback before the snap of the ball. The game officials rule the ball dead to protect the quarterback from unnecessary harm.

uncatchable A pass game officials rule could not have been caught by its intended receiver.

under Refers to a player's positioning on the field relative to other players. An offensive lineman, for example, may line up under a defensive lineman, meaning he is directly across from that player.

unit Any group of 11 players used for an offensive, defensive, or special teams set.

unrestricted free agent An NFL player with the freedom to sign with any team he so chooses.

uprights The name for the two verticals poles of the goal post between which kickers must kick the ball to make a successful field goal or extra point.

veteran A term to define a player who has several years of experience in pro football.

victory formation When one team has the game all but won, and is in possession of the football, they use this formation to finish the game clock. All the offensive players are tight together, and after receiving the snap, the quarterback takes a knee to end the play but keep the clock running.

wedge The blocking approach used on kick returns, placing a couple of players in front of the returner to help create a cushion from him and the coverage unit.

West Coast Offense A term applied to coach Bill Walsh's style of offense that relied on short, low-risk passing routes to open up bigger plays down the field.

wide receiver The player who lines up out wide of the offensive line and primarily catches passes.

wildcat An offensive formation that places a running back in the shotgun behind the center.

wishbone An offensive formation in which three running backs line up tightly behind the quarterback, giving the team plenty of running options on every play.

wrist coach A wristbandlike tool quarterbacks and other offensive players can wear that contains a list of the team's offensive plays and instructions.

yellow flag What game officials throw when one team has committed a penalty.

zone blitz A strategy used by the defense in which select linemen drop into pass coverage and linebackers or defensive backs are sent to blitz.

zone blocking A style of offensive blocking in which linemen are responsible for an area instead of a specific player.

zone coverage A defensive concept that asks defenders to cover an area of the field rather than a specific player.

Resources

We've covered a lot of football info in the previous pages, but if you're still looking for more, you've come to the right place.

General Football Resources

Here are a number of sources that effectively cover a wide range of football topics for all levels. All these sources also offer fantasy football analysis; many of them host fantasy football leagues as well.

ESPN
www.espn.com
Offers a wealth of in-season and off-season football content for pro and college, and covers the NFL Draft better than any other site.

CBSSports.com
www.cbssports.com
CBSsports.com is another well-liked sports news provider with excellent coverage for every football function at every level and one of the most popular fantasy league management tools.

Yahoo! Sports
sports.yahoo.com
Users love Yahoo!'s free fantasy league management service, and the site produces some of the most read football content on the web.

FOX Sports
msn.foxsports.com
FOX Sports offers news and analysis on every football topic.

SI.com

sportsillustrated.cnn.com

The benchmark for sports writing. *Sports Illustrated* (both online and its print publication) still deliver some of the best in-depth feature reporting of any source. *Sports Illustrated* also offers a strong fantasy product.

Sporting News

www.sportingnews.com

One of the oldest-operating sports news providers, Sporting News offers a lot of quick-read analysis.

SB Nation

www.sbnation.com

This blog-based site offers news on every imaginable football-related topic.

Pro Football Resources

The following sources focus on aspects of the professional game.

NFL.com

www.nfl.com

The NFL's official site offers news, analysis, and historical data.

National Football League: Super Bowl

www.superbowl.com

Everything on this site is tied to the biggest sporting event of the year.

Pro Football Hall of Fame

www.profootballhof.com

The official site of the Pro Football Hall of Fame offers feature articles, balloting updates, and profile pages for each member.

Pro Football Weekly

www.profootballweekly.com

This is the oldest source dedicated solely to NFL content (both a print publication and online source).

Pro Football Reference

www.pro-football-reference.com

This database of statistics is both comprehensive and easy to search. The site has pages for every player's statistics, a section for records and league leaders, and pages for team data.

Football Outsiders

www.footballoutsiders.com

A site that analyzes and interprets statistical information differently from mainstream NFL sources.

National Football Post

www.nationalfootballpost.com

Turn here for news and analysis delivered by former NFL insiders with a perspective other sites do not have.

Pro Football Talk

profootballtalk.nbcsports.com

This site focuses on NFL rumors and has a reputation for breaking news.

The Red Zone

www.theredzone.org

This news portal for every NFL team collects stories from a number of local and national sources.

College Football Resources

These resources focus on aspects of the college game.

National Collegiate Athletics Association

www.ncaafootball.com

Part of the NCAA online family, this site covers news for all levels of collegiate football.

Heisman Trophy

www.heisman.com

The official site of the Heisman Trophy includes information on the history of the award and past recipients.

College Football Hall of Fame

www.collegefootball.org

The home of the College Football Hall of Fame includes profiles on every member.

Rivals

www.rivals.com

This site is dedicated to the recruiting process, with prospect updates for every Division 1 college football team.

Scout

www.scout.com

This site focuses on covering the college football recruiting season.

D3 Football

www.d3football.com

This site covers Division 3 football news.

NFL Draft Resources

The following sources cover the NFL Draft, including news on prospects and the positions or players NFL teams may be considering.

Draft Countdown

www.draftcountdown.com

This is one of the few NFL Draft sites committed to delivering year-round content.

Draft History

www.drafthistory.com

Turn here for historical information on every draft and player selected.

Mel Kiper

www.melkiper.com

This is the official site of the original Draft guru, Mel Kiper Jr.

Fantasy Football Resources

The following sources offer assistance in setting up and managing a fantasy football team.

Real Time Sports

www.rtsports.com

At this independent fantasy football league manager site, paying users can customize league settings.

My Fantasy League

www.myfantasyleague.com

This is another independent league manager fantasy football site.

World Championships of Fantasy Football
www.wcoff.com
Check this site for one of the industry's many high-stakes fantasy football competitions.

RotoWire
www.rotowire.com
This all-in-one site delivers tons of daily fantasy football news.

Fanball
www.fanball.com
This site offers online fantasy contests and content and produces high-quality fantasy publications.

RotoWorld
www.rotoworld.com
Turn here for a wealth of fantasy football news, analysis, and feature articles.

Fantasy Football Librarian
www.fflibrarian.com
This blog tracks how successful other sites are at ranking players and projecting data.

Fantasy Football Index
This is one of the industry's most established and respected fantasy football magazines.

Fantasy Football Pro Forecast
This is one of the oldest and thickest annual fantasy magazines on the newsstand.

Committed: Confessions of a Fantasy Football Junkie
by Mark St. Amant (2005)
An author's journey into a fantasy football obsession.

Your Official Guide on How to Dominate Fantasy Football
by Randy W. Giminez (2006)
A step-by-step reference guide for players new to fantasy football.

Coaching and Instructional Resources

These sources can be good tools for those looking to coach.

American Football Coaches Association
www.afca.com
The home of the American Football Coaches Association offers helpful articles, regional contact information, and a clinic calendar.

Football Coaching Strategies (1995)
This book is full of articles and diagrams tackling many of football's most complex offensive and defensive strategies.

The Football Coaching Bible (2002)
This book offers insight from some of the most recognizable names in football coaching.

Books About Football

These books can take readers deeper into the life that surrounds football players and coaches and includes both fiction and nonfiction works.

Paper Lion (1966)
by George Plimpton
This is the story of Plimpton's attempt at cracking a pro football lineup. It's a literary classic.

North Dallas Forty (1973)
by Peter Gent
A former professional football player discusses life inside the locker room. (Also a movie.)

Friday Night Lights: A Town, a Team, and a Dream (1990)
by Buzz Bissinger
A look at high school football in the state of Texas. (Also a movie and a television series.)

Next Man Up: A Year Behind the Lines in Today's NFL (2005)
by John Feinstein
An inside look at how pro football operates by way of the Baltimore Ravens.

Sports Illustrated: The Football Book (2005)
by the Editors of *Sports Illustrated*
This book features stories and pictures to highlight the magazine's first 50 years of covering the sport.

ESPN College Football Encyclopedia: The Complete History of the Game (2005)
edited by Michael MacCambridge
This is a comprehensive source for the history of the college game.

The Blind Side: Evolution of a Game (2006)
by Michael Lewis
Lewis captures the story of a family who takes in a teen and helps him build his football and academic careers. (Also a movie.)

Movies About Football

I gave you a few of the finer football movies in Chapter 29, but here are a few more you might want to check out.

All the Right Moves (1983)
This is the story of high school players trying to use the sport to escape the mill town they live in.

Necessary Roughness (1991)
A bunch of misfits are assembled to keep football alive on a college campus.

The Program (1993)
This fictional story exposes the ugly side of college football.

Varsity Blues (1999)
High school players in Texas band together to make their senior season a success, in spite of their legendary coach.

We Are Marshall (2006)
The story of the Marshall University football program's attempts to rebuild after a tragedy.

Index